You Your First: A Collection of New York Yankees Firsts

MARK ROSENMAN AND HOWIE KARPIN

Copyright © 2023 Rosenman-Karpin
"Topps® trading cards used
courtesy of The Topps Company, Inc."
All rights reserved.
ISBN 979-8-218-25668-5

Press Box Publishing

DEDICATION

To Beth, Josh, Stefania, as well as Liana and J.R., who are my world, and my late father Morris Rosenman who took me to my "First" Yankee game on July 18, 1968, where I got to see the great Mickey Mantle triple in a 4-1 win over the Washington Senators.

Mark Rosenman

CONTENTS

Acknowledgments — ii

Foreword by Michael Kay — v

1. David Aardsma — 1
2. Stan Bahnsen — 13
3. Steve Balboni — 28
4. Ron Blomberg — 38
5. Wade Boggs — 46
6. Joba Chamberlain — 51
7. Rocky Colovito — 58
8. Johnny Damon — 65
9. Al Downing — 77

You Never Forget Your First: A Collection of New York Yankees Firsts

10	Jake Gibbs	98
11	Charlie Hayes	110
12	Mike Heath	116
13	Tommy John	125
14	Tony Kubek	133
15	Jim Leyritz	154
16	Jack McDowell	174
17	George "Doc" Medich	187
18	Mike Pagliarulo	203
19	Fritz Peterson	219
20	Dennis Rasmussen	227

21	Bobby Richardson	242
22	Dave Righetti	260
23	Eric Soderholm	285
24	Shane Spencer	298
25	Nick Swisher	305
26	Stefan Wever	329
27	Paul Zuvella	337
28	The Artists	347

ACKNOWLEDGMENTS

Over my lifetime as well as the last 17 years as host of *SportstalkNy*, I have read thousands of books. Like many others, I do not always take the time to read the acknowledgments. Having now gone through the process of writing nine books, I have a greater appreciation as to how important these pages are to the pages that follow it, for without the names I am about to list, there would not have been a book to read.

First and foremost, as always, is my amazing wife, Beth, who is always there as an endless source of encouragement, love, and support. My son, Josh, his wife Stefania, and my daughter, Liana, and her boyfriend J.R, who by the joy and passion in the way they approach everything they do inspire me to do the same.

My late father, Morris, who took me to all my sports firsts and fostered my love of sports. My late mother, Estelle, who allowed me to buy every sports book whenever there was a book fair at school and always encouraged me to pursue my passions no matter the obstacles or challenges.

My late sisters, Cheryl and Suzie, who always set great examples for their little brother.

I would like to thank the following members of the press who welcomed me into their workspace with open arms and showed me the ropes including but not limited to Laura Albanese, Ken Albert, Christian Arnold, Matthew Blittner, Larry Brooks,

Rick "Carpy" Carpinello, Jim Cerny, Scott Charles, Russ Cohen, Brian Compton, Charles Curtis, Stan Fischler, John Foyole, Bob Gelb, Zach Gelb, John Giannone, Andrew Gross, Shannon Hogan, Patrick Kearns, Chris King, Allan Kreda, Kevin Kurz, Don La Greca, Dave Maloney, Joe Micheletti, Greg Picker, Joe Pantorno, Howie Rose, Dan Rosen, Sam Rosen, Stefan Rosner, Ethan Sears, Arthur Staple, Colin Stephenson, Jesse Spector, Mollie Walker, Cory Wright, and Steve Zipay.

A note of gratitude to the scores of authors who have appeared on WLIE 540am *Sportstalkny* who have inspired me over the years as well as our loyal sponsors Leith Baren, Neil Cohen, Mark Glickman, David and Andrew Reale, Scott Stimel, and my co-host AJ Carter as without them none of this would have been possible.

A tip of the cap to our editor, Ken Samelson, who worked with Howie and I to complete our fourth in the series of "Firsts" books with him.

Thank you to Hadley Barrett and Kit Vogelsang of The Topps Company who were instrumental in allowing to use the Topps® trading cards on the cover of the book.

Last, but not least, my writing partner in this project, Howie Karpin, who encouraged me seven years ago to start writing.

Mark Rosenman

With the number of books that I've written or cowritten, it's been customary to thank my wonderful wife of 40 years, Kathy Block Karpin, for her support and her love. I wouldn't have had this career without her support. I want to acknowledge my son Danny and his fiancée and soon to be wife, Emily, along with my other son, Jake, and his wife, Anita. We have two boys and now we have two wonderful "daughters" to join our family.

My sister, Carol Shore, and her husband, Barry Shore, have been staunch supporters throughout my career. My niece, Wendy Shore

Rosano and her kids, Alex and Rachel and Sharon Shore. We will always have the memory of Sharon's daughter and my great-niece, Melanie, in our hearts.

My family is most important to me and I love them all. Thanks for your support.

To all my friends (and I'm blessed to have a lot of them) I thank you for your continuous friendship.

Howie Karpin

FOREWORD

It's time-honored and tested that you never forget your first. Ever.

About anything.

First girlfriend. First car. First time in an airplane. First time away from home. All of it is indelibly etched in the scrapbook of your mind and as you flip the metaphorical pages, it brings a smile to your face or perhaps a warm feeling to your heart.

Everyone has had a first something and that initial anything will always be special to you. Some people can't remember what they ate for breakfast or the name of someone they met five minutes ago, but can recall, in vivid detail, their first job or first paycheck. These are important touchstones in your life, bookmarks for the big stuff. The stuff that matters.

I remember the first story I ever wrote for the *New York Post*. I was a clerk at the time, essentially getting people lunch or filing photos or compiling statistics, but I wanted to be a writer so I would volunteer to cover events that the paper would not otherwise have covered. And I did it on my own time. The first time I did this I covered a Fordham basketball game and filed the story with the sports desk where the editors did their thing and decided where to place it in the sports section. Driving home that night I was a buzzing with excitement, wondering where in the section they had put my story and how it would look when I picked up the paper in the morning. I couldn't wait. I certainly didn't sleep much that night and told my parents and all my friends that I was going to have a story in the *New York* Post the next morning.

When the sun finally came up, I walked to the corner store in my neighborhood in The Bronx, and couldn't wait to buy the *Post*. I got there, paid the money, and started rifling through the sports section to see my story. I filed a normal length article, say five hundred words, and I couldn't find it. Finally, I noticed the story was chopped down to essentially two small paragraphs. My byline was not even above the story, but was at the end of the story. And here is the kicker: it said By MIKE KAYE. I was crushed. I never go by Mike because my mother always wanted people to call me Michael and the editor added an E to the end of my name! Brutal. As far as firsts go, well, I now remember it fondly, but when it happened, I actually had a hard time walking back home and dreaded hearing from all the people I told. Thankfully, there was no social media and text messages back in 1982, but if there was, I would have been savaged by friend and foe alike.

A much fonder first was the first time I broadcast a Yankees game on radio with John Sterling. My dream since I was nine years old was to be the Yankees' announcer, and although I started in the print industry, the hope was to somehow maneuver my way into the electronic end of the business. Through incredible luck and being in the right place at the right time, I somehow landed my dream gig. Sterling was in his third year as the radio voice of the Yankees but was a veteran of the industry and knew his way around a microphone, with impeccable timing to go with a legendarily beautiful voice.

But despite his credentials, he never made me feel unworthy or undeserving of sitting alongside him for this incredible ride. My first game was in early April 1992 and the Yankees were playing the Red Sox at Yankee Stadium. I was understandably nervous because this was what I had wanted to do my whole life. As first pitch drew closer, I thought I was going to hyperventilate. With about 30 seconds to air, John looked at me and said, "As you embark on this new journey, I have two bits of advice." I leaned forward, anxious to hear these words of wisdom by this master of his craft. I figured he was going to tell me about pacing or maybe speaking from the sternum to not strain my voice, but that was not what he was about to impart. Instead, he told me, "Never ask me my age on the air and I sometimes talk to myself, so don't be alarmed when it happens."

And. That. Was. It. That was the beginning of what, to this point, has been a 32-year run as one of the Voices of the Yankees. And both things he told me served me well. He didn't want me to ask his age because before Google and Wikipedia it wasn't so easy to find out how old someone was and he felt that once you hit a certain age that your age could be held against you, thus costing you a job. And as for talking to himself, well, he certainly did. Between pitches if he was frustrated with someone or something, he would have a dialogue with himself. Sometimes he would do it off mike during an inning when I was doing play by play while I was doing play by play. If he had not warned me before that first pitch, I don't know if I could have handled the shock and surprise. We spent 10 years together and his private dialogue never flustered me. In fact, it would make me smile as I just thought there was a third invisible announcer in the booth with us at all times.

So, as you can see, firsts are a big deal that live on as long as we do, and sometimes longer, if we tell people or write about them. And that's exactly what Howie and Mark have done as they have expertly chronicled many Yankees firsts through the organization's rich history. And they've done the incredible legwork of tracking down many beloved Yankees to tell their stories about their first games, their first hits, and all the important first moments in their lives. If you're a fan of the Yankees, or just love baseball, this book is a treasure trove of firsts that will make you think, smile, and reminisce. You can keep it on your desk or on your bookshelf and at any moment open it up to a certain page that chronicles a certain first and again live that moment with the people who actually lived it in real time.

Please enjoy *You Never Forget Your First: A Collection of New York Yankees Firsts*. And never forget that my last name doesn't have an E at the end of it and never ask John his age!

Michael Kay, 2022

1
DAVID AARDSMA

David Aardsma played nine years in the major leagues for eight teams, including the Yankees. Because of assorted injuries, Aardsma appeared in only one game for them.

FIRST BASEBALL GAME THAT HE ATTENDED AS A KID:

"My Little League in California did a Little League Day at Anaheim Stadium at the Big A. They go out, you walk around the stadium and they kind of get announced. It's kind of neat and it's always during like a Sunday day game. There's not really BP, but [the players are] doing stuff on the field and you see players. I'll never forget a passed ball. Mo Vaughn was at first base for the Red Sox, passed ball [wild throw] and he comes walking over and it went right to my feet and I got to pick it up and throw it to Mo Vaughn and [his Little League team] were the Red Sox so that was like the coolest moment. Remember going to the game and then years later, I'm on the Red Sox, go to Anaheim, Sunday day game and my Little League is at the game doing the walk. I lost it, I lost it. One thing I was always taught really young was to give back to the game in any way possible. Give back to the game. That's not like just throw money at it. You know, take care of the fans, take care of kids, make sure everybody feels welcome, that they would wanna come back. They are the ones that make the game go. The only reason you have an opportunity to play major league baseball is because people want to be a part of it. You don't wanna be a part of it, there would be no major league baseball, so bring them, get them to be a part of it. Every single time in Anaheim, I looked forward to Sunday day games. I hated Sunday day games, except for in Anaheim, and I'd go and I'd give every single kid a high five. None of them cared who I was other than I was a major league baseball player. I wasn't an Angel, man, but I tried to make it special for every one of those kids that were getting the same experience I had. It was a kind of full circle thing. It was really cool."

FIRST BASEBALL IDOL:

"Ryne Sandberg. Rhino man. I grew up in Colorado, moved to California but like almost every kid of my generation, you come home from school, who's on TV, right? Cubbies and the Braves. It was like do I like Chip Caray or Harry Caray? It's not even competition at that point. The lovable Cubs versus the Braves. The [Braves] might be good, but I grew up a huge Cubs fan. Ryne Sandberg was like my super idol. It was crazy. I was never a second baseman. I was a hitter when I was younger, but I always liked pitching, even if I wasn't a pitcher. I liked pitching a little bit more and then became a pitcher, but Ryne Sandberg was my idol."

FIRST DRAFT EXPERIENCE:

Aardsma was a first-round pick (22nd overall) by the San Francisco Giants in the 2003 MLB June Amateur Draft.

"My dad and I took his car and went to a car wash [on draft day] and started scrubbing and spraying it down, scrubbing to completely avoid [following] the draft at all costs. We didn't wanna sit on our computer listening to it. It started at like one [o'clock] Eastern, so we're in Houston so it was like twelve o'clock. Twelve comes, 12:15, 12:30. It's like one now and so we're freaking out at this point. I'm already going, 'Well, I guess I'm going back to Rice [University].' It's like 1:30, like an hour and a half later, I finally get a phone call and I still don't remember who called, what team, anything about the phone call. All I remember is you're selected in the first round, that's all I heard. So I get done with the phone call. My dad's like, where did I go. 'I got picked,' and he's like 'Where?' I go, 'I think the first round,' and he's like, 'By who?' I go, 'I don't know,' (laughs).

"At the time, Bobby Evans was the assistant GM and [Brian] Sabean was the GM. Immediately call my mom and she's freaking out. She goes, 'We just heard.' I'm like, 'Who did I get drafted by?' She goes, 'The Giants.' So that was an amazing experience. So I get drafted by the Giants. I finally sign, I fly up to San Francisco. Bobby Evans drives me down to San Jose. It's like 45 minutes, an hour, or whatever, right in the car. The whole time he's like, 'Hey, just so you know, until you pitch in your first game and you walk on that mound, anything can happen. You're going to High A, that's a really big deal for us. That's a big deal for any drafted player to be going straight to High A and skipping the short-season teams. You're not even going down to Arizona with the rest of your draft.' He goes, 'No matter what, always be prepared for something to happen until it happens.'"

FIRST SPRING CAMP:

"Talk about walking into a locker room of just superstars, right? Your first experience, obviously Barry [Bonds]. I'd gotten to meet him once when I got drafted. I went up to the San Francisco and Jose Cruz Jr. is there, who's a Rice guy. Jose Cruz Jr. when I walked in the door, 'Aardsma, congratulations.' He introduced me to Andres Galarraga, who was a Rockie. I loved the Rockies growing up in Colorado. You meet J. T. Snow and all these guys. Then, to walk into the locker room with all the pitching staff and there were some guys like Kirk Rueter on that team. Dustin Hermanson, [Brett] Tomko. Not many huge superstars. Jason Schmidt. Schmidt was the only superstar pitcher they had, but they had a really good staff. Then, Bonds comes. I remember we were having a big meeting in the clubhouse and Bonds goes, 'What's going on?' and everyone's like, you just see everyone roll their eyes. He came in with just this huge personality and all that stuff. Then, Marquis

Grissom comes in and [Ray] Durham comes and all these dudes come. Dude, like this is wild, right?

"What I decided was I did not care what anybody thought of me. I didn't care what they thought of me as far as like my preparation, me being ready every single day. They can think I'm an idiot, think I'm crazy but I'm gonna be prepared to pitch and plan on making this team. Day one, when I walk into spring training, one of the trainers came up to me and said, 'David Aardsma, nice to meet you. I'm the trainer at Double A, I'll be having you this season.' I'll never forget that moment. In my mind, I didn't say this, I'm not a dick but, no you won't. You can think all you want. Like they might have whatever plan they have for me, I'm gonna write my own plan. They had a locker room at the old stadium.

Scottsdale Stadium had two rings. They had an inner ring and they had this outer ring. Most spring training locker rooms are set up like this because you just have so many players in one room and that wasn't built for that many players. Inner ring, that's all the dudes. Outer ring is the invitees. You figure out really quick when you're sharing a locker with a guy in the corner that you're an invite. Like, okay, why does Barry Bonds have three lockers? I get it. They're not planning on having us there that long. We're renting this space. They own it, we're renting it. I also made a decision. I wanted them to see me. I wasn't just gonna be in the background and maybe later on people notice me. You will see me, you will notice me. I'll have the biggest smile on my face. I'll be quiet, but you'll notice me. So, every run we did, every BP we did, ever PFP (pitchers fielding practice) we did, I was first in line.

"I started throwing and I was throwing the shit out of it. I felt like I was getting a fine rapport with the team just doing my thing. I think they all think I'm a little standoffish. I think they viewed me as a little bit of a threat and rightfully so. I wanted them to think that. I wanted to be the nicest threat possible. I wasn't making enemies, but I wasn't making friends by any means. So, the outer ring starts slowly dwindling. I'm sitting in the corner so keep going and I'm starting to pitch against more legit batters and I'm still dealing. That outer ring's disappearing and then pretty soon there's no one left besides me in the little corner. I'm literally the only guy left on the outer [ring]. I think the clubhouse guys came in one day and were planning on moving all the lockers out and rearranging and putting the guys in the normal lockers and having a real normal locker room. They go, 'Dude, we didn't even know you're still back here.' I go, 'Yeah.'

"We go up to San Francisco to the exhibition games. I'm planning on making the team, but in all reality, I'm like, I don't know. We're playing Oakland, I don't pitch the first game. Don't pitch the second game, so I goin' for the third game. This is the day they're making cuts. Like this is the final day. They're making the roster. So I go in to pitch, it's like they gotta make the roster. I went in against a very, very good Oakland A's team and I was throwing, like the best game I'd ever thrown. Just lighting up, throwing 99, 98 every single pitch. Then, I remember Jermaine Dye and he comes up and it's like fouling off, fouling off. I'm throwing 98, 99, just foul, foul, foul. I finally pumped and I was a little higher, a little harder and got to strike him out. I'm coming into the dugout and Rags (pitching coach Dave Righetti) sits me down. He goes, dude, that was insane. He goes, 'You pitched great in a big moment, congratulations.' He goes, 'I'm gonna be the first one to tell you right now, Dave. You just made the team. When the game's over, they're gonna call you in the office and officially tell you, congratulations, you just made the team.' So they bring me in there. Sabean's in there and like Rags obviously in there. [Giants manager] Felipe [Alou] is in there. They're like, this is a very hard decision. [Sabean] goes, 'It was an interesting decision just to bring you to spring training, let alone a very hard decision here, but you're gonna make the team.' He goes, 'Our first opening game is in Houston. I know you're basically from Houston, so we would like to help you eliminate any distractions possible.' He goes, 'We'll get as many tickets as you need and we'll handle all that. Just pitch and do your thing.' I've got very high respect for Felipe, but we didn't really interact a whole lot. When you're pitching, especially as a reliever, you don't deal with the manager too often. Felipe, I'm sure was dealing with the hitters a whole lot more. It was really our bullpen coach, we had a great relationship. I'm pretty sure Felipe didn't know my name. I'll be honest.'"

FIRST MAJOR LEAGUE GAME: April 6, 2004 vs. Houston Astros at Minute Maid Park

Aardsma tossed two scoreless innings in relief and was awarded the win as the Giants defeated the Astros 7–5.

"Andy Pettitte just signed down there and he's a Houston guy. Gonna watch him make his debut. That was just incredible within itself. When we lined up on Opening Day, I'll never forget. I get lined up on the side and Brad Lidge, who went to Cherry Creek High School, was always kinda my hero from high school. He runs down and he like pointed at me. Then, Lance Berkman was a nice guy. When he runs down and he pointed right at me so that was like, this is cool. I started warming up in the bullpen in Houston. The bullpen on the visitor side felt it was like a dungeon but the problem with that is when you throw the ball, it's like boom. So you start overthrowing trying to hear that sound. It's kinda like they put a giant radar gun right next to you. I'll never forget, I'm hearing the sound boom boom and we played there at Rice, so I kind of knew what to expect. It's a little different when you're hearing 60,000 people and the sound and the energy. The opening day or second game of the season. So I run out there, I'm nervous as can be and you gotta face [Craig] Biggio, Hall of Famer and then Bagwell. Berkman, who could arguably be a Hall of Famer in the right argument. Then it was like, [Jeff] who I believe is a Hall of Famer. I mean, it was incredible. At the same time, you realize quickly, this is my job. I can't think about the moment. I can't think about how cool it is pitching to Craig Biggio. Craig

Biggio is stopping me from being a major leaguer. I have to get Craig Biggio out. It's your job at that moment. Such a big learning experience. If you can't do your job, they're gonna find somebody else."

FIRST TIME SEEING HIMSELF ON A BASEBALL CARD:

"I believe it was Topps, it might have been Upper Deck. They had a little card deal so they sent me a bunch of cards to sign. That was the first moment, like opening a box and like, oh, I have to sign all these. It was surreal 'cause I was a big card collector, huge card collector. Everybody, I feel, in my generation went to stores and bought your sets. Upper Deck and Donruss and all those. That was one of the many, kind of "made it" moments. You're like, 'Wow, this is real.' Like, no matter what happens, I got this that says I made it or at least I'm there. I had my cup of coffee and not many people get this. Now, everybody gets baseball cards, even in college. But that was that moment of what I used to love to do is collect baseball cards. Now, I'm seeing it and I have it."

FIRST EXPERIENCE WITH THE YANKEES:

While playing for the Seattle Mariners, Aardsma had hip surgery after the 2010 season and underwent Tommy John surgery shortly after that. In February 2012, Aardsma signed a one-year contract with a club option for 2013.

"The Yankees offered me great terms, awesome terms. They had a whole lot of incentives to come back and incentives that would play into next year. So, it's the Yankees, man. That's pretty cool, like I love playing for historical teams. The contract negotiations were really easy 'cause I understood from their standpoint, they're gonna want me on a minimum [salary]. I had just come off of two great seasons and an injury, so we put in a lot of incentives to make a lot of money and become a Yankee, so I liked everything about it. The only weird thing that happened was they told me we agreed to the terms, but they said we can't sign the contract because the moment we signed the contract, we have to put you on the roster. They said they had a bunch of injured guys coming into spring training that they need to shuffle around on the roster. They said once the season starts and they can set everybody, they'll sign me. Like the contract is basically signed without being signed. Me and my agent took a little chance and trusted the front office. They fly me to New York to go get my MRIs. So I gotta get an MRI on my shoulder 'cause I'm a pitcher because I just had Tommy John. I land in New York, it's like six in the morning, seven in the morning, I'm walking into my hotel room, like the lobby to sign in. I had just taken a red eye and my wife tells me she's pregnant. That moment, like, I'm signing with the Yankees, wife tells me she's pregnant.

"We do the agreement like three days into spring training and I'm at home and [the Yankees are] like, 'By the way, we're totally fine. We're gonna sign the contract. We want you to get on the plane tomorrow. We actually misinterpreted a couple of the rules. We can bring you in and we don't have to put you on the 60-day [DL at the time] yet. Then, I go down there and I'm throwing on the rehab process and like the first day, my throwing partner is Andy Pettitte. Andy Pettitte's just showing up to spring training just to help. He wants to see if he wants to come back, so he's my throwing partner and I'm like, 'Andy, come on, dude. You're not playing, aren't you?' He ends up signing like a couple of weeks later.

"I walk in the locker room, every locker's taken, right? 'Cause I'm late to spring training, every locker's taken except for one and it's Derek Jeter's extra locker for all his mail and bullshit. They're walking me through the locker room and they're like, 'Yeah, you know it's tough, but we got one locker for you, right here.' I go, 'No,' and Jeter's standing there. I go, 'No, put me in the training room, put me in the weight room. I'm not gonna take Derek Jeter's extra locker.' I go, 'Derek, I've got the utmost respect for you and your career. We've played against each other now for years. Dude, you're good man. I'm just the rental.' He's like, 'No, dude, it's no big deal.' Eventually, they gave me his extra locker and then that was incredible. Derek Jeter was my locker mate for spring training. It was an amazing experience."

FIRST TIME PUTTING ON THE YANKEES UNIFORM:

"Absolutely [it] means more 'cause when you're talking about major league baseball, you cannot have a conversation without the Yankees. You're talking about the greatest players of all time. You can't have a conversation without the Yankees dominating it. Being a part of that franchise, being a part of that team, it just means something different. The reason I liked Rice was that it was business, but it was fun business. You come here, we're gonna have a great time but we're here to work and we're here to be major league baseball players and win every game along the way. When you go to the Yankees, it's business. It's like great, congratulations on your career. By the way, the dude who had your locker before you are a Hall of Famer. Like you don't matter. The Yankees matter, that was felt throughout the locker room and by me. Cool, I'm next to Derek Jeter. Well, you know what? Derek Jeter, by the way, wasn't even the best Yankee to be here. You're not special, he's not special compared to those guys. That's not saying Jeter's not special, but in their eyes, 'Hey, is he the Babe?' So unless you're Babe Ruth, you don't matter.

"One of the coolest things I've ever experienced was there's a lot of rumors, just like there always are in Yankees camp and there was a bunch of rumors about them trying to make some trade, trying to move some guys, trying to get a little better roster. Some players were starting to speak or stuff to the media. [Yankees GM Brian] Cashman came in and had a closed-door meeting with us. He was kind of fired up, kind of pissed off about it. He goes, 'Guys, I don't wanna hear another word from anybody in this locker room about what we're trying to do in the front office.' He said, 'My job, what I am being paid to do, is to the make the New York Yankees the best team they can possibly be.' He's like, 'Your job is to make yourself the best baseball player you can possibly be, whether you are on the Yankees or you're on another [of the] 29 other teams.' He goes, 'You are either gonna be on this team and help us or you're not and hopefully you're helping somebody else, but that's your job. My job is to determining whether you're the one that's gonna make this better or not. Let me do my job and if you're doing your job, you'll be making money.' I loved it. It was like, I'll do my job, you can do your job. Don't give a shit about what I'm doing, I won't give a shit about what you're doing as long as we're both doing it. So yeah, putting on that uniform, like it was business, but I loved it. My entire goal after hip surgery, after elbow surgery, and everything I'd gone through was just get back on that mound and do my job and wanna do it as much as humanly possible."

FIRST GAME WITH THE YANKEES: September 27, 2012 vs. Toronto Blue Jays at Rogers Centre

Aardsma pitched the eighth inning of the Yankees' 6–0 loss to the Blue Jays.

"Well, it's not like rehab goes perfect. I was supposed to be back earlier and I had a little doubt in my elbow. Basically, right when we started throwing sliders and splits again, I had to get shut down for a month, so that kind of killed me from the contract standpoint. So there's lots of self-doubt, plus I had torn my groin. The team didn't know. I think the team did know but I wasn't telling anybody. It wasn't hard to see how much I was getting worked on it. I've got a wrap around my groin. I was taking stuff every day just to try to fight through that pain, just for that moment. So when you're talking about self-doubt, like nonstop self-doubt. Middle of a pennant race, rehab was a mess. You're back on the mound after all that stuff. I had doubt about my arm, but it was also like doubt in my subconscious 'cause my stuff was not the same. I was 92, 93 [mph], now I wasn't a hundred. I was always a hard-throwing guy. I understood everything I went through was to get there in that moment and then to continue it. This moment isn't the end all, be all. This is the start of a new road. I always looked at that as like, I need to get to this point to keep moving forward. I can't not get to that point.

"I gave myself like 20 seconds. Warming up in Toronto, warming up and then run to that mound. I warmed up ready for the inning. They throw the ball around and whenever I get it, I gave myself like 15 seconds and just enjoyed it. All the stuff I went through like all that process to get to this moment.

Immediately when that moment started the road to move forward and started that next journey. Here we go right now, first pitch of my next level. This is just one more pitch and then I gave up a home run. J. P. Arencibia, son of a bitch. I saw him after the game and I was like, 'What the fuck!' It was like the second pitch of the at-bat or something like that. He goes, 'Dude, I know you too well, I am not gonna get to your off speed [pitch]. I had to jump on a fastball as soon as I could get one.' Hit a base hit, why did it have to be a home run? But I think I got everything in there. I give up a home run, think a walk, a hit, a strikeout, a [groundout]. Got it all outta my system."

David Aardsma by Hideshi Yokoyama

2
STAN BAHNSEN

Pitcher Stan Bahnsen played parts of five seasons with the Yankees. In 1968, Bahnsen went 17–12 with a 2.05 ERA and was named the 1968 American League Rookie of the Year. He pitched in four games in 1966 and then four straight seasons for the Yankees from 1968 to1971. The right-hander was 55–52 for some poor Yankees teams during his tenure. In December 1971, the Yankees traded Bahnsen to the Chicago White Sox in a controversial deal for third baseman Rich McKinney, who never panned out in New York.

FIRST BASEBALL IDOL:

"I'm from Council Bluffs [Iowa], and they had a Triple-A team for St. Louis. My name's Stan and Stan Musial, he was with the Cardinals but that was a Triple-A team for the Cardinals so I kind of followed Stan Musial. Almost every weekend the Yankees were on the Game of the Week. I certainly admired the Yankees and I followed the Yankees and everybody followed the Yankees. I mean, they were the dominant team, when I was a kid, in the American League."

"We didn't have a major league team in Iowa. So, Des Moines [had] a Triple-A team and Omaha had a Triple-A team and there's lots of minor league teams around but everybody looked at the Game of the Week. I would say 60, 70 percent of the time it was a Yankees game. So, I followed the Yankees. I had nothing against the Yankees except they dominated so much that you felt sorry for everybody else. I followed Stan Musial because of my name and I followed the Yankees 'cause they were on TV most of the time."

FIRST DRAFT EXPERIENCE:

Bahnsen was selected by the Yankees in the fourth round of the 1965 MLB June Amateur Draft out of the University of Nebraska-Lincoln.

"I had just pitched one year in Nebraska and I had a really good year. This was the first year they were gonna have a draft in baseball and I went to the Basin League. The Basin League was a big league for college players. We had another pitcher, Gary Neibauer. We were both going to Rapid City, South Dakota, which is about 450 miles from where I lived. I had a car and we went up to Rapid City and about three days later, they had the draft. I had pitched two innings in the game because I'd turned my ankle. I couldn't start for a week or so, but I pitched and then my dad called me. He got a hold of me. I had a message to call him and I called him and he said, 'The Yankee scout is here.' I didn't even know I'd been drafted. Communication then, it wasn't like now where everything is covered, but [his father] says, 'The Yankees drafted you and they really want to sign you.' I talked to the scout but I had a sprained ankle so I thought, 'Well, I'll just go back a few days and see what happens.' Rapid City didn't care, they were all for me going as far as I could. This was the first year of the draft. It was my first year in college baseball. I was a sophomore but you couldn't pitch as a freshman on the varsity, so the scouts weren't allowed to talk to the players before. The year before, I'd had scouts talking to me after every game, probably. I had a couple come up to me and ask me if I'd sign if I was drafted. That's all they asked me 'cause they would've got in trouble, especially if they tried to negotiate or anything. So it was all new to me, so I was surprised.

"I never knew there was a scout at the game from the Yankees. I read the head scout's paperwork. Somebody sent me, or maybe he even [sent it] 'cause he had me number one on the draft choice because they didn't know if I would sign. They didn't wanna waste the draft choice. You don't wanna throw away a number one draft choice, so they took Bill Burbach, who made the big leagues. He didn't last that long, but he was a big kid from South Carolina somewhere. He had a good arm, but everyone's got a good arm in the big leagues.

"I drove back all the way. It's like 450 miles from Rapid City to Omaha, Council Bluff. I'm from Council Bluff, which is on the other side of Omaha. We were a suburb of Omaha. We played all the big Omaha schools. I had good competition in high school and I played all three sports. Got hurt real bad in football, concussions two years in a row and I couldn't play my senior year, which I was so happy for. I wanted to kiss the coach. I mean, the doctor said if you have another concussion, you may die now. I was unconscious for like a whole day. So I signed [with the Yankees]. Nobody knew what was going on with the draft. The year before, I'd have probably gotten three or four times the money I did 'cause the guys had the same numbers I did, before me. That's why scouts weren't allowed to talk to you because they didn't wanna, but I did have scouts asking me if I would sign if I was drafted. They didn't identify themselves as scouts. They probably didn't want to get in trouble, but I know the Yankee head scout had me rated as a first pick. The scout that came to me was not their head scout, he was a Midwest scout. They offered me $30,000. I was a kid, I didn't have any money, hardly anybody did in those days. My dad worked on the railroad; he made a decent living but we didn't splurge on anything. I got thirty grand and the first thing I did was buy a new Corvette."

"They sent me to Double-A ball, Columbus, Georgia, which was their first-place team in the Southern League and it was funny 'cause I wasn't well received there because I was a college kid. These guys had all played three years in a minor league, almost every one of 'em. The first guy I met at the hotel which I checked into Columbus, Georgia, was one of the players and he said he was waiting for me. I'm not gonna say his name but he was another pitcher. He came up, says, 'You Stan?' I said, yeah, 'Well, you're going down to Fort Lauderdale, a rookie league.' 'Well, they didn't tell me that,' but I went the other way. I went to Triple A and then the big leagues. After I pitched, they all thought, 'Okay, he belongs.' I can see the resentment, but I didn't know where Columbus, Georgia, was, but it's where Fort Benning is. Weekends were crazy 'cause everybody, all these young army guys were out but I was only there for about a month, 'cause half that time I was on the road. The Southern League's a good league and Double-A ball is good baseball, but I knew nothing about minor league baseball. We had Roy White on that team. We had Frank Fernandez, Steve Whitaker. We had several guys on that team that made the big leagues."

FIRST TIME HE SAW HIMSELF ON A BASEBALL CARD:

In 1967, Bahnsen was on a rookie card with Bobby Murcer.

"I'd figured I'd be on one. Bobby and I came up together. Then, the Rookie of the Year card, the bigger one that was (1969), that was a nice card. That's a separate card from the other card. That card I get in the mail a lot, you know, sign it. When I do shows, a lot of people want that card to sign, but that's nice at this age to still be remembered. People collect Rookie of the Year stuff. They collect MVP stuff, they collect all kinds of stuff. I get mail every day, several letters a day. One guy, he was from the Bronx, he sends me like an envelope every month with 17 cards in it with the same story, like he was giving these cards to kids and stuff. Then, there was a guy, said he worked in a firehouse and he did a big collection. He did a big charity fundraiser. You hear all kinds of stories, just tell me the truth. You're selling them. I know you're selling 'em or trying to. Some people get excited when they get autographed baseball cards. I would've too. I never thought of it when I was a kid."

FIRST PROFESSIONAL NO-HITTER:

Bahnsen threw two no-hitters while in the minors. On July 17, 1966, Bahnsen tossed a seven-inning no-hit, no-run game for the Yankees' Triple-A affiliate at Toledo as he beat Richmond. The no-hitter didn't become official until after the game as a call that was originally ruled a hit was changed to an error on third baseman Mike Ferraro. On July 9, 1967, Bahnsen was pitching for the Yankees Triple-A affiliate at Syracuse when he tossed a seven-inning perfect game against Buffalo.

"They changed the [ruling]. There was an error that they gave a hit. When they looked at it later, they decided, I guess it was an error. It didn't really matter to me that much, I was just glad we won the game, but yeah, I remember they changed it."

FIRST TIME BEING CALLED UP BY THE YANKEES:

"I was in Toledo. We had a good team up there. I had heard I was probably gonna get called. I was having a good year [in 1966]. Tom Seaver and I, he was with Jacksonville, I was with Toledo. We both were having really good years. Usually, from Triple-A ball, if you have a good year, you'll get called up at the end of the season. It's only a month and everybody expands their roster so they don't have to let anybody go or make a trade or anything. I had heard rumors that I'd probably get called up for the last month of the season, which I did. So you get called. I don't remember, who said what."

FIRST MAJOR LEAGUE MANAGER: Ralph Houk

"Ralph liked me because I had ROTC [training in] high school and he was a big military guy. He talked to me about his experiences in the war. [Houk served in World War II and reached the rank of major and that became his nickname.) So he used to call into his office once in a while 'cause I had three years of ROTC in high school. I went in the military with Bobby Murcer, Thurman Munson, we were together for the whole time. I was with the Yankees and we went to Fort Dix two weeks every summer, which was kind of tough, but you just did it. We had Frank Fernandez, Frank Tepedino, Joe Verbanic. We had like five guys in Army reserve. You were lucky if you'd get in a reserve. If you didn't, you were gonna get your ass kicked. Ralph was real good. He was a catcher and I think catchers make the best managers cause they're used to seeing the field. They can tell when a pitcher's losing it and they can tell when a pitcher's throwing alright, but not having any luck. He very seldom, I thought, made any mistakes about taking a pitcher out because of a circumstance. You know, like somebody drops a ball, a double play ball and two runs score and so they take the pitcher out. That's stupid, you know."

"Ralph would chew tobacco, which was one funny story. I had a play at first base. I beat the runner but the umpire called him safe. So I'm arguing with him and [Houk] pushes me out of the way. Ralph pushed me out of the way to not get me thrown out of the game for arguing. Because he chewed tobacco, he knew how to chew it one and then he knew how to argue with the other way. He would spray like a spray gun and I'm standing there watching this argument and all of a sudden, I start laughing. The reason I was laughing was because the umpire had so much tobacco all over his face, that was unbelievable, and it was a young umpire. I thought he was gonna start crying, but Ralph was good. I thought he was fair. It was tough managing. Every team has about four or five guys in reserves [who] had to go to summer camp for two weeks. So Thurman and I went to summer camp, but it was at Fort Dix, New Jersey. We had eight o'clock games at night. The reserves would let you out when you're done at five o'clock and we'd get up real early. Thurman would try to make night games when they were at home. He would work at 5:30 in the morning and then get back at probably one o'clock in the morning and get up again. I pitched that was a few times, but it never worked. I was just too tired."

FIRST SPRING TRAINING:

"When I went to spring training [in 1966], I assumed I was going to minor league training camp. Hollywood [where the minor league camp was located] is just south of Fort Lauderdale. I flew into Fort Lauderdale on a flight from Omaha and the guy picked me up and took me to the ballpark. I didn't know I was at the major league camp until I walked in. I got there real early 'cause the flight got in early. It was in the afternoon before they had a night game that night in Fort Lauderdale. The clubhouse guy came out and took me in and I'm walking and I said, 'Boy, that's a nice clubhouse.' I look and I see all these names. 'They put the minor leaguers with the major leaguers in here.' The guy said, 'No, you're in a big league clubhouse.' I said I was amazed because I'd never pitched an inning in the minor leagues. I was the last player cut. Johnny Keane was there and Ralph took over from Johnny Keane later on. The last two games in spring training, they pitched me in the ninth inning both games. I should have figured out what they're doing. They want me to be their closer. All the cuts that were made and I'm still there. Couple guys are injured but I'm a rookie and I'm not gonna say anything. Johnny Keane was there, he actually called me in. I think [general manager] Lee MacPhail might have been there but they said, 'We really love your arm. Our starting pitchers are set.' He said, 'We want you to be our closer,' and I said, 'I can't do it. I can't throw every day. I can't throw this hard every day, I'll be done in a year. They said, 'Okay, we respect that but we're loaded with starters. We need a closer.' They said, 'Okay, we'll send you, you'll go to Triple-A' at Toledo and we had a good year. Then, they called me up. The first time they brought me in, I came up in September with a couple other guys."

FIRST MAJOR LEAGUE GAME: September 9, 1966 vs. Boston Red Sox at Fenway Park.

Bahnsen pitched scoreless ball over the final two innings in a 2–1 win to earn the save in his major league debut.

"We had a flight to Boston. I hadn't pitched yet. A flight to Boston, I thought we were gonna crash because we had to fly by the tower twice to see if our landing gear was down. I said, 'Oh, great. Here's my big chance and I'm gonna get killed in an airplane.' We're only there for three days and then Boston is coming to New York. Ralph called me in the office. He said, 'We're gonna pitch you Monday against Boston in New York. I want you to stay in the dugout, watch the game and then get your throwing in later in the game 'cause we're going back to New York and you're due to throw. I'm watching the game. Fred Talbot was the starting pitcher, he was having the game of his life. He had a shutout going, he's probably given up two hits. The pitching coach [says], 'We'll get you throwing in the seventh inning 'cause we want you to get your throwing in before you start next Monday or Tuesday,' so I said, 'Okay.' So I go down there. I never heard some of the names called me in the world, other than that Boston bullpen. I thought it was exciting. I thought, 'I'm not gonna pitch in this game but they're all yelling at me, you know you're gonna get killed.' Jake Gibbs is warming me up, just throwing. Then, it's the eighth inning and

Jake points to in. I said, 'I'll go in after the game. I'm not gonna walk across the field.' He said, 'No, you're in the game.' I didn't know what to do, I was like, frozen, but it was good because I would've worried about it the whole game. So I went in, I was like so hyped up. I struck out the side on 10 pitches, all fastballs. I think it was [Tony] Conigliaro, yeah, [Joe] Foy, [Carl] Yastrzemski. I still got one more [strikeout] in the last inning."

"At the end of the game, everybody's excited. Everybody's patting me on the back. Mickey [Mantle] comes over and says, 'Why not take that ball over to Carl and have him sign it? He'd probably love to meet you right now.' So I'm thinking, 'I'm gonna get killed.' Mickey had that drawl and everybody just cracked up laughing. They wouldn't have let me go but I had the ball in my hands and I was almost in shock. I'm sitting in the locker, looking at the ball and thinking, what just happened in the last 20, 30 minutes. My wife, she's from Maine and Conigliaro was her favorite player so I had to relate that to her, but that was an unforgettable game. I've seen other managers do that with pitchers. They don't want them sit and fret about it a whole game. If I'd had sat worried about pitching all these guys for two hours and then have to finally go in the game. I thought I was just going to get ready for a start three days later, which I did. That game, Carl hit a home run off me so he got even."

FIRST EXPERIENCE WITH NEW YORK CITY:

"New York was different. They put me in a hotel right down in Manhattan. I walked outside and here's a guy with a giant snake wanting me to take a picture with his snake. I'm walking, looking for something to eat and a girl comes up to me, stupid me. She says, 'Hey boy, do you wanna date?' I said, 'I don't even know you. Why would I want to go out with you?' It was all good, you know. The money now. I remember the minimum salary was $7,500 for the year. They make that in less than one pitch now. I can't believe how things have changed in baseball."

FIRST TIME HE HEARD HE HAD WON THE 1968 AMERICAN LEAGUE ROOKIE OF THE YEAR AWARD:

"I think the Yankees called me and told me. I thought Reggie [Jackson] was still a rookie. I didn't even think about Rookie of the Year when I was playing all year, 'cause I thought Reggie was a rookie. He played too many games the year before. I didn't know that because it didn't enter my mind. I was excited."

FIRST INTERACTIONS WITH MICKEY MANTLE:

"Sometimes he showed the power and the speed and I thought, I saw him on TV when I was a kid. To be there and see this every day had to be amazing. The closest thing I had was Richie Allen when I was with the White Sox, he had one year [1972] like that. I was in Oakland with Reggie, but Reggie didn't have years like that when I was there. Mickey, you could see signs of his talent. I lockered right across from him, he was a mess. Both of his legs were totally wrapped with Ace bandages. He did it a lot just to get on the field. Sometimes fans didn't appreciate that, I didn't think, because he didn't have to do that but he really wanted to play. He thought he made a lot of mistakes. I went out with him a few times. He wanted to go out to dinner with me, just to talk to me. He said, 'Don't make mistakes like I did.' He was out there amongst the crowd in New York City a lot. It was funny when he and Roger [Maris] lived together for a while and Roger was totally different. Roger was real quiet. He wasn't a party guy at all but Mickey, you could see signs of things he could do, once in a while. When I was a kid, he did this all the time. It must have been amazing to see how far and above he was above everybody else in baseball as far as speed, power, arm.

"The other thing, the funny thing he did with rookies. Mickey had a great knuckleball. I don't know how many people know that. He would say, 'Rookie, you wanna throw?' and I'm like, 'Oh, yeah!' You throw in the outfield and back and he starts throwing knuckleballs and you couldn't catch 'em. They'd beat you up, they'd hit you. He'd be laughing. I played with Wilbur Wood, [Mantle] had a knuckleball as good as Wilbur Wood's knuckleball. There's no way Mickey Mantle is going to be on a pitching mound, but he could've. He might have played 10 more years. He asked me to go out and have dinner with him a few times. That was exciting. He said, 'Don't do like me. Don't be like me. You got a great arm. Just take care of yourself and you'll have a good career.' Which I did."

FIRST TIME HE CAME WITHIN ONE OUT OF A NO-HITTER: August 21, 1973 as a member of the Chicago White Sox vs. Cleveland Indians at Cleveland Stadium.

With two outs in the bottom of the ninth, Chicago's Walt Williams singled to spoil Bahnsen's bid for a no-hit, no-run game. Bahnsen retired Chris Chambliss to complete the one hit shutout.

"Walter was with us the year before in Chicago. He was a good hitter, a good contact hitter, you couldn't strike him out. Bill Melton came up to me, he was the third baseman. He's like, 'I'm gonna play in on the grass, and I said, 'Why?' He said, 'In case he bunts." It was two outs. I said, 'Walt and I are friends, he's not gonna bunt. Whatever you think.' So he played up on third base where the grass cuts the dirt in case [Williams] bunted. I threw him a curveball. He hit a little ground ball and Bill missed it by about four inches to his left. If he'd been playing back, I'd had it [a no-hitter] easy. I half agreed with him but now I kick myself in the butt for not telling him. I should've probably said, 'Well, if he's gonna get a hit, he's gonna have to earn it.

"I had a perfect game going against Minnesota one year. Eighth inning with two out and I think it was Bobby Darwin. I think that was the name, yeah, it was Bobby Darwin. Hit a rocket off the left field fence. Richie Allen on first, he's yelling, 'He missed first,' and Darwin knew he missed first base. He was already to second, almost and he turned around, running back, slid and he just beat the throw, 'cause he'd been out 'cause he hadn't touched first base yet. I got the next hitter out. I would've had a perfect game. I would've had a no-hitter. I think I had a walk in that game [Bahnsen gave up a second hit in the ninth inning but completed the shutout]. [Darwin] hit that ball, I thought, this ball's gone. It was a rocket. He deserved to get a hit. I didn't mind him getting a hit. I was glad it didn't go outta the park."

FIRST EXPERIENCE WITH THE "ORANGE BALL"

In March 1973, Oakland A's owner Charles O. Finley convinced baseball officials to use an orange- colored baseball in a spring training game. Offense was down and pitchers were dominating the game. Finley associated that decline with the hitter not being able to clearly see the white baseballs. While pitching for the A's in 1976, Finley tried to get Bahnsen to use the orange baseballs to warm up before a start.

"We were playing a Monday night game against Kansas City and I was pitching. [Finley] was professing [using] that orange ball. He said the hitters can see the ball better, the batting averages are going down and the pitchers are dominating. So I'm starting against Kansas City and we're in a pennant race. This was like a week left in the season and we're on national TV and I'm getting ready to go out [to the bullpen] and the bat boy comes over, hands me an orange baseball. I said, 'What's this?' He said, Mr. Finley wants me to warm up with this. I said, 'Why?' 'Because he wants the TV people to catch on to it. So I said, 'Let me see that ball,' and it was a dime store ball and it was lightweight. I don't know where he found it. It was painted orange, it wasn't orange, so I gave it back to the kid. I said, 'You're kidding me, with this line-up? I'm gonna warm up with this thing and I have to pitch to [George] Brett and all these guys?' So I sent it back. He was really upset, but I didn't care. Charlie was always about Charlie, he was a character. I liked him; he was kind of tough to deal with sometimes but that was funny."

FIRST TIME IN A SENIOR LEAGUE:

In 1989, Bahnsen pitched for a Senior Professional Baseball Association team in Florida called the Gold Coast Suns. Hall of Fame Manager Earl Weaver managed that team. In 1990, Bahnsen pitched for the Daytona Beach Explorers.

"I live in Pompano. Earl Weaver called me. He lived down there and he says, 'Stan, I'm gonna manage a team in the senior league here in Pompano.' He said, 'You wanna play on it?' He told me what it's about. He told me he had a lot of big-name players and he said, we'll play like two or three games a week. We'll give you like $10,000 a month. I said, 'God, that more than I made any month as a rookie.' We only played three games a week and nobody went to [the] games. We had some people, it didn't draw well. Some places it did actually draw decent but you didn't even know we were playing. It wasn't in the paper. It was never a success, really."

FIRST TIME PITCHING IN HOLLAND:

In 1992, Bahnsen accepted an invitation to be a player-coach for a team in the Danish Baseball League.

"My orthopedic surgeon had been in Europe a lot. My arm was okay, it was healed up, but I wasn't throwing. I saw him once in a while. He said, 'How's your arm?' I said, 'Why?' He said, 'I have a friend of mine, owns a team in Holland. They have like three or four different leagues and they have a few minor leaguers play.

They play like three or four games a week. They have regular ballparks, like our spring training facility in Fort Lauderdale. I wasn't doing it but the [team owner] offered me $10,000 a month to pitch like four games a month. So I went over there for three months and we had a good team. It was very interesting. Each team had a few minor league players from America, maybe one or two. I helped coach the pitchers. They had a few guys with talent. We had a catcher that was the MVP the year before. I didn't play with him, that was the year before, but the Phillies drafted him. It was a pretty good league. Some of the teams drew well, others didn't, but it was fun. The guy gave me my choice to live on the beach or in town, a nice apartment, gave me a brand-new car. [Danish players] didn't have the drive, they didn't get upset, they didn't have the fire in them like the American players do. It's kind of passive but they didn't get mad if somebody hit a home run off them. It was just different."

Stan Bahnsen by John Pennisi

3
STEVE BALBONI

Steve Balboni was a slugging first baseman who was nicknamed "Bye Bye Balboni" for his home run prowess. Balboni had two stints with the Yankees and played five of his eleven major league seasons in New York. Balboni was traded after the 1983 season but returned to play with the Yankees in 1989. In his second stint with the Yankees (1989-90), Balboni hit 34 home runs with 93 RBIs.

FIRST BASEBALL IDOL:

"I love baseball. I was a Red Sox fan. I grew up in New Hampshire, so I was a Red Sox fan. I liked watching the power hitters, but Carl Yastrzemski was probably, I would say, the first. I liked watching them all, but I mean he was the best player. He could pretty much do everything, you know, hit for average, hit for power."

FIRST MAJOR LEAGUE GAME HE ATTENDED AS A KID:

"It was the Red Sox game. My father took me. I was young so I don't really remember a lot. I remember, the shock walking into the stadium. It was just amazing. The green and size of it. I remember being overwhelmed by the stadium. We walked in, 'cause I had seen it on TV and it just was different."

FIRST COLLEGE EXPERIENCE:

Balboni attended Eckert College in St. Petersburg, Florida.

"It was something new. I grew up in New Hampshire, especially Manchester, it's a big baseball town. It wasn't like we're up here skiing and in hockey and everything, I mean baseball was big but when I got down to Florida, I mean it was a lot different. The coach I had, Bill Livesey, was incredible. It really taught me how to play the game, but it was so much more intense and at a higher level than I'd ever experienced before."

FIRST TIME PLAYING AT FENWAY PARK:

In 1977, Balboni played in the prestigious Cape Cod League and was named an All-Star. The All-Star Game was played at Fenway Park and Balboni was named the MVP.

"It was incredible to just play there. I mean, that was exciting in itself, but just hitting one home run. Two would be even better, but even just hitting one was incredible. I mean, growing up, watching the Red Sox play in that stadium. Seeing that Green Monster and just going in there and actually hitting it and it was really nice. My family was there. My sisters and my parents and it was a great experience."

FIRST DRAFT EXPERIENCE:

Balboni was chosen by the Yankees in the second round of the 1978 June Amateur Draft.

"I was home so the people I talked to were my family. Jack Butterfield was in charge of the scouting and everything. My coach, Bill Livesey, was working for the Yankees at that time. He had left the school in my junior year and started working for the Yankees so he was actually the scout I think that signed me. Jack Butterfield was in charge of scouting and player development and everything. He was the one that called me and told me. Yeah, I was excited, even though my family wasn't thrilled. I mean, Red Sox fans, being signed by the Yankees, but I was excited because it was the New York Yankees. No matter what kind of fan you are, the Yankees are the Yankees."

FIRST PROFESSIONAL EXPERIENCE:

Balboni began his professional career with the West Haven Yankees of the Double-A Eastern League in 1978.

"I was there and they wanted me to learn how to catch. So Stump Merrill was the coach there and they wanted me to go there, not to be a [starting] catcher, but just as another position. I went there for a couple of weeks but I wasn't playing much. Then, they decided to send me down to A-ball so by the time I got to A-ball, I really hadn't played much so it was kind of like, starting over. I started off really slow and it was kind of a weird experience for me because I wasn't starting at the Double-A level. Two weeks later, going down and now I'm playing every day but I really wasn't in great baseball shape to jump into the middle of the season. I did struggle the rest of that season."

FIRST REACTION TO GETTING THE CALL TO COME TO THE BIG LEAGUES:

Balboni was called up in April 1981.

"I started off a little slow in Triple A. I wasn't swinging that good at that time. Marshall Brant was probably doing a little better than I was and so they called him up but they had released him in that offseason, so he wasn't eligible to get called up at that time. I don't remember all the details but they couldn't call him up. I guess they found that out, so they called me up right after. It was kind confusing because [Brant] went up and then all of a sudden it was like, no, he's not going up, he can't.

"I was excited. I mean, it was an opportunity. I knew it was going to be a short time. It was just going to be because someone got hurt, but it was like this is an opportunity. You find out quickly in baseball, you really have to take every advantage of every opportunity because you don't always get that many."

FIRST TIME PUTTING ON A YANKEES UNIFORM:

"It was incredible. I mean it's hard to put it in words. It was just an incredible feeling. I think getting a lot of press, [announcers] Phil Rizzuto and Frank Messer really took a liking to me. So as I was coming up, Double A, and Triple A, they would keep talking about me and everything. So when I got there, a lot of Yankee fans already knew who I was and everything. It was pretty incredible.

"When I went up for the first time, I mean, it's hard to actually remember it because it's all kind of like a blur because I was really concentrating on walking up to the plate. The funny thing is, though, we were playing Detroit and I had faced the pitcher coming up through the minor leagues, so I was the only one who knew the pitcher. So guys were asking me what he threw. That was nice to know I was facing someone I had faced before."

FIRST IMPRESSIONS OF YANKEE STADIUM:

"There was nothing like the old Yankee Stadium. I mean, walking into Fenway was incredible, but Yankee Stadium. They have on the board all the history. They got old clips of Babe Ruth. They make sure you can see all the history there but it's pretty incredible. Walking out there for the first time. Playing there for a while, you see other players, especially that came from the National League or something. It's the same feel, it seemed like it was the same for everybody who walked in there the first time you walk in there. You look around. It's just not, it was different than any other stadium."

FIRST BIG LEAGUE HIT/FIRST RBI: April 22, 1981 vs. Detroit Tigers at Yankee Stadium

In his first major league at-bat, Balboni hit a booming triple off Tigers pitcher Howard Bailey in the third inning. In the seventh, Balboni walked with the bases loaded for his first run batted in.

"I don't remember what the count was, but I faced [Bailey] before and I knew he had a pretty good curveball and changeup. I wasn't going to do anything but look for a fastball and he [threw] me a fastball. He was trying to get inside and he left it over the plate and I hit it. Not as good as I could but I hit it really good and I remember it bounced. I hit like 400 [feet] and it was 430 to left-center and it bounced and hit the fences. So I hit it about 425 and I had to run it out. I ended up with a triple.

"That [first RBI] was a walk. That same game. I got up to the plate, I mean, I had chills. I think it might have been one of the most incredible feelings I've ever had in baseball because I had hit the triple. Then, my next time up, I think the game was tied or something. It was a close game and I got up with the bases loaded. I just remember the place going crazy. It was hard to think. Obviously, you want to hit a home run but I just remember I wanted to hit the ball hard. I didn't want to strike out, I just wanted to have a good at-bat.I ended up walking which wasn't easy. I wasn't looking for a walk. That was the last thing I was looking for." (Balboni's walk gave the Yankees a 3–2 lead during a five-run seventh inning as they defeated the Tigers, 7–2.)

FIRST OLD-TIMERS' DAY:

"We were playing I think in Toledo, Ohio, or something when I was at [Triple-A] Columbus. It wasn't easy to get to New York but they wanted me up there right away. I had to get up real early to get a flight. It was kind of a long day so it wasn't a direct shot. It was from one airport to another. I think I had to go through Pittsburgh and wait for hours. So I was really tired. When I got to Yankee Stadium, I went right to the stadium. I hadn't even checked in the hotel yet or anything and I was exhausted. So I just went into that player's lounge and fell asleep. Laid on the couch and fell asleep. When I woke up, they were all there, it was Mickey Mantle, Joe DiMaggio, everybody was there. It was like I was dry. I was just in baseball Heaven. It was strange because I'm laying there and they're all walking around. You know, it was embarrassing but it was kind of incredible."

FIRST HOME RUN: May 13, 1982 vs. Oakland Athletics at Oakland-Alameda County Coliseum

Balboni hit his first major league home run, a two-run shot off A's pitcher Tom Underwood in the top of the first inning.

"It was in Oakland. It didn't seem like a big ballpark but the ball really didn't carry great there. You had to hit it. It was a great feeling. That's what my whole career was, I mean, that I had power. It wasn't just home runs. To me, the most important thing was RBIs. I didn't go up there looking for home runs, especially with guys on base. I definitely didn't even think about home runs, it was mainly getting the runs in and trying to hit the ball hard. That was one thing. When I was young and I got into the Instructional League, my first couple of years, the biggest thing they impressed on me was don't try and hit home runs. Just try to hit the ball hard. Jack Butterfield told me, "What we want you to do is try and hit the ball hard once again. If you can do that, you'll have a good career.' That's kind of what I tried to do, just go up there and just try and hit the ball hard. Not really think about home runs but I've always had power. I've always had this swing, where if I did hit the ball good, usually in the air, usually was a double or a home run. Fortunately, I didn't have to do anything. It was just the swing I had, it was just a matter of making solid contact."

FIRST GRAND SLAM HOME RUN: July 26, 1983 vs. Texas Rangers at Arlington Stadium

Balboni cleared the bases with his first grand slam home run off Rangers pitcher Frank Tanana.

"It was in Texas. It was funny because we had guys on second and third. I was hitting behing Lou Piniella and it was so hot there. It was like 105 [degrees]. It was incredibly hot. Lou had heat stroke. Billy Martin was the manager. [Piniella] comes in and he's like in real bad shape. They're gonna take him out of the game but he's up that inning. Lou was a mess. He basically dragged his bat, but they really sent him up because they're gonna walk him obviously to get to me. He went up there and walked intentionally, went to first and they had to take him out of the game, but he was a mess. Then I came up and hit a homer. A grand slam off Frank Tanana."

FIRST TIME HE SAW HIMSELF ON A BASEBALL CARD:

"When I signed, Topps was the first one there and Rawlings. I liked their gloves. My first spring training, I signed all of them. I know I was impressed. I know it was something special because when you're a kid, you're collecting baseball cards. Now you're looking at that, you want a baseball card. I think my first one was that rookie card with Andre Robertson and Andy McGaffigan."

FIRST HAND VIEW OF THE "PINE TAR GAME":

The famous "Pine Tar Game" took place on July 24, 1983 at Yankee Stadium. Royals third baseman George Brett hit a two-run homer in the top of the ninth off Yankees reliever and fellow Hall of Famer Rich "Goose" Gossage to give Kansas City a 5–4 lead. Yankees manager Billy Martin claimed Brett had used an illegal bat because the pine tar on it exceeded the limit specified in the rule book. Home plate umpire Tim McClelland ruled the bat was illegal and called Brett out, negating the home run. Brett famously stormed out of the dugout to get at McClelland. American League President Lee MacPhail upheld the Royals protest and ruled the game to be resumed from that point it was stopped. The game resumed three weeks later with the Royals prevailing in a 5-4 win. Balboni was 0 for 2 in that game before Don Mattingly pinc hit for him in the seventh inning.

"We were in Kansas City and everyone saw the bat. George [Brett] was using that bat. He didn't wear gloves and used pine tar. His bat wasn't real fat at the top. It wasn't a real top-heavy bat, so he put pine tar in the middle. Every time he put the [weighted] donut on, it would drag the pine tar down towards the top of the bat. I mean, you could see the pine tar went up pretty high. They knew if he does anything, we're going to check the bat. Nothing happened in Kansas City. When we went back to New York and he hit the home run, the plan was to do it. It wasn't like it came out of nowhere. They were just waiting for him to do something so that they could check the bat. I didn't know George at the time and when I saw him coming out of the dugout, I thought he was gonna hit me. I had no idea who he was. He looked like he was gonna attack them."

FIRST TIME BEING TRADED:

In December, 1983, the Yankees traded Balboni and pitcher Roger Erickson to the Kansas City Royals for pitcher Mike Armstrong and minor league catcher Duane Dewey.

"[Royals manager] Dick Howser called me. I had met him in spring training but I didn't know him. It was mixed feelings because it was hard to get a shot with the Yankees, but it was such a great experience being there. I didn't want to leave, but after talking to Dick Howser on the phone, I was really excited about going to Kansas City. When I got there, I was going to a really good organization. They were a winning organization. They were there every year going through those late '70s and early '80s with the Yankees. It was really exciting for me to go there, especially after talking to Dick Howser and all the confidence he had in me. It was pretty special. It was after they had all the drug problems and they were kind of [rebuilding]. They had a lot of young players coming up because a lot of veterans were now off the team. I felt like it was a great situation to go into but there was still a part of me that was sad to leave the Yankees."

FIRST POSTSEASON EXPERIENCE:

1984 ALCS with the Royals vs. Detroit Tigers. Kansas City lost all three games (ALCS was a best three-of-five series in 1984). Balboni won a World Series with the Royals a year later.

"It was great. That's what you play for and looking back, it was really the most fun you can have in baseball. You weren't thinking about stats, you weren't thinking about numbers or anything else. All you really cared about was winning. That started in late September. We were fighting to get to win the division and all those games mattered. I just remember it being a lot of fun. I think being such a young team, I think we were excited that we made it, but we did have veteran players, Hal McRae, George Brett, Frank White. They wanted to win, so we wanted to win. We thought we could, but Detroit had a really good team. We played them well during the season but they were just a really good team."

Steve Balboni by Eric Raleigh

4
RON BLOMBERG

The Yankees made Ron Blomberg the number one overall pick in the 1967 MLB June Amateur Draft. Blomberg was highly recruited in three sports at Druid Hills High School in Atlanta, Georgia. Being of the Jewish faith made for a good match with the large Jewish population in New York City. Blomberg had a left-handed swing that was made for Yankee Stadium but his career was cut short by a number of knee and shoulder injuries.

FIRST DRAFT EXPERIENCE:

Blomberg had scholarship offers to play basketball for the legendary John Wooden at UCLA or play football for the legendary Bear Bryant at Alabama, but he signed with the Yankees.

"The only way I would've signed to play football or play basketball if I was not drafted by the New York Yankees. The Yankees had the number one draft pick because they had the worst record [in 1966]. If they started winning, I would not have been the number one draft pick. Well, not by the Yankees. The Chicago Cubs already told me if the Yankees did not draft me, they're going to draft me number one and they drafted number two. I already made up my mind if the Yankees were not going to draft me, I was going to sign and play basketball or football."

"That [signing] was a no brainer for me being a Jew, coming up to New York City. I became a role model to so many kids up in New York. The greatest part about it back then, we made no money. We made no money whatsoever so everybody had second jobs. My second job during the offseason, I was related to every Jew and I did every wedding. I lit every candle. That was my secondary job every weekend on a Saturday. If not real religious, of course, Sunday. I did every wedding, every Bar Mitzvah, Bat Mitzvah [for girls] so I was related to every Jew in New York City. It was really fun. The people were unbelievable to me, even to this day."

FIRST TIME MEETING THURMAN MUNSON:

"What made us so good together, because we came from different background. I was the number one draft choice in '67, he was the number one draft choice in '68. I got to meet him in '69 down in Fort Lauderdale in spring training and he loved to play golf. He loved to fish and he loved to eat. Those are the three kickers that I loved. I come from Georgia and Atlanta. Back then, Atlanta was a Southern town. Of course, Thurman came from Canton. Ohio. That was a Midwest, blue collar town and we just hit it off. The greatest thing in the whole world to be part of the New York Yankees, to be able to talk to people like yourself and the greatest thing to me was rooming with Thurman and to really get to know a person who was our team captain and who was a guy that we would do anything for. Thurman was the best of the best and he deserves to be in the Hall of Fame and I'm going to do everything I can to help promote him to get him in."

FIRST TIME BLOMBERG INTRODUCED MUNSON TO JEWISH FOOD:

"It's very simple. Because we trained down in Fort Lauderdale, of course, Miami is just 45 minutes away from Fort Lauderdale. Me being a Jew from the South, I knew about all the matzo balls, the pastramis, the corned beefs but we didn't have the good stuff like we have in New York. The second biggest Jewish city in the country was Miami. I got to know a lot of the delicatessens down there because I used to eat down there and bring them pictures and baseballs. So, when Thurman and I became friends, because he loved to eat and I loved to eat, I took him to quite a few delis down in Miami. He loved them. He never knew what a matzoh ball was, he never knew pastramis, corned beef, half sours [pickles]. He never knew Dr. Brown's [soda], he never knew about the potato salad and cole slaw. When I talked to him about a bagel, he said, 'Yeah, we get Lenders down in Canton.' Once we became friends, he said, 'I'm going to take you to one of the best places we're going to eat.' He took me to White Castle hamburgers. I'm taking him to the expensive Jewish food, so he takes me to the nickel White Castles, but we got along so well and he was such a wonderful man. He was such a wonderful family person. That's what I want the people to realize what type of person he was and what type of general he was out on that field. As soon as he put that uniform on, he had that 'it' factor and you knew right off the bat that he's going to do something and he's going to lead. He was the team captain as soon as he put on that Yankee uniform."

FIRST TIME MEETING JOE PEPITONE:

"This guy was so talented on the field and off the field. Number one, he was a great ballplayer when he wanted to and when he showed up for the game, because a few time Joe would say, 'Well, I'd rather fish than play in a ballgame this weekend.' He was so talented, I mean, he could run, he could throw, he could field and he could hit with the best of them if he wanted to. Number two, Joe was always a party type of person. We used to frequent his place, his establishment. You probably don't even know this, Joe could sing. Joe could dance and tell stories with the best of them. Thurman was always upset with him because he never gave 120 percent every time he was at the ballgame. He would look up at the stands, trying to find somebody to party with. Thurman was a guy that whenever he was on the field, he gave 120 percent. When Thurman did not see somebody that really, actually gave 120 percent, he gets a little bit upset and he had a few words with Joe a few times.

"I was just a young kid and the people that really got on him was [Mickey] Mantle, [Joe] DiMaggio, Yogi [Berra] and all those guys. Clete Boyer, Phil Linz, all those guys always [got] on him because you had no idea what hairpiece he would have, like a blonde streak on the back of the back of it. Even back then, that was a big deal. Then he'd have it flushed up and it looked like a birdcage. It looked like he had like four or five birds in it and he was just so funny. You used to watch him. It was so fun to watch him fluff it up. Back then a hair dryer was a big deal because nobody had any idea what a real hair dryer [was] and he used it. Even when he was out on the field, he used to come in and used to blow dry. He used to fluff up his hair in his hat."

FIRST CONFRONTATION WITH GEORGE STEINBRENNER OVER LENGTH OF HIS HAIR:

"We get into the clubhouse. It was Thurman, it was Catfish [Hunter], I think it was [Graig] Nettles so there was an envelope [at some lockers] and there was like four or five guys who just picked up the envelope and it said they wanted to see us in George Steinbrenner's office up there. I'm hitting .400, Thurman was hitting over .300, [Lou] Piniella was hitting the ball extremely well. Catfish was pitching real well and the team was just coming up a little bit. We knew they're not going to trade us, we didn't think so we come to the ballpark, we went up there. First thing, George had a barber up there and he said, 'You know the Yankee rule and your hair is too long.' The first thing I said to him, I said, 'Screw you. I mean you can release me now and I'll get picked up,' and I didn't have no idea what I was saying. Thurman did the same thing. So we go downstairs. We left there, we yelled at him, he yelled back at us and we said, okay, there's two things, we're gonna be traded, we're gonna get released. You can't release us and we all get traded at the same time together. So we come back the next day and there was another envelope. I said, 'Oh no, I got my walking papers,' and all these guys got theirs and I said, it couldn't happen. So I opened it up, it was a hundred dollar bill and he said to us, 'I really respect sticking up for yourself.' We respected him, we yelled at him, he yelled at us. We told him to screw himself a hundred thousand times, but that's the type of relationship that we actually had."

FIRST IMPRESSION OF BILLY MARTIN:

"When Billy was a manager, how many times I'm sitting on the bench or getting ready to hit and there's a phone call from upstairs, George said, 'I want you to put this guy in. I want you to put this guy in,' and Billy would always say, 'Hey, I'm not taking any more phone calls from you. Don't call me up anymore.' And he hangs up the phone. We said, 'Okay, Billy's gonna be going again. He is going to another team and we're gonna be getting another manager.' [George] respected Billy too. He respected him in a sense where he got rid of him back and with three, four times and he had to pay him, three, four times. Jill [Billy's widow], she's still getting paid from all [these] contracts."

FIRST DESIGNATED HITTER IN BASEBALL HISTORY:

Blomberg made baseball history when he was the first player to bat in a major league game as a designated hitter. On April 6, 1973, at Boston's Fenway Park, Blomberg came to bat as the Yankees' designated hitter and walked with the bases loaded in the top of the first inning.

"It's unbelievable because, when the DH came out in '73, nobody had any idea what it was going to contribute. Nobody ever thought it's going to last. They looked at the DH, to be honest with you, as a glorified pinch-hitter. We joked about it down in spring training because everybody wanted to be the DH. People will call me back every single year to talk about the rule but I think it's great for the game of baseball.

"When I came up as a DH, it was a mistake because I hurt my leg. We were not conditioned to be the DH, they just threw us in, just go hit it. If you look at the guys now, they are weaned to be the DH. You got Little Leagues, you got high school baseball, you got college, you got majority of minor league baseball. When we played, we had no idea how to really warm up before the ballgame. During the ballgame, we sat on the bench. These guys nowadays, they got their own hitting cages. They got their own computers. They watch everything so it's really a specialized position. In '73, I was coming off a pretty good year in '72 and they wanted somebody to get on base, to drive in runs. I played gap to gap. I hit a few home runs but mostly my game was gap to gap, get on base, drive in runs. That was me.

"For myself, being the DH, it was hard to adjust to that position because it is a position. People say, 'Well, you just get your bat and go up there and hit.' It's not like that because you got to watch the pitcher, how he pitches. Then you gotta go sit on the bench for maybe, two, two and a half innings. That is very difficult to do When I became the first DH up in Boston, up in Fenway Park, they had such a small little runway where you could get yourself into shape to really stretch your muscles. It was 34 degrees and Luis Tiant was pitching. I mean, he was throwing about 96, 97 miles an hour. We had no runway to get yourself in shape. It was very hard. Back in those days, Fenway Park did not even have heaters. It was really hard to adjust to that, but nowadays, these guys, they got the whole world. They got everything."

FIRST THING THAT COMES TO MIND ABOUT HAVING HIS BAT IN COOPERSTOWN:

The bat that Blomberg used in the first plate appearance as a designated hitter is displayed at the Baseball Hall of Fame in Cooperstown, New York.

"That they can never take it away. The good part about it is, being the DH and that's where my book Designated Hebrew [with co- author Dan Schlossberg] came out and being a Jew, coming up to New York City and your bat's in Cooperstown and you got [millions of] Jews following you and stuff. I go up to Cooperstown almost every year. We go up there, sign autographs and stuff with the Hall of Famers up there. I have a New Jersey camp. It's the largest

Jewish sleepaway camp in the country. I go up there in July and August and we always take a trip. I always take my kids to see my baseball bat and you know what? They can never take it away. I got in the Hall of Fame, the back door. All those other guys got into the Hall of Fame, the front door, but it's still something there. It's a new era in the game of baseball in '73 and I started it. A Jewish guy from the South coming up to New York, wearing the Yankee pinstripes and being the first DH in major league history. I mean, it's an honor. It's been great. I have such a great time with it."

Ron Blomberg by John Pennisi

5
WADE BOGGS

Hall of Fame third baseman Wade Boggs played 18 seasons in the major leagues, five with the Yankees, where he was part of their 1996 world championship team. Boggs played a key role in the World Series win. In Game 4 in Atlanta, the Yankees rallied from a 6–0 deficit to force extra innings against the Braves. With two out and the bases loaded in the 10th inning, Boggs was sent up as a pinch- hitter and drew a walk on a 3-2 pitch to force in the go-ahead run as the Yankees tied up the series at two wins apiece. They went on to win the Series in six games.

FIRST DRAFT EXPERIENCE:

Boggs was a seventh-round pick of the Boston Red Sox in the 1976 MLB June Amateur Draft from H. B. Plant High School in Tampa, Florida.

"I guess a Kansas City scout, when he scouted me here in Tampa, it was for two games or something. It was one of those that, you shouldn't draft this kind of guy. He said a lot of things but George [Digby, Red Sox scout] saw that there was something in my swing that was conducive to other people he's seen play the game. So with five and a half years in the minor leagues and the seasoning that I had once I got to the big leagues in '82, I was ready."

FIRST REACTION TO PLAYING IN THE LONGEST PROFESSIONAL BASEBALL GAME:

In April 1981, the Pawtucket Red Sox beat the Rochester Red Wings, 3–2 in 33 innings, the longest game in professional baseball history. The game began on April 18 and carried over to the early morning hours of April 19 but was suspended with the game tied after 32 innings. The 33rd inning was played later that season on June 23. Boggs, who was the third baseman for Pawtucket, was 4-for-12 and tied the game in the bottom of the 21st inning after Rochester had taken a 2–1 lead in the top of the inning.

"Probably [remember] all the cracked bats that we were burning in the dugout to keep ourselves warm. It was freezing that night. It was one of those games after about the 15th or 16th inning that you just sort of looked around and said we could play forever and no one score. It just kept going on and on and they tried to get a hold of the league president and kept calling his house. Back then we didn't have the use of cell phones and things of that nature. Just tried to keep trying to get a hold of him and then finally they did and the last pitch was thrown about four that morning."

FIRST MAJOR LEAGUE GAME: April 10, 1982 as a member of the Boston Red Sox vs. Baltimore Orioles at Memorial Stadium in Baltimore.

"[Went] 0-for-4. I remember the trees in Baltimore had a huge white house in centerfield. Early in the season in Baltimore, these trees wouldn't fill in so the white house sort of came into play. With [Orioles pitcher Dennis] Martinez's change up, you really couldn't tell the difference. It wasn't the kind of debut you hope you would have. One of those times that you jump in and get your feet wet. Coincidentally, the first major league game that I ever saw, I played in."

FIRST EXPERIENCE PLAYING FOR THE YANKEES:

After spending his first 11 seasons with the Boston Red Sox, Boggs signed a three-year contract with the Yankees prior to the 1993 season.

"I wanted to stay in the American League and I wanted to stay on the East Coast so my father could stay up at night and watch games. I was familiar with the American League, didn't want to change leagues and have to learn new pitchers and things of that nature, so that sort of made an easy decision to become a Yankee.

"I had the best of both worlds. I got to play for two organizations that are so rich in history and going to New York and starting their rebuilding process. New York, they were sort of [floundering] in sixth and seventh place. When I went over there, the mentality changed and started building players around like personalities like the Spike Owens, the Jimmy Keys, Paul O'Neills, and mixing in the young guys.

Derek Jeter, the Bernie Williams, the Jorge Posadas. They started filling all the positions and then we really took off in '94 and '95. In '95, we run into the buzzsaw, [Hall of Fame pitcher] Randy Johnson, in Seattle. Then, '96, wound up getting Tino Martinez to take Don Mattingly's place. That's when every piece of the puzzle fell into place and wound up winning a World Series that year. It was a tremendous, enjoyable time that I had in New York. I loved playing for the Yankees as much as I loved playing for the Red Sox. Like I said, the best of both worlds."

FIRST YANKEES MANAGER:

"I had Buck Showalter the whole time, '93, '94, '95. Then, Joe Torre in '96 and '97. Buck's a little field general. Preparedness is probably his strong suit. Joe Torre's more of a laid back, kind of let the guys go ahead and do their own thing. So that made it really easy because we had so many veterans on that ballclub. Then we just policed ourselves and nothing really ever got outta hand."

FIRST REACTION TO WINNING THE WORLD SERIES IN 1996:

After the Yankees beat the Atlanta Braves in Game 6 at Yankee Stadium to win the 1996 World Series, Boggs was seen riding horseback with an NYPD officer who was part of the crowd control detail that was on the field to keep fans from trespassing.

"I was going nuts and we were doing the dogpile on the mound and we decided to take a victory lap. 'Till this day, I've never looked at the video or gone back and really saw how I got up on this horse. The next thing I know, I'm in center field on the back of a horse and [I'm] not a big fan of horses. Yeah, it was one of those impromptu, how in the heck did I get on the back of this horse kind of thing and riding around. A lot of pictures were taken and got to home plate, got off the horse, thanked the police officer and then went into the clubhouse for the champagne fountain and that was just absolutely spectacular."

FIRST TELEVISION ACTING EXPERIENCE:

Boggs made an appearance on the TV sitcom Cheers in 1988. Boggs appeared as himself and was accosted by the regulars in the cast who thought he was a fake. Boggs was also one of the baseball players whose voice was used in the "Homer at the Bat" episode of the classic cartoon, The Simpsons.

"The Simpsons was just a voice-over, did it in LA when we went out to play the Angels. On set with the cast [of Cheers] and doing all the prep work and learning lines and going over various things and meeting everyone and sort of getting your feet wet in the industry and go to one of the top episodes of all time, Cheers. We had a blast doing that and it turned out great."

Wade Boggs by Maz Adams

6
JOBA CHAMBERLAIN

Joba Chamberlain was a highly touted prospect who pitched seven seasons for the Yankees.Expectations were high when Chamberlain made his debut in August 2007, but injuries and indecision on whether he should be a starter or a reliever plagued him throughout his career. When Chamberlain first came to the majors, he was operating under the "Joba Rules" that were designed to keep him healthy by not using him on consecutive days and giving him a day off for every inning pitched.

FIRST DRAFT EXPERIENCE:

Chamberlain was a first-round pick of the Yankees in the 2006 MLB June Amateur Draft from the University of Nebraska-Lincoln.

"Well it was a long day 'cause I just had my son, so I was walking him around and the phone calls are going. You're supposed to go here, you might get drafted here, well, they'll take you at this time. Then you just kind of wait and we didn't really have what they have today as far as the draft goes during

normal years. So it was kind of just on my phone and walking my son back and forth and then just checking the computer. Finally, once we got the call and the Yankees [drafted me], then it was kind of a media circus of going to school and doing the interviews with everybody. Obviously excited to be drafted by such a storied franchise."

FIRST PROFESSIONAL EXPERIENCE:

Late in 2006, Chamberlain made his pro debut with West Oahu of the Hawaii Winter Baseball League. In 2007, Chamberlain, who was rated one of the top prospects in the Yankees system, moved quickly through the system as he played A-ball in Tampa, was promoted to Double-A Trenton and finally with Triple -A Scranton/Wilkes-Barre.

"I think my goal was originally to get to Double A in my first year. I thought if I can get there, that's a great start and we'll continue to move forward from there. Initially, that was my goal and that ended up getting there quick, going to the Futures Game and then getting called up again. I think I spent less than three months in the minor leagues before I got the call, so it kind of happened all so fast that I didn't really have time to think about it."

FIRST PITCHING COACH:

"Scott Aldred, I had him in Hawaii and then obviously got to be with him in Double A. He was, first of all, so easy to talk to and he could get his message across and make me understand it 'cause I'm a very visual person. If he tells me to do something, sometimes it's hard, but he was just so good at breaking everything down and just an unbelievable pitching coach and a great man. It was somebody that I think when I looked back on it, I'd reach out to him if I was struggling and he would kind of watch some video and fire back some stuff."

FIRST MAJOR LEAGUE GAME: August 7, 2007 vs. Toronto Blue Jays at Rogers Centre

"Well, we were in Toronto and we actually cleared benches twice that day, so it was an interesting first day for me. The first time wasn't a good look. I was nervous and I just happened to be in the bathroom and we cleared benches the first time. So I'm coming out, getting ready to go to the back of the bullpen and all of a sudden my pitching coach, Nardi Contreras, [said] you better get out there and I'm like looking at the TV and I'm like, gosh, this is not the first impression they run out of the bullpen. Here I am in the bathroom, now I look like an awful teammate. [We] had some older veteran guys, so that walk back to the bullpen, oh man, they let me have it for sure."

FIRST MAJOR LEAGUE MANAGER: Joe Torre

"Just a great man. Obviously, an unbelievable name in the game of baseball. I was fortunate enough to play for long enough to have some really good managers, most of 'em were catchers. The way he went about his business was just so methodical, but there was always a method to the madness. It was awesome to be able to say you played for him in the old Yankee Stadium and just the storied history that he has as a player and manager. It was one of those things as a baseball fan, you never think you're gonna be able to play for a man like that and that's your first manager. So it's really cool."

FIRST EXPERIENCE WITH "JOBA RULES":

"Honestly, you're just happy to be in the big leagues. I mean, I was 21 years old and my dream had come true to get to the pinnacle of where it was, especially with the Yankees, so I didn't really think about it. I mean, shoot, if they'd asked me to fold towels, I'll stay in the big leagues, I'd have done whatever. I think it was just one of those, the competitive side gets a little frustrated because obviously you're succeeding, you wanna be out there as much as you can and it was something that was just pushed right there. It was really the only thing I knew so I didn't know any different. I'd obviously never thrown out of the pen before so I'm trying to watch guys and put cream on and take an Advil or like, I didn't know what to do, so I'm just trying to watch guys and do that. So when I got up there, it was kind of, hey, you throw one inning, you're gonna have a day off and throw two, you're gonna have two days off. So it was the only thing I really knew. Then, as you get older and you become a veteran guy, you can kind of see, you know, the good and bad about it."

FIRST POSTSEASON EXPERIENCE: 2007 AL Division Series vs. Cleveland Indians

Chamberlain made his postseason debut in Game 2 of the American League Division Series against the Cleveland Indians. In the bottom of the eighth, Chamberlain was plagued by a swarm of midges (similar to mosquitoes) and threw a wild pitch that allowed the tying run to score from third with two out. The Indians went on to win the game and eventually the series in four games.

"I came in to get Andy [Pettitte] out of the inning in the seventh and there was normal nighttime bugs, nothing crazy. Then, coming back out for the eighth and all of a sudden, I'm just like, what is going on here? So they come out, they spray, which as we now know, it did not work. I mean, it's hard enough in that situation. You know, it's your rookie year, you're in the playoffs, it's a big game and it's hard enough to get outs against these guys. They're the best in the world, let alone having a million midges around your face. I mean, you're in the moment so you're trying to stay focused as much as you can. I remember having a conversation with Derek [Jeter] after a few years. I was like, man, why didn't you come help? He goes, 'Dude, every time I got closer to the mound, it got worse.' I was like, thanks, I appreciate that. I guess when I finally saw it on TV, yeah, it was bad. Then I was digging 'em outta my ears and my eyelids. At the end of the day, I didn't do my job. That was the most frustrating part of them bugs."

FIRST WORLD SERIES EXPERIENCE: 2009 vs. Philadelphia Phillies

"It was a different feel. I mean, '07, I mean these guys have already won. They know what they're doing but then you get '09. It's a new stadium, new beginnings, we make a bunch of free agent deals and so a little bit different buzz and it was just something that felt right. When we started getting the walk-off wins, you could kind of feel it. There was a vibe about like this is special, this team's really, really good. I remember trying to get to record the last out, but I just ran and I was at the bottom of the stairs and I was just hoping I didn't get punched in the head by a swinging fist celebrating. It just kinda all happened so fat. You run out on the pile to celebrate. It was definitely a cool moment."

FIRST IMPRESSION OF MARIANO RIVERA:

"Just his routine. Like it didn't matter it if was a boat race, he did the same thing. He grabbed [the] ball, he stretched, he did his stuff. There was always something that he told me. He goes, remember, you get eight pitches to warm up when you get in the game. He goes, so save some here because you don't need to let it all out here. You gotta go in the game. So it didn't matter. He never panicked. He never like, okay, you got the next hitter. Did not matter. He still went out, grabbed [the] ball, did his stuff and got his pitches in. There was never a panic like, hey, I need to hurry up and get this going. I think it's just the way he was able to always stay calm, no matter what situation."

On Rivera's famous cutter:

"It's not that easy. I mean, he made it look easy, but the crazy thing is he always had that little hiccup during the year where he would blow one or two saves and everybody would lose their minds. Like, he's done. I remember one time where he asked me to stand in and [Bullpen coach Mike] Harkey's catching and [Rivera's] throwing. You see it on TV but until you actually stand in the box and see what that pitch does, it's incredible. It literally gets to you, says, hold on, I'm gonna go ahead and take a left. It's unbelievable. Like playing the Xbox [or] PlayStation. It was crazy. Just to watch him and be able to play catch with him and then actually just be in the box even though it's a flat ground, it's not like he's really going a hundred percent. When you actually get to see it, it's incredible and everybody tries to do it. Some are good, some aren't. I'll never forget when they got all over him at the All-Star Game when he was showing 'Doc' [Hall of Fame pitcher Roy Halladay] how to do it. I'm like, oh man, Doc's already good enough. Don't let him get another weapon."

Joba Chamberlain by John Pennisi

7
ROCKY COLOVITO

Rocky Colavito played for six teams during his 14-year major league career. Colavito was born and bred in the Bronx, where he attended Theodore Roosevelt High School, but dropped out after his sophomore year to pursue a career in baseball. In 1968, Colavito's final season in the majors, he was released by the Los Angeles Dodgers in early July and the Yankees signed him a few days later. Colavito played in only 39 games for the Yankees but he was a two-way player for them in one game. On August 25, 1968, the Yankees hosted the Detroit Tigers in the first game of a doubleheader. Colavito was not in the starting lineup but he came into the game as a relief pitcher. He pitched 2 2/3 scoreless innings, giving up one hit with two walks and a strikeout.

FIRST SPRING TRAINING:

Colavito was playing semipro ball when he was invited to join the Yankees' minor league camp in spring training in 1951 without a contract. The Cleveland Indians had an offer on the table, so Colavito chose to go with Cleveland.

"It really wasn't that tempting [to go with the Yankees] and I'll tell you why. [Cleveland was] willing to give me money. Actually,

I wasn't going to spring training with the Yankees. They offered me to go to spring training [at] the minor league facility, so I didn't think that was very good. Why should I go to spring training with them, even though I was a Yankee fan, when the Indians were willing to give me a $3,000 bonus —$1,250 when I signed, $750 if I lasted 30 days, and another thousand if I lasted 60 days. I gave my father a thousand. I gave my brother, Dominic, who didn't want to take it, a hundred dollars because he always gave me money more than anybody. I just felt like let me get them something."

FIRST PROFESSIONAL EXPERIENCE:

Colavito was 17 years old when he made his professional debut for the Daytona Beach Islanders, the Class-D Florida State League affiliate of the Cleveland Indians.

"I loved it. I never felt like a big city boy in a small town and that type of thing. I never felt that way. Every place that I played, it seemed like they liked me. I had a nice following at Daytona Beach my first year. I led the league in home runs and I had a nice following. The people, when you hit a home run at Daytona, they passed the can around and the people would put change in it or whatever they could afford. At the end of the night, you got half of it and half of it went into a till to split up with the whole team at the end of the season."

FIRST MAJOR LEAGUE GAME: September 10, 1955 as a member of the Indians vs. Boston Red Sox at Fenway Park.

Colavito made his major league debut as a pinch-runner and scored a run.

FIRST MAJOR LEAGUE HIT: September 24, 1955 vs. Detroit Tigers at Briggs Stadium

In the second game of a doubleheader, Colavito entered the game as a pinch-runner in the top of the first inning for Al Smith, who had singled. Colavito went on to get his first major league hit, a double off Tigers pitcher Ned Garver in the third inning. He went 4-for-4 in that game with two doubles and two runs scored. In the fifth inning, Colavito got to display his outstanding throwing arm when he gunned down Tigers first baseman Earl Torgeson, who was trying to take third on a fly ball to right.

"Earl Torgeson is a good guy. I played against him a lot of times. Torgeson told that story all winter long. He was one of those banquet speakers, he liked to do that. I remember them telling me about it. He'd say that he was on second and I was in front of the 415 [feet] sign. It was way out there, between right-center [field] and center. Torgeson tagged up and was going to third and the third-base coach was telling him, get down, get down, you know, slide. He said, what is he nuts, this is Torgeson telling this thing. What is he nuts? No way he'll throw me out and God willing, I threw him out. He was shocked to death, but he told that story all winter long."

FIRST TIME HE HIT FOUR HOME RUNS IN A GAME: June 10, 1959 vs. Baltimore Orioles at Memorial Stadium

Colavito became the second player, at the time, to hit four consecutive home runs in a single game. Colavito walked his first time up and then hit a home run in his next four at-bats. He had six runs batted in as Cleveland beat the Orioles, 11–8.

"There was a beat writer who followed the club for the Cleveland Plain Dealer, his name was Harry Jones, who I later worked with on TV. Harry was the beat writer and we're standing around the cage taking batting practice, it was on the road. He says to me, 'Hey, Rock,' and Harry wasn't the guy to laugh all the time or anything like that. Pretty stone faced, not ugly, just stone faced and he says to me, 'Hey, Rock. So when the hell are you gonna break out of this slump?' Now slump was not in my vocabulary. I never used the word slump and I said, 'What are you talking about, Harry? What slump are you talking about?' I said, I have no slump and he said, come on. Just like that, real serious and I said, 'Yeah, that's right. Just what I said to you,' and he said, 'When do you think you're gonna break out here?' I said, 'Harry, you'll never know. It just might be tonight.' That was my exact words. Not knowing anything else, didn't make any adjustments, just went up and did what I always did. Lo and behold, four in one game. So that was something I've always been very proud of.

"I almost did it twice. I hit three in one game in Cleveland for Detroit (July 5, 1962 as a member of the Detroit Tigers playing against his former team) hit three consecutive home runs, two off Pedro Ramos, one off their right-hand closer, Frank Funk. I hit the third one off of him. [Cleveland] brought in a guy who later had much more success at Minnesota by the name of Bill Dailey. Anyway, I have three in a row and I come up for the fourth time and nobody has ever done it (four home runs in a single game twice). I knew that and it was in the back of my head, not that I was really going for it. When I get to that point, I wanna get a base hit. I'm gonna hit the ball as hard as I can somewhere. So I hit this shot in the upper deck and it went foul about 15, 20 feet. It went foul right at the end. It hooked, but it was in the upper deck. I hit it as good as any of them. Then, the next pitch he threw me a sinker, low and away. That was his deal. He was a sidearmer so to speak and it sunk a lot and he threw the ball away from me and I hit the ball well, just [to] the right side of second [base]."

FIRST TIME PITCHING IN A MAJOR LEAGUE GAME: August 13, 1958 as a member of the Cleveland Indians vs. Detroit Tigers at Cleveland Stadium

Colavito entered the game in the seventh and pitched three scoreless innings against Detroit in his major league debut as a pitcher and received a no-decision in the Indians' 3–2 loss. Colavito did not give up a hit and retired Harvey Kuenn, one of the better hitters in the American League, for whom he would be traded for less than two years later, twice. Ten years later, Colavito made his second appearance as a pitcher for the Yankees.

"I like Harvey. I always thought Harvey was a good player and a decent guy. What was said, I got all the publicity a lot more than he did. I never felt any animosity towards Harvey. As a matter of fact, I wanna strike 'em all out, but it didn't happen. I just liked doing it. I did it as a favor. I told [manager] Ralph Houk, when I joined the Yankees, that was the second time [that he pitched], that's the one when I won the game. The first time, I didn't win the game, I relieved [Hoyt] Wilhelm. The second time I was pitching for New York, both times was against the Tigers."

FIRST TIME BEING TRADED:

On April 17, 1960, two days before the season opener, the Indians made a controversial deal when they traded Colavito to the Detroit Tigers in exchange for Harvey Kuenn. Fans were outraged that the popular Colavito was traded. Indians GM Frank Lane exacerbated the situation when he said, "What's all the fuss about? All I did was trade hamburger for steak." Colavito learned of the trade while he was playing an exhibition game.

"I'm kind of honored that they still talk about it. That means they still remember you and they still hate the trade as much as I did. In those days, you didn't admit anything like that. I mean, you would never give them the satisfaction of admitting that you were sad that you didn't want to be traded and I definitely did not. I definitely was upset and I can say it now, it just was horrible to me because here I am with the Indians, having a pretty good spring, which is highly unusual for me. I homered first time up in Memphis, Tennessee, and I was really feeling good. I hit a shot to the third baseman the second time up and it handcuffed him, but he forced the guy at second and they didn't get me at first.

"Anyway, here comes [Indians manager] Joe Gordon from the dugout, walking towards me kind of fast. Herb Score was sitting against the light towers right by first base. [Gordon] comes up to me and he said, 'That's the last time you'll ever hit in a Cleveland uniform.' I just looked at him and he said, 'You've been traded to the Detroit Tigers for Harvey Kuenn. I wish you all the luck in the world.' They put a runner in for me and I go past Herbie and I said, 'I'm going back to the hotel, I've just been traded.' He looked at me and said, 'Come on, just like that? Don't fool around like that.' I said, 'No, I've been traded to the Tigers for Harvey Kuenn.' He repeats, don't fool around like that, because we were very close. We were all like brothers, roommates. I said to him, 'I'm serious.' I thought at first when [Gordon] was coming out, he was giving me the rest of the day off."

FIRSTHAND EXPERIENCE WITH THE PINE TAR GAME:

In 1983, Colavito was a coach with the Kansas City Royals when they played the Yankees in the infamous "Pine Tar Game." Colavito was ejected for arguing when the umpires overruled George Brett's famous home run in the ninth inning.

"George hit a bullet into the upper deck off of [Rich] Gossage. Wasn't the easiest guy to hit. He was a great reliever. George really got into one, hit the upper deck and he rounds the bases, comes home and then Billy Martin comes out of the dugout. I'm watching this whole thing 'cause I played with Billy and he put up his usual fuss. Then, they announced that the bat was too far up the pine tar. It's too far up towards the sweet spot. Now that was so stupid that it almost made you throw up because if anything, if the ball hit the pine tar, it would retain it. It would like stick to it a little bit and might stop it from going a long ways. It wouldn't last long 'cause I'd be so quick but still it wasn't even close to being, to hurting anything."

(On the ejection)

"I said, 'I'm only a peacemaker here.' I said, 'I'm not doing anything. I'm not fighting. I'm not arguing,' and they just threw me out anyway. I told [American League president Lee] MacPhail, I'm not paying [a fine] and they never forced me to."

***Rocky Colavito* by John Pennisi**

8
JOHNNY DAMON

Johnny Damon spent four seasons of his 18-year career with the Yankees and was a consistent offensive performer. During his Yankee tenure, Damon slashed .285/.363/.458 with an OPS of .821 while averaging more than 100 runs scored and just over 23 stolen bases while wearing the pinstripes. Damon was the starting left fielder on the 2009 Yankees world championship team.

FIRST BASEBALL IDOL:

"My first baseball idol was George Brett. Being born outside of Kansas City and watching him hoist the trophy in 1985. I knew I wanted to be a baseball player and that was the only thing I really wanted to do. Nothing special on my end, but to be a great teammate, eventually, but to be around a group of guys who can work together to accomplish an amazing feat that only one team gets to do every single year."

FIRST BASEBALL GAME THAT HE ATTENDED:

"The first baseball game I went to as a child was at Tinker Field [in Orlando, Florida] and it was spring training. It was the Minnesota Twins with Kirby Puckett and the Baltimore Orioles showed up with Eddie Murray and Cal Ripken and I was able to get autographs from all three of those guys and it was absolutely amazing. It's not as crazy as the card seekers now or the amount they want. One autograph to me was golden. I remember that to my playing days. So that's why I always gave back to the fans because I was a fan when I was a kid, so I made a lot of people happy over the years taking my time, even when there wasn't much time before a game, I would go over and try to sign a couple and just explain to them sometimes you guys just and like. Okay, I'm busy, but if you talk to them, like normal people, they totally get it and you try to get them later or hopefully, down the road. I've signed a lot of autographs and made so many people happy."

FIRST EXPERIENCE BEING HIT BY WARREN SAPP DURING A HIGH SCHOOL FOOTBALL GAME:

Damon attended Dr. Phillips High School in Dr. Phillips, Florida, near Orlando and played football against Pro Football Hall of Famer Warren Sapp, who attended Apopka High. Damon sustained his first concussion as a result of colliding with Sapp during a play.

"I remember that. Looking across the line, I'm a free safety and Warren Sapp is a 280 pound All-American tight end. So obviously, they're going to go to him, so we collided and he definitely got the better of me. Rung my bell and back then, you kind of just keep going. It wasn't as major as the one that I received playing for the Red Sox, but definitely rang my bell. He felt it a tiny bit, but the most important thing, we were talking about that a couple of days ago. I had to remind him that we actually won that game 6–3 and he denies it, so maybe that concussion hit me too hard or I actually hit him hard enough."

FIRST DRAFT EXPERIENCE:

Damon was chosen by the Kansas City Royals in the first round (35th overall) in the 1992 MLB June Amateur Draft.

"What I remember about draft day is I had a really tough senior year. Every hard-hit ball that I hit found a glove or was called an error. So my numbers did not look well. I lost some weight due to food poisoning during that year. So my stock dropped from being the number one [prospect] in the country to eventually 35th, but I knew I had a lot in the tank and I was a lot better than what that year was and I'm resilient. Growing up as an army brat, being around a lot of tough guys growing up, I knew I could bounce back and it was only a three-month period of my life when I struggled in baseball. That day, I was actually out playing golf, trying to get my mind off of it. I wish they had the format that they have today. Like that special day for the families and the kids getting drafted. It was a little bit different but getting that phone call from the Royals. [Senior advisor to the general manager] Art Stewart, [executive] Allard Baird, I mean it was just absolutely amazing. Allard was right. He told the Royals, you cannot lose with this guy and Allard's career [took] him to being a GM and being a very respected man in the game. I appreciate him for having my back and I'm glad that I was able to do them well."

FIRST PRO MANAGER:

In 1992, Damon reported to the Royals' affiliate in the Gulf Coast League and played for manager Mike Jirschele.

"He was the perfect coach to walk in with. He would joke, he had some young kids that he brought with him down to Florida and we just had a good old time and we enjoyed ourselves. They're always told to put a certain vibe out there and you know, he did it and it was a special year. I bounced back from that horrible high school season and won the MVP of the league and also won a championship. So I have that championship pedigree from back in high school, like winning a couple of summer national championships and winning a couple baseball tournaments. I also had a guy like Mike Jirschele, who had my back. After we won that year, I was able to go up to High-A that year and play a couple games in the playoffs and held my own. So, the following year, guess what happens? Mike Jirschele had a great year and he goes up to Rock-ford, Illinois, with me and we have a really good year. We just don't finish the job that year."

FIRST TIME HE LEARNED HE WAS BEING CALLED UP:

"Back then [1995], there was a strike going on so I never had a major league spring training, so I don't know these guys. They don't know me, but all of a sudden, there's three popular players for the Kansas City Royals who are being released. Vince Coleman was one of them. Chris James another and I'm not quite sure about the other, but it was surreal. We were in Midland, Texas, and I show up to the ballpark and I'm not in the lineup. I was off a couple of days earlier and I play all the time, so I'm throwing a little hissy fit, not really knowing when. I want to play, I don't know what's going on. So I asked the manager, 'Is there something I did wrong?' He goes, 'Hey guys. Some of you guys don't get to play all the time but John is complaining about having a second day off in four days. Johnny, just to let you know, the reason why you're off today is because you're going to the show' and this is Ron Johnson, bless his soul. Ron Johnson [Damon's manager at the Royals' Double-A affiliate at Wichita] said you're going to the show and I was like, cool. Going to? I didn't quite grasp. Triple-A, that's my next level and he goes, 'You're going to Kansas City tomorrow morning,' and I'm thinking Kansas City and he's like, 'Yeah, you're going to the big leagues,' and right there I shook hands with everybody. I tried to call tons of people and nobody picked up, so got a flight back to Wichita early next morning, loaded up the car and drove to Kansas City, hoping I wasn't going to face Randy Johnson in my big league debut. So many emotions going on. Nowadays, they put me on a plane and just ship me to Kansas City. Great time for myself, for all my family and a dream come true. That first game still had a bunch of nerves."

FIRST MAJOR LEAGUE GAME: August 12, 1995 as a member of the Kansas City Royals against the Seattle Mariners at Kauffman Stadium.

Damon got his first hit in his third at-bat, a leadoff triple in the fifth inning off of Mariners pitcher Tim Belcher.

"That meant the world to me. I was so proud of my rise and my accomplishments. I probably really wasn't prepared for it. I was always thinking Triple-A's the next step. I wasn't thinking the big leagues. I was kind of going, 'Wow, this is a big move.' I went over to my first at-bat, a little tentative on swinging the bat. Good thing Tino Martinez was playing [first] base, so I hit a slow roller down the first-base line and with the wills I had and still have, I was able to lay out three [bases] and a first big hit. It seems like Tim Belcher has given up a lot of first major league first hits. I know Derek Jeter is another one and I'm sure there's a couple more."

FIRST TIME HE FOUND OUT HE WAS TRADED:

In January, 2001, Damon was traded to the Oakland A's as part of a three-team, multi-player deal.

"I was actually horseback riding in Hawaii and left the phone in the car. I come back and I have 20-plus voicemails. I don't think text messages were too easy to send back then. I started jumping on the horn trying to figure things out because I always kept hearing, Seattle was going to be a team [rumored] to get traded to and also the Yankees. So, I'm making calls and finally I get traded to the Oakland A's. They always were under the radar so I kind of forgot they made the playoffs the year before. I'm thinking, is this is a good team I'm going to? We probably only played them a couple of times a year before and I was actually suspended for three of those games for getting into a fight. So yeah, I get traded to Oakland. It's just totally different. My head's spinning, I've got to pack, I gotta find a new place to live. I got to do this and get ready for spring training in Arizona for the first time. I know my now ex-wife was not happy about me getting traded to Oakland. I was like,

'Well, I can't control anything until next year.' That was a very difficult start to that offseason. Going to spring training without my little kids. They were just a year and a half at the time, so that was tough. Then, I go join a bunch of rowdy boys over in Oakland, a bunch of guys who should still be in college and they're just a very talented bunch. I'm looking around and going, man, these guys are legit. They know how to have fun playing baseball because in Kansas City that felt like you're looking over your shoulder and like you have one bad game, you might not play the next so I know I got past that point. My first couple of years in Kansas City it was like, they'd go and pinch-hit [for] me [against] a lefty who I hit very well. Everything changed when Tony Muser got to Kansas City. That instilled a lot of confidence. He told me, 'You're going to be in the lineup every day unless you can't go,' so I broke a Kansas City record at the time of playing in 305 or 300 consecutive games. I was a version of an ironman, but getting to Oakland and finding out how to play winning baseball, I was the catalyst of the team, didn't have a great stat year but I made everything easier for the guys around me. I took pitches and I could battle and battle and 102 wins for a wild-card team, not to shabby."

FIRST TASTE OF POSTSEASON PLAY: 2001 ALDS as a member of the A's vs. Yankees

The Yankees rallied from a two-games to none deficit to beat Damon and the A's in five games.

"There's a huge difference [in postseason baseball] especially when you're facing Roger Clemens at Yankee Stadium. Another one of my idols back then and still to this day and to be able to go for that first game. Not too many balls were hit very hard but we got the job done [in the] first two games. Unfortunately for me, everything I hit from Game 4 to 5 found the glove. Wasn't that I was struggling but doesn't help either when your four and five guys, [Eric] Chavez and [Miguel] Tejada, I believe 0-for-19 each, big part of our lineup. Our pitching staff was so good. Seattle didn't want to play us. We beat Arizona earlier that year, three games to nothing in Arizona, so we had a scrappy team who could play defense very well because we were horrible at the beginning of the year. They started me in left field thinking I was only going to be there for one year. Once they made that move to put me in center, then we just steamrolled teams."

FIRST TIME HE HAD THREE HITS IN ONE INNING: June 27, 2003 as a member of the Boston Red Sox vs. Florida Marlins at Fenway Park.

Damon tied a major league record by getting three hits in one inning. In the bottom of the first inning, the Red Sox scored 14 runs, en route to a 25–8 win over the Marlins. Damon led off the inning with a double and scored on Todd Walker's single. Damon later tripled to drive in two runs and scored a second run on another Walker single. Damon came up one more time and singled in the 14th run of the inning before Bill Mueller was thrown out at home trying to score to end the rally.

"Looking back, it was really weird because at the start of the game, I'm in center field and I see a bright light behind home plate, which some people were talking about, like filming upstairs that I kind of stopped the game for. It feels like five minutes, it could have been 30 seconds. Who knows? That delay could have been the whole difference. I believe in all that stuff, things happen for a reason so I remember that at the start of the game. Then, coming up to bat, it's always great to get on base and get the team rolling. Get the base hit and see. We have a saying, 'If Johnny gets a hit. It must be easy.' Like we always joke [the pitcher] must be nothing if Johnny gets a hit. So I get that hit and our lineup just kept moving. Come up the second time. The guys who make an out, they really don't want to come up to bat a second time. So we had some guys on our team going, 'Not me, not me.' So, get that second hit and we're still rolling. They keep changing pitchers. I've never seen anything like that, not even in T-ball or Little League. Then, come up for a third time. Hit a nice pitch to left field. Unfortunately, our guy gets thrown out at home because maybe Todd Walker has a chance to get three hits as well. So I think about that, definitely would have been a amazing feat if you have a couple of guys who get three hits. Great inning. We took it to the Marlins and they eventually loaded up and put a great team together for the stretch run and win the World Series."

FIRST ALL-STAR GAME: 2002

While playing with the Red Sox, Damon was named to the American League All-Star team for the first time. In his first All-Star at-bat, he singled and scored a run.

"I deserved to be on the team. It's unfortunate that I've only made two All-Star Games. Looking back in my career, I've been asked by managers is it okay if we left you off, so we can take our guy. I was like you don't have to tell me, I love that three or four days off that I get. There's no bonus in my contract. So, I'm like yeah, I'm good to go home and relax and get my body some rest. Being voted in by the fans was a tremendous honor. Didn't realize how much work it is to get to the All-Star Game. You walk in and you're signing 500 baseballs so they can pass out to everybody, all the parties leading up to it. I've never been a guy who likes to go to these clubs and stand like this. So there's a lot of stuff that happens with the All-Star game, but it's definitely a great honor to say you made the All-Star team. I knew we were having a great year and we should have made the playoffs. I was told on the scouting report that this guy doesn't throw over to first base, left-handed pitcher so I get a big lead. This is at the end of August, early September. He throws over the first and I dive back into the bag and dislocated my finger. At the time, I was getting hot again, one of the hottest players and all of a sudden I can't grip a bat but I want to play. So I continue to play but our team just went through that September down spill that they're used to and we didn't make the playoffs."

FIRST EXPERIENCE WITH THE YANKEES:

In December 2005, the Yankees signed Damon to a four-year free agent contract.

"I didn't think it was gonna happen. Our last game was getting swept by the White Sox in the Division Series. I thought I was going to come back, there was never a contract talk before the year. After 2004, they told I was going to be there for a long time and the contract was going to come in spring training and contract extension, never happened. So playing the season, and having a great year, I think everybody thought I was going to go out and party too much and not be ready for the season, but that's the one thing that I prided myself in because I enjoyed winning that championship so much. I wanted to do everything I can to get back there. Yeah, I'm still going to have fun on the baseball field. I'm not going to get too crazy serious, but I'm going to be ready to do my job. So after the season, which ended early October, for six weeks, the Red Sox are the only team that can have contact with me about a contract. You would think during those six weeks, something would possibly get done. [Red Sox general manager] Theo Epstein's a free agent as well and you're going, so who's gonna negotiate this contract? Well, Theo didn't because he wanted to take care of his contract because he didn't want to be in charge of me leaving, the fan favorite. So I actually didn't think that the Yankees were going to be the team. I made a call to Detroit. They just lost 120 games and I knew they were close. Close or better than that, but they have a young kid named Curtis Granderson who they were going to give a shot to. So I shifted my thoughts to the LA Dodgers. They needed a center fielder, leadoff guy, second guy, but they just signed Rafael Furcal for four years so they didn't have money back then either.

"The only teams that really needed a leadoff hitter and center fielder were the Red Sox and the Yankees. When Jacoby Ellsbury got drafted [by the Red Sox] years before I was the guy, they brought him to the clubhouse and I was the guy that said, 'Do your best. I know you're going to come and take my job one day and I get it, so don't worry about me. This is going to be your job in a few years. Sure enough, there was no contract from the Red Sox and I know a lot more now because you like to try to dissect everything. So I started talking to the Yankees and the contract negotiations went quick because they said, if you don't take this contract right away, they're going to pull it. I was like, 'Man, four years, 52 million dollars] from the Yankees and zero from the Red Sox. I know if the Yankees pull it, the Red Sox can come back to me with a one-year deal and Jacoby ready to go. Took the contract, sent shockwaves around the baseball world. I was like, 'Man, what just happened?' Like, this happened so fast. We let a bunch of our friends know and they were shocked. They were crying. They were disappointed that they weren't going to see us as much as we saw each other in the past. After I agreed to the Yankees, I get a contract offer [via] FedEx in at my house that says, here's a four-year, $40 million dollar contract offer and it's a little bit too late. I really wanted Boston to come up to four year, $44 million. You know, not robbing the bank but I let them know that I had a substantial offer. I was gonna take it and they just thought I was bluffing. Unfortunately, I'm not a guy [who] lies about certain things. I wear my heart on my sleeve and try to be as honest as I can about anything possible."

FIRST YANKEES MANAGER: Joe Torre

"Calm and cool and did a great job with the Yankees. Just he had a great team that he inherited and he put the certain guys together like bringing in Dwight Gooden, bringing in Darryl Strawberry and bringing Cecil Fielder and all these guys and making them mesh so I knew he could bring a team together and that's exactly what we had. I mean, we had a powerhouse in 2006 and we were thumping people. Unfortunately, come playoff time, a lot can happen and a lot did happen that year." [The Yankees were upset by the Detroit Tigers three games to one in the American League Division Series.]

FIRST GAME AT YANKEE STADIUM AS A MEMBER OF THE YANKEES: April 11, 2006 vs Kansas City Royals.

"It was absolutely amazing. Just lots going through my mind because, 'How did we get here from six months ago?' I put on the pinstripes at my press conference. Just being around the guys most of spring training, because we had the World Baseball Classic, that I got to spend time [with] A-Rod [Alex Rodriguez] and Jeter. Just putting it on and some fans are still upset with me about 2004. George Steinbrenner wants the best and, at the time, I was the best."

FIRST YANKEES CHAMPIONSHIP: 2009

Damon is one of two players to have won a World Series as a member of the Yankees and the Red Sox. Damon batted .364 in the 2009 World Series with six runs scored in the six-game victory over the Philadelphia Phillies. In Game 4, he set up the winning rally in the ninth inning by stealing second and third on the same pitch and then scoring the go-ahead run in a pivotal 7–4 win.

"There's only been one other who's done that and it's Babe Ruth. When you look at the history of the game and yes, the Red Sox hadn't won in 86 years when we accomplish the feat, but being able to make it worth my while going to New York because it would have been horrible if I had left Boston [and didn't win a title with the Yankees]. I know [the Red Sox] spent money in 2007 to win the championship, and we did the same thing in 2009 with the Yankees. We had to get better starting pitching and we did. A. J. Burnett, CC Sabathia, I recruited them very hard and I told them it's a really great place to play and they listened. I was like, at least listen to what they have to say. I'm telling you it's not as much pressure as you think. Playing in Boston was a lot more pressure. Like I said, everybody will be on you if you're not doing great. In New York, yeah, they'll get on ya, but it also motivates you in New York. Like they're telling you, 'Get going,' in Boston, they're telling you that you're trash."

Johnny Damon by John Pennisi

9
AL DOWNING

Lefthander Al Downing was the first African American pitcher in Yankee history. A native of Trenton, New Jersey, Downing played parts of nine seasons with the Yankees and was 72–57 with an ERA of 3.23. Downing attended Muhlenberg College in Allentown, Pennsylvania, and Rider College in Lawrenceville, New Jersey, and played 17 seasons in the major leagues with the Yankees, Oakland A's, Milwaukee Brewers, and Los Angeles Dodgers. In 1971, Downing was with the Dodgers when he won 20 games for the only time in his career.

FIRST EXPERIENCE WITH THE YANKEES:

Bill Yancey, who was one of the first African American baseball scouts, is credited with signing Downing.

"Bill Yancey first saw me when I was in junior high school. Bill Yancey, his nickname among the players in the Negro Leagues was "Yank," because he played some 20 some years in the Negro Leagues for the New York Black Yankees. He was a shortstop. Bill also happened to be a basketball player. He was a point guard for the Harlem Rens.

"Bill became like a father to me. My father was still alive, but

[Yancey] told all the guys who he liked that he scouted, call me Uncle Bill and call his wife Aunt Louise because they had no children. Bill played most of his professional career at baseball and basketball in New York and his wife was a dancer at the Cotton Club. He lived in New Jersey, little town called Morristown, which is about 20 some miles out of Philadelphia. When Bill went into organized baseball, he became a scout. When I say organized baseball, I'm talking about integrated baseball. Bill went to work for the Milwaukee Braves, that team that in '66 moved to Atlanta. They're going from Boston to Milwaukee to Atlanta and his general manager was Roy Hamey. At that time, in 1958, the best high school team in the country, not in the state, in the country, was Montclair, New Jersey. We were playing at that time the Greater Newark Classic. They picked certain high schools in New Jersey to play in this. In '58 they picked us. We had like 4,500 students. Montclair, I think, was the same size and they were in that tournament but remember, they were the number one team in the country. We were supposed to play a game against them up in North Jersey in the first game of the Greater Newark tournament and everybody figured we're going to play 'Clair. They're gonna hand us our hats, right? So we go up there and I'm playing first base and our best pitcher is a fellow named Charlie Columpar. He was our ace pitcher, he was right-handed. I was left-handed and we rotated. When he pitched, I played first and when I pitched, he played first. So, he started that game.

"Charlie was, I wouldn't say he threw hard for a kid his age 'cause he was so big, but these guys were just hammering him, hammering him, boom, boom, boom. They kind of like ambushed him right out of the gate. So we got to the second, third inning. Our coach called timeout and he said, 'Charlie, get your first base mitt, Al you get your fielder's glove, you're gonna pitch,' and I shut Montclair down for the rest of that game. After the game, this gentleman comes up to me. He says, 'My name is Bill Yancey and I work for the Philadelphia Phillies and I was watching you.' And he said, 'How old are you?' I said, 'I'm in junior high school and I can't talk to you.' So he started talking to our coach, Mr. Palumbo and Mr. Palumbo said, 'Yeah, he's a junior but next year, he'll be back again.' So [Yancey] says, 'Well I'll be back next year looking for him.' He couldn't talk, he couldn't make contact with me because I was underage. The next, year, the senior year, they had something. That was the year '58. They remember the Dodgers and Giants had split [to move to California] so in honor of those teams leaving, let's have this all-star game. North and South Jersey. The liner demarcation was going to be New Brunswick, but they were in our conference so we knew the New Brunswick players. The players from North Jersey were kids above that. So kids like Jeff Torborg was from Westfield. New Jersey always had a lot of good players. South Jersey was more of a football territory. Football and basketball.

"I was picked to pitch for the team because I was considered to be, at that time, the best pitcher on our team. Charlie had gone on to Rutgers so I was chosen to pitch. I was a senior coming out of high school. One of the players on our team was a guy named Lefty Robinson. You remember Dave 'Lefty' Robinson, a football player out of Moorestown, New Jersey. [Robinson is a former Packers linebacker and member of the Pro Football Hall of Fame.] Mr. Yancey said, 'I came to see Lefty.' Then he saw me. He said, 'Aren't you that kid I saw last year?' I said, 'Yeah.' He said, 'You're gonna pitch here.' I said, 'Yeah.' So they bring me in the game at about the fifth inning and I pitched two innings. When I came up to bat, I got a base hit and I'm standing on first base and I look behind me and the first baseman is talking to the second baseman. He is about 30 feet behind me and I stole second base. After the game, Yancey said, "Can I ask you a question?' He said, 'Why did you steal second base?' I said, 'He wasn't holding me on.' That was the thing that made him understand that I was a baseball player, not just a pitcher because I could separate the two.

"[Yancey] didn't try to sign me. He asked me what was I gonna do next year. I said, 'I'm gonna go to college.' He said, 'Where?' I told him, 'Muhlenberg College.' 'Oh, what are you gonna do?' I said, 'I'm gonna play basketball now.' He really liked me, I was a basketball player also. He said, 'Let me know when you decide you wanna play, when you want to sign.' He still worked for the

Phillies at the end of the '60 season. The Yankees cleaned house. They fired general manager George Weiss, they fired manager Casey Stengel. They only kept the scouting department and the front office people, so Roy Hamey was brought in as the general manager from the Phillies to the Yankees.

"Mr. Yancey says, 'Al, I have something good for you. At the end of my freshman year in college he asked, "Don't go back to school in the fall because if you go back to school, I can't sign you until the spring and it's too late. I want you to go out next year and play.' I said, 'Okay,' so I went back home. I didn't say anything to anyone. I think it was November ninth, was the day he came to our house. He says, 'Okay, now I'm working for the Yankees. I wanna sign you for the Yankees.' That's how it happened."

FIRST PROFESSIONAL MANAGER:

Downing was assigned to the Binghamton Triplets, the Yankees' Class-A affiliate of the Eastern League. Jim Gleeson was Downing's first professional manager.

"Jimmy Gleeson was a big man and he was a hero at Rockhurst College in Kansas City. Jimmy was about six foot-two and Jimmy had been a shipmate of Yogi's [Berra] in the Navy. So Jimmy is the manager of this Class-A team and he said to me, 'Welcome, welcome.' In those days, I was the only African American. We had a kid from Panama, from Santo Domingo. There were four players of color we had on our team, 'cause you had to have an even number. [If you had an odd number], somebody would get a room by themselves and they didn't want that, right? First two weeks of spring training, we did a lot of running and most of the guys on our team were guys who had been through college. These guys were like 22, 23 years old here. I was 19, hadn't even turned 20 then. So Gleeson says to me one day, 'Would you like to pitch batting practice tomorrow?' I said, 'Yeah.' 'Okay, tomorrow you pitch 15 minutes batting practice.' Fortunately, I always had great coaches all coming up. And one, Mr. Palumbo particularly told me, 'Learn every facet of the game. They asked you to do something, do it, don't ask why.' He said, 'Batting practice is for the hitter, it's not for the pitcher,' and that stuck in my head. So, batting practice, I'm throwing strikes and guys hitting line drives all over. When I come off, Gleeson giving this wink, 'Way to go.' Two days later, I'm pitching batting practice again and all the guys are saying, 'Well, they lit you up in batting practice,' and I just laughed. That's my indoctrination into what players thought. They thought batting practice was to show people how good your stuff was.

"One day after I pitched batting practice a couple of times, Mr. Gleeson asked me, 'Hey, Al, I wanna take you over to Lakeland because they have this field, I don't know if you've ever been there and they can play eight games,' I think it was about eight games at one time. He said, 'They have a tower and they have these different field that radiated out of the tower. They called it 'Tigertown' so I wanted to take you over to pitch a game. I think I pitched against their B-team and I pitched about five innings and they got one run. After the game, he kind of just winked at me. Three days later he said, 'We're going back to Lakeland. You go pitch against their A-team,' and I go and I pitch five innings, give up about one or two runs. He says, 'Okay, we're gonna have an exhibition game against our Double-A team, which was Amarillo, which happened that year in '61 to be the team in the minor leagues in Double-A ball and [Joe] Pepitone was on that team. [This] right-handed pitcher, kid out of Puerto Rico, he says, 'You're gonna pitch against this team and it's a night game in Barto.' He said, "You only got one guy you have to worry about, 'Peppy-tone,' he called him Peppy-tone and I said, 'Who's Peppy-tone?' 'He's a skinny guy, got a left-hand stance like Stan Musial.' He said, 'You gotta watch out for him. He's quick, he doesn't look like it, but he's quick.' I threw a couple of pitches and I threw a fastball, which I thought was on his hands and he hit it about 400 feet against the light tower in right field, and I said, 'Oh, that's Peppy-tone.'

"I think in that game, I pitched about six innings, gave up two or three runs and about a week later, we were breaking camp. Gleeson says to me, 'Look, I'm gonna do something that a lot of people in this organization don't agree with. I told them I wanted to take you up as one of the three players we could take up for 30 days and just give you a chance to see what it's like in A-ball because eventually we're gonna send you down to B-ball, which was Greensboro. I said, 'Okay, fine. Whatever he asks me to do, I'll do and that's how my first initiation with the Binghamton Triplets.

"I didn't come up there to pitch. I came up there to observe because I'm only gonna be there 30 days. We had all these guys, who were 24, 25 years old and I wasn't really a hard thrower. I was what you call, a two-seam fastball guy, which I don't know why every left-hander doesn't throw it. They got 'em all throwing four-seam fastballs, straight as a string. That's why guys are hitting so many home runs. Fastball doesn't move. Fastball's supposed to move. I remember one time one of the players from the Reading team, he said, 'You throw everything on the corner, everything on the corner.' I said, 'Chico, if I throw it down the middle, you're gonna be hitting line drives. This way, you're hitting ground balls.' Next thing you know, I'm pitching a game in Reading and Reading was [in] the Indians' farm system, lot of fastball hitters and I'm throwing fastballs that are sinking and they're hitting ground balls to shortstop and second base. When we go to Binghamton, we're opening the season in Springfield. Springfield was the defending champions, Giants farm team, good farm team again with a lot of guys, 25, 26. I don't know anything about customs. We get off the bus and go into the locker room and the ball's sitting on my stool, the baseball on the stool. One of the players come up to me to say, 'You're pitching today.' I wound up pitching a two-hit shutout against the defending champions. Now, when I get on the bus, guys are whistling. 'You sure you're only 20 years old?' 12 games later [Downing made 12 appearances at Binghamton and was 9–1 with a 1.84 ERA] they called me up to the Yankees. You know, I didn't expect it. I was 9–1, had great numbers. I had a few more walks (50) than I should have but I had a lot of strikeouts (96 in 98 IP). I had a strikeout an inning, which was very impressive to a lot of scouts. Of course, a lot of people were saying, 'How do the Yankees hide this guy?' and that's the story."

FIRST TIME BEING CALLED UP TO THE YANKEES:

"When I pitched a game that Friday night against Reading, I beat them pretty handily. I think they got one or two runs and I was jamming a lot of right-handers 'cause they were looking for fastballs out over the plate and I was jamming guys. The next day, Jimmy Gleeson came over to me, he says, 'I got good news for you.' They were gonna play the All-Star Game that Monday in Springfield. He says, 'You're going to New York." I said, 'Well, I'm going to New York for what?' He says, 'No, no, no, you're going to New York. The Yankees have called you up. I have a picture of me packing my bag and the guys all wanted their travel bags with the names on to get in the picture because some of them said, this is the closest we'll ever get to the big leagues. What they're saying is like, 'I've been in this business for four or five years and gotten no higher than A-ball. This guy comes up there in like three months. He's in the major leagues.' The guy most proud of me going up was Jimmy Gleeson. I never forgot that because he said, 'You know, you worked hard to get here now. Just do the same things you've been doing here and everything will be okay.'"

FIRST EXPERIENCE WITH THE YANKEES:

"My first interaction was with Hector Lopez and Elston Howard because I was told to go to the Lord Baltimore Hotel, look up a fellow named Bruce Henry. Bruce was the traveling secretary and Bruce will tell you who you're rooming with. I was rooming with Elston Howard and Hector Lopez. So I went to the hotel and met these two guys and they became like my big brothers in baseball, my mentor, my confidants. I couldn't have picked a better place because there were two, not only great guys, great family guys, great veterans, who had been around the game. Elston had played in a Negro League, Hector played through the Caribbean leagues and played with Kansas City. They took care of me and they made sure I was indoctrinated into the big leagues and understood life in the big leagues was more than just playing. You had to be a good upstanding citizen also and you had to represent yourself and your team well."

FIRST MAJOR LEAGUE GAME:

Downing made his major league debut on July 19, 1961 against the Washington Senators at Griffith Stadium. Downing started and gave up five runs in an inning-plus. After a scoreless first inning, Downing faced five batters in the second inning and did not record an out.

"They [Yankees] said, 'You're gonna pitch the second game of a doubleheader against the Washington ballclub.' Bud Daley was pitching the first game so you can stay in the hotel until I said, 'No, I'm going out there on the bus 'cause I don't know how to get around this town. So I go out there on the bus and I sit on the bench for like five innings with my uniform on. Then I go lay on the table for a while. When I woke up, Bud was sitting in the training room with me. I said, 'Bud, what happened?' He said, 'Man, they racked me.' I'm thinking, this guy's a veteran, been in the big leagues almost 10 years and they knocked him out, what's going to happen to me? So I go out the first inning and Yogi's catching me and says to me, 'Al, the first inning, the first time around the lineup, we're gonna see how they react to your fastball. I was a fastball pitcher but my fastball had a lot of movement on it. For some reason, the adrenaline level went up, I mean, it went through the charts. I was throwing fastballs that he had to jump up and catch. Yogi [asked], 'Wow, your ball always moved that much?' I said, 'Yes, but not that much.' I had never had a fastball like that. I don't know if it was adrenaline or what, but I was throwing harder than I'd ever thrown in my life. That's one of the reasons I got in trouble in the second inning because I started trying to throw hard and now, I had no command of my fastball. I was getting behind and then I had to try to just get it over and then guys were hitting balls and they knocked me out in the second inning."

Downing had a firsthand look at the Maris/Mantle home run chase in 1961

"When I came there, I think Roger had 40 and Mickey had 39

or vice versa. Mickey got an infection in his hip. He got a cold and the guy gave him a shot and I think the needle broke off in his hip. That's when it became infected, then he couldn't play. He didn't play like the last three weeks of the season or the last two and a half weeks of the season, but people don't understand that ballclub hit 240 home runs. There was like five guys that hit 20 home runs on that team. [Bill] Skowron, Yogi, Ellie, [Johnny] Blanchard hit 20, then Mickey and Roger. There's five guys so that team was basically a team that was put together well and that was the old Yankees because you had the bench and everything. Even if you lost a guy like Mantle, we had guys like Jack Reed who could play center field. He would come in the late innings and play center field 'cause he could. I mean he was like the Garry Maddox of his age. He ran down everything but they always said, 'Good field, no hit.' And then you had Hector [Lopez] who could play shortstop, third or left field and you had Blanchard who could catch and play first. It was a very diversified team and very talented team. We won the pennant and went into the World Series against Cincinnati."

FIRST TIME HE GOT TO WEAR NUMBER 24:

"When I joined the ballclub, I was on the road and I had a gray uniform. Gray uniforms were like sail cloth. If it was hot, you slaughtered. I mean, there was no sweat things in there, no sweat holes. I joined the ballclub and got this gray uniform. I don't even remember what the number was, it was high like in the forties or something like that. When we got back home, I go to my locker and Pete Sheehy was the equipment manager. He had grown up in upper Manhattan and he was a big time Giant fan. So Pete had these trunks, he sat in the back of the clubhouse, so when you come in, walk straight ahead, Pete would always be sitting on these trunks. So I came home, I'm looking for my number, I'm not looking for my name. I'm looking for my number and I see my name. I said to Mr. Sheehy, 'You gave me the wrong uniform.' He said, No, come over here and sit down next to me,' on his trunk. 'I gave you that number because a great number 24 [Willie Mays] just left here two years ago. I think you're gonna be a great pitcher in the Yankee organization.'

"That was the second thing. The first thing was when I got knocked out of the game in Washington and all the writers came to me. We had these old-time writers and they were great guys. I mean, good bunch of guys, but they were all lockstep in what was said (laughing). It was basically, we don't think a black guy can be a good pitcher in the big leagues or you definitely can't have a black catching the pitching, right? Well, they wrote that for years. They wrote that for a long time. So, I got knocked out and I'm sitting on my stool and all these writers are gathering around me. [The writers were asking] 'What happened here?' and [a] head comes through the crowd and its Yogi and he says, 'Tell you something nice about him, he's gonna be here a long time.' That changed the whole tenor of the interview. From that moment on, whatever Yogi said, these guys listened to because Yogi's one of the greatest baseball minds ever. We make him out to be some buffoon, which he never was. He was a baseball genius and a great judge of talent. The writers, all of a sudden looked at me a lot differently. I didn't pitch that much that year, but those two conversations what Yogi said with Big Pete [Sheehy] said, gave me a lot of confidence that maybe I can pitch up here."

FIRST MAJOR LEAGUE WIN: June 10, 1963 vs. Washington Senators at Griffith Stadium.

Downing tossed a complete game, two-hit shutout to beat the Senators, 7–0.

"It was a twilight double header and I shut out Washington. I remember telling Ralph [Houk, Yankees manager] I wanna go get my car. He said, 'Where's your car?' I said, 'Richmond.' He said, 'Well, go get a train and go down to Richmond and get your car and we'll meet you in New York.' I took the train down to Richmond, got my car, and drove back to New York to drop my car off in Trenton. Took a train up to New York. By that time, when I won my first game, I guess you could say I was reinvented because I had gone to Richmond in '62 to get back on track from where I was in '61. When I did, it took me half a season to do that because

I had to all of a sudden figure out what went wrong. What had gone wrong was that I had forgotten how to pitch. I had become a thrower. Because I had become a thrower, I no longer was able to have that good movement on my fastball. So my fastball would straighten out and because I was getting behind too many batters, the guys were hammering me. We had a fellow named Billy Chance was one of our catchers, Bobby Chance's brother and he said to me, 'Al, you know I know what's wrong with you. You pitch to the catcher but then you're afraid to tell the catcher how you want to pitch. When you warm up, next time I want you to warm up and tell me what you want me to do.' I said, 'Bill, I would like you to get down on one knee, because that way, that makes me keep my arm above the target. That way, I'm throwing down as opposed to throwing up and that was the middle of the '62 season to the end of the '62 season in Richmond. I was like, night and day. [The Yankees] even said that, if you hadn't turned it on the second half, we weren't going to put you on the 40 man roster the next year.' So they put me on the 40-man roster.

"I remember pitching one inning in September [for the Yankees] then I had to go Army reserves. When I came out, I was late for spring training. Because I didn't get out until March and spring training started like early part of February. So, they said, 'We're gonna send you back to Richmond.' That's when I met my second gift, which was a fellow named Preston Gomez. Preston was one of the old fellow Cuban guys who everybody understood. Everybody knew Preston in baseball. He's a genius. Another Yogi. Genius. He not only understood the game of baseball, he understood people. He could understand talent. He knew how to evaluate talent and how to make talent fit together to make a good ball club and the Yankees had hired him to be the manager of the Triple-A team. When we started the season, it was like the first week in June. I was like 3–2. I had a pretty good earned run average but the record was 3–2. [Gomez] came up to me one day, we were in Columbus, Ohio, he says, 'I called New York, I told them you didn't belong here.' I'm thinking, 'Oh God, they're gonna send me down. I said, 'What do you mean, Mr. Gomez?' He said, 'No, no, no. You're going back up to New York. You don't belong here.'

They told me, when you got control and command of your pitches, it's something I knew I could see it coming, but he saw it long before I saw it. All of a sudden, my fastball had zip on it and [pitching coach] Johnny Sain taught me something. Today, they call it a cutter, throwing the ball from left to right to a right-handed batter. That goes with the normal fastball, which would go from right to left to a left-handed batter. I had two fastballs right there. My curveball is just a show pitch and then I had a great changeup, which they didn't want me to throw. If I started throwing that in '63 or '64, who knows what might have happened, 'cause it was probably one of the best changeups I've ever had during that time. So, when I won my first game, I felt like, 'Wow, this is great,' but then you gotta keep it up. The old saying was, 'It's easy to get to the big leagues. It's hard to stay there,' and I never forgot that. Never forgot that every time I walked out on the mound."

FIRST WORLD SERIES GAME: Game 2, 1963
World Series vs. Los Angeles Dodgers at Yankee Stadium.

Downing gave up three runs in five innings pitched in a 4–1 loss to Johnny Podres and the Dodgers. Eight years earlier, Podres shut out the Yankees in Game 7 at the Stadium to give the Brooklyn Dodgers their only World Series title.

"We had a lot of veteran pitchers on the team. We had [Bill] Stafford, [Bud] Daley, [Bob] Turley, Ralph Terry. Whitey [Ford] was gonna pitch the first game. Who pitched the second game was up to Ralph and Jim Hegan, who was the bullpen coach and pitching coach Johnny Sain thought was the guy we should have out there. They came to the decision that we want a left-hander out there, Downing. If I made any mistake, it was underestimating Maury Wills because I knew Maury could run. I didn't know Maury was as good a hitter as he was and hit one right between my legs. Bam! I said, 'You little...,' he hits the ball between my legs. Now, he's on first base and I know he's going on first pitch. [Joe] Pepitone was our first baseman. I throw over to Pepitone. Pepitone throws and Maury throws a hook slide and steals second. From then on, we were looking up because they were just running every time they got a chance. But it was a great thrill. Number one, to pitch in the pinstripes and the World Series. If anybody says, oh, my greatest thrill was putting on the pinstripes, yes, that's only part of it, but when you're pitching in the World Series and wearing those pinstripes, there's a different connotation because even the players around the league look at you differently. They look at you with respect."

FIRST TIME LEADING THE AMERICAN LEAGUE IN STRIKEOUTS:

In 1964, Downing led the American League for the only time in his career with 217 strikeouts. He was 13–8 with a 3.47 ERA.

"I was very disappointed because I thought that I still hadn't reached a point of being a good pitcher because I think I had 217 strikeouts, something like that and I probably should have had 240 strikeouts, but I was trying to strike guys out as opposed to pitching. When I was getting guys is because I was jamming guys, I was getting them to hit ground balls. Then I would fire a fastball, letter high and boom, all of a sudden, the guy was swinging and missing. The team was behind, the team was that good. I could have won 15, 17 games, but I thought there were some games I just threw myself out of the games because I was trying to throw too hard and try to strike guys out. I also led the league in walks (217)."

FIRST ALL-STAR GAME: 1967

Downing pitched two scoreless innings in the All-Star game in Anaheim. The National League eventually won the game, 2–1, in 15 innings.

"Well, the first thing I remember is the night I got in, we were staying at the Disneyland Hotel. I was walking around and I see this guy walking around and I say, 'Hey, how are you doing? My name's Al Downing.' He said, 'Hi, my name's Rod Carew.' That started the whole weekend. We started talking. We're two young guys, first All-Star Game and we decided to walk around Disneyland and enjoy the sights and we'll see you in the locker room tomorrow. A friendship that still to this day, I cherish. The thing I remember most is when we got there and you walk in the locker room, you saw the epitome of baseball, the greatest players in baseball because that's who was on the All-Star team. In those days, people weren't coerced to vote for certain guys. People looked at your stats, they said, who belonged? Well, everybody knew who was going to be the outfield for the National League, right? [Willie] Mays, [Hank] Aaron, [Roberto] Clemente. There are guys like Billy Williams, Curtis Flood, and Frank Robinson until he got traded to the American League. I mean, those guys were overlooked every year. I remember our manager that year was Hank Bauer and Hank came up to me and he said, 'Al, can you gimme two innings?' I said, 'Yeah, sure,' because, remember the pitchers were chosen by the manager. Okay, little did he know that we were gonna play 15 innings. Poor Catfish [Hunter] had to pitch the last five innings 'cause there was no other pitchers. These teams were so evenly matched and at that time it was that pride. You know, American League, National League, American League, National League. Then, they brought in one guy who basically epitomized that whole thing and that was Pete Rose. He said, 'We're not gonna lose, we're gonna beat you.' I remember the story they were telling [one year] when [the manager] gave Willie the lineup and told Willie, 'Write up the lineup. Put yourself anywhere you want to put yourself.' Willie had himself leading off. Willie says, 'I put myself leadoff because I wanna start us off and we really wanna win.' He didn't trust anybody else. I think that permeated through all the guys. 'Hey, this is a big game, a big-time game. Make it that.'

FIRST IMMACULATE INNING: August 11, 1967 vs. Cleveland Indians at Cleveland Stadium.

An "immaculate inning" is when a pitcher strikes out the side on nine pitches. In the bottom of the second inning, Downing became the first Yankee to throw an immaculate inning when he struck out Indians first baseman Tony Horton, left fielder Don

Demeter, and catcher Duke Sims.

"It was an inning on which I got three outs on strikeouts. Nobody called it anything other than that."

FIRST TIME BEING TRADED:

After the 1969 season, the Yankees traded Downing and catcher Frank Fernandez to the Oakland Athletics in exchange for first baseman Danny Cater and infielder Ossie Chavarria.

"I thought it was inevitable that I was gonna be traded because it all started in '67. Not only did they lose confidence in me, but I think they were waiting for me to do something. I think they felt I was becoming a clubhouse lawyer because we had a lot of young guys. I had become like the senior colored guy as they [said] in those days. All the young guys coming up. Whether it was Horace Clarke or Roy White or Bill Robinson, Ron Woods, Jerry Kenney. They would all come to me for advice. 'Hey, Al, what do we do about this?' and everybody thought, 'Why is everybody going to him?' Well, I had been there the longest and they knew this is the guy you talked to. You wanna get a haircut, you wanna go buy some clothes or something like that. Go talk to him. That's what guys did for me when I came up to the big leagues. All of a sudden, I think they thought I was becoming too vocal."

FIRST TRADE TO A NATIONAL LEAGUE TEAM:

On June 11, 1970, the A's traded Downing and outfielder Tito Francona (Terry's father) to the Milwaukee Brewers for outfielder Steve Hovley. Less than a year later, Downing was traded from Milwaukee to the Los Angeles Dodgers for outfielder Andy Kosco.

"I go to Milwaukee and I'm pitching in Milwaukee and now we're on a ballclub that basically had been an expansion team from Seattle. They moved to Milwaukee because management lost the team. People in Milwaukee came in and they started looking at who they wanted to [get rid of]. They knew all of us were on the chopping block. That's how you got on an expansion team. I was one of the guys but I was pitching a lot. Oh, I had a 2–10 record. We had some guys there like Ted Savage. Davey May was there. Tommy Harper was there, Hank Allen, Dick's brother, was there and we would sit there and talk about it after every game. These guys would all say to me, 'Oh, you can really pitch.' I hadn't lost confidence in myself but it was nice to hear that come from your teammates. When the season's over, everybody goes home and I don't think anything about it. I said, Milwaukee probably won't bring me back. Frank Lane had taken over as general manager of the Milwaukee ballclub and he calls me. He said, 'I know you're only 29 years old, but we got some young pitchers we wanna look at and we figured you're expendable and we can get something for you. I said, 'Okay, well what's the deal?' 'We got a chance to make a trade.' It's the first time a general manager ever called me and said we have a chance to make a trade. He said, 'We want to give you a chance to make a decision to go to St. Louis or Los Angeles.' I said, 'St. Louis is a wonderful town, but I don't like Astroturf.' He said, 'Good, I'll call [Dodgers general manager] Al Campanis in the morning.' That's how I wound up with the Dodgers."

FIRST TIME HE GAVE UP A RECORD-SETTING HOME RUN: April 8, 1974 at Atlanta Fulton County Stadium.

Downing gave up Hank Aaron's 715th home run which broke Babe Ruth's career record.

"I'm not linked to the moment. I just happened to be the pitcher on the mound at that point. If you look at the history, [Commissioner] Bowie Kuhn, if he hadn't opened his mouth. Remember, Hank said I wanna break the record in Atlanta. Bowie Kuhn wasn't wise enough to understand the significance of what Hank was saying. When the Braves had moved to Atlanta in '66, they were coming from Milwaukee. Atlanta was a football town and you go in and you bring major league baseball into Atlanta. Major league baseball didn't catch on in Atlanta until like '74 after Hank hit the home run. Until then, they were playing second fiddle to football teams. [Aaron] said, 'I wanna break this record in front of the people in Atlanta who have accepted us.' He knew that wasn't the whole town. He told then when he hit the [record-tying] home run off [Cincinnati Reds pitcher Jack] Billingham on Opening Day, 'I want to go home and I wanna play Monday night.' Bowie Kuhn was saying, 'You can't do this for the integrity of the game.' Crap, crap, crap. Bowie Kuhn didn't even show up for the ceremony. He sent Monte Irvin and he never explained why he sent Monte Irvin. If he had been wise, he would've said Monte is an old compatriot of Hank's and this would be an ideal moment for the two of them and everybody would've understood. [Kuhn] basically [was] saying, I don't condone this. Well, Hank broke the record.

"[The Dodgers] said, 'You're gonna pitch the first game in Atlanta.' I was supposed to pitch Sunday in San Diego. I go out there and I had never struck Hank Aaron out and still haven't struck him out to this day because I know one thing about Henry. With two strikes, he's gonna make an adjustment, he's gonna put the ball in play. That's the type of hitter he was. That's why he was a .300 hitter, so I knew I couldn't strike him out, so I had to make sure I made good pitches to get him out on. Good hitters feast on good pitchers because they know you're gonna be around the strike zone. It was a pleasure. I'm so proud to be a part of that moment. I'm proud to be in the big leagues pitching against Willie Mays, Henry Aaron, Willie McCovey, Orlando Cepeda, Harmon Killebrew, Al Kaline, because I'm a major leaguer.

"I think it was '94. We were at a luncheon in Atlanta and one of the writers tried to get slick. We're sitting next to one another, talking, laughing and one of the writers says to Henry, 'Henry, I bet you wore Al out.' Henry says, 'No,' always a diplomat. He looks at me and says, 'What I'd get, two or three home runs off you?' He knew how many he'd gotten. Then he said, 'Al was a very good pitcher. You can't take that one moment and try to make that epitomize his whole career, 'cause he never was a guy who was going to give into you if he made a mistake. Yeah, you're gonna jump on it, but I faced him when he threw hard and it was much more difficult to do that.' The guy had to shut up because I think, even to this day, we look for villain and the hero. We don't look at the fact that these guys are all professionals."

FIRST TIME BEHIND A MICROPHONE AS A BROADCASTER:

Downing was a color analyst on Dodgers cable-TV and radio broadcasts in the 1980s. He later worked for CBS Radio and was a broadcaster for Atlanta Braves games in 2000.

"We had a guy named Bud Furillo. He was a writer here, used to call him 'Steamer' and he worked for the [Los Angeles] Examiner. Great guy and he was like the old guy in radio. Really deservedly so because he had been around the longest. He had seen [Los Angeles] become a Triple-A city and then a major league city. Bud got sick and they said, 'Bud's gonna be out awhile, have you ever done any radio?' I said, 'I did some radio in high school and stuff like that. 'Oh, no, have you ever done?' 'No,' I said, 'just interviews in New York. They said, 'See if you can do this talk show,' and that's how I got into talk radio. When Bud came back in '84, he was there a brief period of time, then he got very sick. Eventually, they put me on late night when the team was on the road. Then, when Bud retired, they asked me to come back in '87. 'What would you like to do?' I said, 'I'd like to do weekends because I know on weekends, I was going to get two and a half hours pregame and an hour and a half postgame every Saturday and Sunday. That's more than I get during the week. So I did Saturdays and Sundays, talk radio from what, '83 until '91. I did CBS from '95 to '98."

In Downing's first game as a broadcaster, he worked as a color analyst.

"That was my forte. I love that because Tony Kubek, we would sit on the bench [when they were playing] and Tony would say, 'Okay, I'll take the top of the inning and you take the bottom of the inning.' He would take the top of the inning. He would go through it and really do the play-by-play. Then, I'd take the bottom of the inning because [his teammates] said I fell asleep on the bench and they wanted to keep me awake."

FIRST ACCOMPLISHMENT THAT STANDS OUT THE MOST TO HIM:

"Being able to play in arena that I never thought I'd ever be in, because as kids growing up, we fantasized as being major league players. You played games with your friends and they say, Okay, I announce Duke Snider is up or announce Stan Musial's up but we never fantasized being on the mound, pitching in the majors. Not me. I was a little kid, so when you say, what is the thing I'm most proud of is not only being to go out and perform in that arena, but to hold my own, because I never felt in any time I went out on the mound that I was gonna lose. That was just a mentality I had. One of the things that was most disappointing to me was not being able to grasp control of the situation in my first start. I let it get away from me very quickly because I tried to be something I wasn't but when I got it together a year and a half later, and it took that long because it doesn't happen overnight. All of a sudden I felt like, okay, now I'm getting this.

"I'm making up for lost time and now I know the guys I can strike out. Anybody would say, 'Who do you fear?' I fear anybody who swings the bat, but especially guys who hit the ball through the middle. There were two guys in particular, Frank Howard and Willie McCovey because everything they hit went through the [middle], if they hit the ball through the middle, I'm done. I'm playing one day in Washington's old DC Stadium in '70. I'm with Milwaukee and it's a 1–0 game and we're in the bottom of the sixth inning. Frank Howard comes up. I get him two strikes, but that's when I didn't have my great fastball anymore, but I had a fastball. I could come up and in on him and back him off the plate. I threw him one of my best curveballs and I swear, this thing was almost like ankle high and he had one of those one-hand swings and the ball went in the center field mezzanine. I said to myself, 'I'm back in the big leagues.' Then, I come in and the manager says to me, 'How could throw him that pitch? How could you throw him that pitch?' I said to myself, 'I have a manager who doesn't understand the big leagues. Big leagues, good hitters hit those pitches."

Al Downing by Maz Adams

10
JAKE GIBBS

Jake Gibbs played his entire 10-year career with the Yankees. He was a standout athlete at the University of Mississippi in football and baseball. Gibbs was a backup catcher and became the starter after the Yankees traded catcher Elston Howard to the Boston Red Sox in August 1967. He eventually lost the job to Thurman Munson towards the end of the 1969 season.

FIRST BASEBALL IDOL:

"There's probably a number of people. One was probably Dizzy Dean, the old pitcher for the Cardinals. Of course, everybody knew about Babe Ruth and Lou Gehrig back in those days when they hit a home run. Probably, that was the early one. After that you got people like Mickey Mantle, Joe DiMaggio, Ted Williams, people like that. Great ballplayers."

FIRST COLLEGE CHAMPIONSHIP:

Gibbs played on the baseball and football teams at the University of Mississippi. He won his first championship when he led the baseball team to its first SEC title in 1959. As a senior in 1960, he was the quarterbacked the football team to a 10–0–1 record. After winning the Sugar Bowl, Gibbs and Ole Miss was recognized as the national champions by the Football Writers Association of America. Gibbs was named the SEC Player of the Year and was named to the 1960 College Football All-America team. In 1995, he was inducted into the College Football Hall of Fame.

"I guess just very fortunate to choose Ole Miss. It was a great school. I had good programs in baseball and football. I was just surrounding myself with a bunch of good athletes. Fifty-nine was the first season, which was my sophomore year, to win the SEC [baseball] championship outright. That's in the spring of '59, in the fall of '59, the football team scored 329 points, gave up 21. We did not win but we were chosen the team of the decade and we beat LSU in a rematch game in the Sugar Bowl. That's all in '59, in '60, we win the baseball championship again and then we win it in football. Back-to-back years, I don't know if anybody's done that before."

FIRST PROFESSIONAL DRAFT:

Gibbs was selected by the Houston Oilers of the American Football League and the Cleveland Browns of the National Football League in 1961, but he decided to sign with the Yankees.

"I got a phone call, in January, I guess. It was a scout for the Philadelphia Eagles and he said, 'Norm Van Brocklin is retiring and we are thinking about making you a number one draft choice. I said, 'Well, that's crazy, that's fine but I tell you what, I'm not going to make a decision until my baseball season is over in the spring,' and he said, 'What?' I guess he didn't know I played baseball. Before he hung up the phone, now I went from a number one draft choice to maybe getting picked somewhere down the line. I found out Cleveland had drafted me, I can't remember, either sixth round or the eighth round [actually, ninth]. Houston Oilers got me in the sixth, but I had actually made up my mind by then. I was gonna go for baseball."

FIRST YANKEES CONTRACT:

Gibbs got a $100,000 signing bonus to join with the Yankees in 1961.

"Roy Hamey [Yankees GM], Atley Donald [former pitcher] and Jack White [scouting director] all came down. I signed at a little small hotel in my hometown, Grenada, Mississippi, on the 25th of May, 1961. I left the next day and flew with them guys up to New York. We left and flew into New York. About an hour and a half after we got there, I was in the Yankee locker room."

FIRST MINOR LEAGUE EXPERIENCE:

After signing his contract, Gibbs reported to the Richmond Virginians, the Yankees' Triple-A affiliate in the International League. He began his professional career with five hits in a doubleheader and an eight-game hitting streak.

"I always had a feeling I could play in the pros, but you never know what to expect. I spent 11 days with the Yankees, batting practice, infield, get to know the guys. They flew me down on [Yankees owner] Dan Topping's airplane, me and Jesse Gonder. We flew down to Richmond together. It was baseball, you knew you had to suit up and play. You knew that was another level and Triple A was good back in those days. I just got dressed and started playing. I didn't think a whole lot about it, tell you the truth. That's what I wanted to do is play. I said 5-for-7 is lucky as hell. I don't think I hit a ball hard that night, but they did fall in. That was the first game of a doubleheader and I don't think I pulled the ball. I had five hits but I didn't any of them hard. Just lucky."

FIRST YANKEES MANAGER: Ralph Houk

Gibbs first met Houk and some of the players during his 11 days with the team.

"I was impressed by the whole deal. You walk in that Yankee

locker room for the first time, you know the players in there 'cause you watch them on TV, [hear them on] radio interview, newspapers but to walk in that locker room for the very first time as a member of the Yankees. It's very impressive, I just couldn't believe it. I met Ralph Houk, he came over and was very cordial and welcome, glad you're here and that kind of thing. Then a lot of the other guys, Mickey came over, Yogi came over, Moose Skowron came over, most of all the guys and they made me feel at home the first two minutes I was in that locker room. That is a good feeling to have when you're 1,300 miles away from home and in a strange place to start a new life. To have those kind of guys come over and visit with you, congratulate you and talk to you, it just made me feel really welcome. It was a great feeling for me."

FIRST TIME HE PUT ON THE YANKEES UNIFORM:

"They told me where my locker was. I went over there and started putting on the uniform. You put it on and you feel good. You feel right. Top of the world. Putting on a Yankee pinstripe, everybody knows what they are. To put on that uniform and knowing any instance you walk out to that playing field, it's just breathtaking. You have to be there and go through it. You have to be there to understand the feelings that you have inside, but it was a good feeling, proud feeling, very honored to do that. I was very appreciative of everything that people had done for me. All that goes into your thinking, but you can't wait to put it on and you can't wait to go through the locker room. You get to the clubhouse and go out to the dugout. Once you get to the dugout, you look out there on the field, the Yankee field and you can imagine what goes through a kid's mind. You know it's real but you don't know it's real 'cause you are there. It is so impressive that I knew then that I had made the right decision 'cause I was a free agent. We didn't have a draft, so I could choose whoever I wanted to play with. It got down to where there were other good offers, but when they got down to it I said, hell, I'm gonna play with the Yankees. We won at Ole Miss in football, we won at Ole Miss in baseball, and the Yankees win every year. If I made good, I'll make the team. If I don't, hell, I'll go somewhere else, but that was my feeling. Very honored to be a Yankee.

"You just look around, you look up in the stands, you look at the field, you just take everything in. It's the first time ever and you just say, 'Here I am. God, I'm in Yankee Stadium.' Get ready to take batting practice, just a lot goes through your mind but it's a joy. It's just a ton of joy and I was proud, I was happy. I knew then I had made the right decision and I knew it was gonna be hard because they had great ballplayers. It isn't like your gonna step in and take over. You're going to have to earn your job. If you ever got there and play, you're gonna have to earn it. Of course, that's what you do. You put that in your mind. You got that feeling of being proud and you wanna be number one. So you know it's just gonna take a lot of hard work and a lot of patience and good coaching. That's gonna take a lot go get you there and that's what you do every day. You set your mind to go to the ballpark and do the best you can. That was my whole philosophy. Baseball is a fun game and it should be played as a fun game. That's what my feeling was, just come out here and play. My daddy always told me he never played ball in his life. He told me, 'Do your best, but don't overdo it.' What the hell does he mean? I found out later what he meant. Go out and play and do the best you can. Go out there and do your best but don't overdo it."

FIRST EXPERIENCE AS A CATCHER:

In 1963, the Yankees asked Gibbs to move from the infield to catcher. He played second, third and shortstop during his minor league career before moving behind the plate.

"I was in Fort Gordon [Georgia] doing my basic training for the Army. So we was in a theater one Saturday morning and this army captain comes up to me and says, 'Jake, do you belong to the Yankees?' I said, 'Yeah.' He said, 'You gonna be a catcher when you go to spring training.' I said, 'Captain, you pull rank on me but I ain't gonna be no catcher, I'm an infielder.' He said, 'No, you gonna catch. I have a good friend who knows and he knows what you going to do. I just kind of shook it off. How would an Army captain know? Nobody told me a word about it. I get outta the man's army, I go home. I got my wife and baby. My oldest, my son was born in September the 22nd of '62, so he was pretty young. We went to my hometown, spent the night and got up the next morning and went to Florida. In those days, you gotta look for your own place to stay. We got there early, we spent a couple of days in a hotel on the beach and looking. Finally, it was time to go to practice. I walked in about eight o'clock at Fort Lauderdale Stadium and you have to walk right by Ralph Houk's office. I walked by, he hollered and said, 'Jake, come in, let me talk to you.' I said, 'God, it's the first day. What's going on?' So I go in and he gets right to the point. He says, 'We've been thinking all winter about making you a catcher.' My thoughts went back to that army captain. He knew what he was talking about. I didn't know a thing about it.

"I'm 24 years old. As a quarterback, we were taught always thinking ahead. One play after the next, this play don't work, you know what will work. So I'm always thinking ahead and I'm telling myself, 'Hell, I'm 24 years old. They want me to catch. It's gonna take me two years to learn how to be a good catcher. Hell, I'll be 26. That's pretty old to be a rookie.' I didn't say that to Ralph, but I'm just thinking that. He said, 'I'm gonna tell you why.' He says, 'We think you're the only person in this organization can make this move and make it quickly and do it because of your football background, being the quarterback, running, calling the plays, running the team, that kind of thing. We think you're the one guy can make the change and do it quickly.' I didn't know what to say, really. He said, 'What do you think?' I said, 'I don't know.' He said, 'Let's try it for one week and if you don't like it, we'll put you back in the infield.' I said, okay and I went and bought a new mitt. For three days, I didn't do anything but warm up pitchers in the bullpen. On that third day, my legs were so slow and so tight and hurt from all that squatting you know. I wasn't used to it. The fourth day, they said, 'All right, it's time to go catch batting practice. Put your gear on.' I got back in. The first day, somebody fouled off a ball and I turned my head and they said, 'Keep your head still. Don't move your head.' After the first week, [Houk] called back and said, 'What did you think?' I said, 'I don't know, Ralph. It's kind of different.' He said, 'Let's try it for another week.' I said, 'Okay.'"

FIRST TIME HE SAW HIMSELF ON A BASEBALL CARD:

"If you signed with Topps, you could pick three or four different items that you wanted. I think maybe I got a TV from Topps. The other one was Hillerich and Bradsby, signed with them too. That's where I got my golf clubs. That was the bat company. I signed with them and they gave me a set of golf clubs and they were really good. I used them but I didn't know much about golf coming up. I never played a game of golf, but I figured that'd be a good time to get a free set. After four, five, six, seven years, I gave those clubs to my old baseball coach."

FIRST TIME AS AN ASSISTANT COACH AT MISSISSIPPI:

After the 1965 season, Gibbs returned to Mississippi to become an assistant coach and a mentor for quarterback Archie Manning, a Heisman Trophy finalist.

"The season was over. I came back, I lived in Grenada, Mississippi. I told my wife, 'I'm gonna go up and watch football practice on Wednesday.' I came up to watch practice and I was up on a hill where our football field was used as a playing field for a baseball outfield. So I was standing on the hill and below on the practice field and it was [an] offensive drill with the backs and the ends and I'm just standing there watching. They was doing sprint out passes and that kind of stuff. So somebody noticed me standing on the hill and coach waved me down. So I went down the hill and he introduced me to hisself, receivers, quarterbacks. All of a sudden, he says, 'Jake,' I had on a light shirt, cufflinks, street shoes, I'm dressed up and he said, 'Get under center and show these guys how to run a 36-slant, which was a slant pass. I said, 'Coach, I ain't thrown a football in five years,' and he said, 'Jake, I don't give a damn. Get under center.' He said, 'You guys, watch this.' So I took my cufflinks off, I rolled my sleeves up, got under center, snapped the ball, sprint out and I told the guys I had seen what they were doing. They would wait too damn long to throw the football. I told the receivers, I said, 'Y'all look quick.' I sprinted out and about the fourth or fifth steps and I hit him. So the coach said, 'Run it again. Run it again.' I went seven times, worked up a sweat.

"Then Archie came along in '67. Archie was tall and lengthy and skinny, but you could tell that he had good feet, good hips, you could tell he had good coordination. So he was a real pleasure to work with and we had a great understanding of each other for four years. Today, he'll call me and we'll talk four or five times during the year. Just talk about baseball, Arch was a good baseball player too.

"When Peyton [Manning] went to Tennessee, we were going through a coaching change here [at Ole Miss] and Arch and all those people didn't know who in the hell our offensive coordinator would be. Of course, David Cutcliffe was a coordinator at Tennessee. Tennessee was a pretty good outfit back in those days. All of a sudden, Peyton says, 'I'm going to Tennessee.' You know, he just pissed off the Ole Miss family. Archie went through a lot of crap for a year. I think Arch let Peyton dictate where he wanted to go. Wasn't any doubt about Eli [Manning] at Ole Miss."

FIRST IMPRESSIONS OF MICKEY MANTLE AS A TEAMMATE:

"It was just a pleasure. It was an honor to be on the same team with Mickey, 'cause Mickey was a leader. He was a quiet leader, but everybody followed him. He wrapped his own legs every day. He'd get work and he'd go out and play the game and never complained. Sometimes he was hurtin', the way he ran, but he never let on and everybody respected him from the way he approached the game, how he played the game, how he loved the game and that made you play better. Mickey made each guy play better and I think that's a point that probably hasn't been said too many times. That year [1968] he was hurtin' a little bit more. The Yankees had gone through a transition of young players and Mick was probably the oldest player there. So they had traded away Elston Howard in '67, Roger [Maris] was gone, so we didn't have a lot of old players. Mickey was a professional. He wanted to play well all the time and I think it hurt him when he couldn't. It wasn't a good year for Mick in '68. He struggled and he knew it was time for him to get out of the game. Mick and I had become real good friends."

FIRST TIME WINNING A CHAMPIONSHIP AS COACH OF THE OLE MISS BASEBALL TEAM:

Gibbs piloted the Ole Miss baseball team to the SEC Championship in 1972 and a berth in the College World Series. Gibbs was a two-time SEC Baseball Coach of the Year. In February, 2020, Gibbs's number 41 was retired by the school.

"I never said I was going to be a doctor or a lawyer or whatever. I knew I was going to coach. I loved sports and I figured one day I would be a high school football coach. That was my thinking way back in the old days that I was going to coach. I went to Ole Miss, physical education was my degree so I knew I was going to coach. Having that opportunity I did, what helped me a lot was sitting in the bullpen with Jim Hegan, my catching coach and we would study the game. Look at the game. Jim was really a good friend of mine, a great man, a great catcher. When you in the bullpen, if you're paying attention to what the hell is going on in the game, you can learn a lot by watching. What you do is, you put yourself in the other manager's shoes and certain situations, what would he do. Instead of sitting in the bullpen and dreaming, you watch the game and that's what I did. I'll watch the game and I'll watch the moves a manager would do, what players would do. You can learn a lot. When I was catching with the Yankees, I used to watch the opposition catchers. I saw how they squatted, I saw how they move their feet. I thought you can learn a lot about watching other players.

"At Ole Miss, I just said, 'Go out, play hard and have fun. Just enjoy yourself. We didn't have a deep team in pitching at all [in

1972], but we just got hot and our players got good attitudes and hell, nobody could beat us. We were 15–1 going into the last series against LSU and got beat down there twice 'cause we had it wrapped up, but it was fun. What people don't realize, that '72 team and my '77 team, they still get together and do things together. They call on me all the time, so it's a wonderful feeling to have a player that played for you and stay in contact and call you up and come by and visit."

FIRST INTERACTIONS WITH DEREK JETER AND MARIANO RIVERA:

Gibbs was a minor league manager for the Yankees' Class-A team in Tampa in 1994 and 1995. Hall of Famers Derek Jeter and Mariano Rivera both played for Gibbs in 1994.

"I think I met Jeter, seemed like spring training of '93, he came to camp for a day or two. In '94, I'm getting him at shortstop and they were a little concerned about his errors. After the first two or three weeks of the season, I could see where he was making his errors. He covered more territory at shortstop than anybody I ever seen. Going in, going to his right, in the hole, coming up, throwing, going behind second base. Catching the ball, turning his hips, throwing and that's where a lot of errors was coming from. Not because of the glove but because of not turning proper and getting his hips turned and making that throw. So that's what we worked on from when you get there, you gotta turn those hips and get lined up to throw the ball. You can work on it; you can do it and that's what he did. I just had him for three months in '94 and he was one of the young guys that I had on a steal situation. I had a couple of guys I would give the daylight sign to run. You run when you think you got a chance to make it. He was one of the guys I gave a daylight sign to when he got on first base. We had a sign that he could pick his pitch. That year, he stole 22 out of 23 bases. The only time he got thrown out, it took a perfect throw from the catcher that just barely nailed him at third base. I always kinda wondered why they didn't run him more in the big leagues 'cause he was a smart kid. He understands the game and he played hard and wasn't a big talker. He just showed up and played.

"Mariano was coming off an elbow surgery. When I got him, I could pitch him, say tonight, I could pitch him in relief as a stopper for 20 pitches. That's 20 pitches, go get him. The next night, you couldn't get him up at all, so he pitched every third night. I had him for like two and a half months and he was still throwing that cutter. I remember Stick Michael coming by one day, 'What do you think about Rivera?' I said, 'Hell, I can fish. He's got that cutter.' Now he's going to get right-handed hitters out. He knows where to put it. That's the difference in throwing a cutter, knowing where to put it. He had to figure that out."

FIRST REACTION TO BEING INDUCTED INTO THE COLLEGE FOOTBALL HALL OF FAME AND HAVING HIS NUMBER RETIRED BY OLE MISS BASEBALL:

"Well, it was a great honor. I think anytime you can get your uniform retired, it's a great honor and you really appreciated it, but I never made a big deal out of it. Ole Miss has never been known for retired numbers. You don't have that many numbers in football that are retired and baseball is only two. I think there's only one in basketball here and you got Archie and Eli and Charlie Conerly. I never thought my number would be retired."

Jake Gibbs by Eric Raleigh

11
CHARLIE HAYES

Third baseman Charlie Hayes played two separate stints with the Yankees. Before the 1992 season, they acquired him in a trade with the Philadelphia Phillies. Hayes was left unprotected after the season and was selected by the Colorado Rockies with the third pick in the expansion draft. In August 1996, the Yankees reacquired Hayes from the Pittsburgh Pirates to platoon with Wade Boggs. In Game 4 of that year's World Series win over the Atlanta Braves, Hayes had three hits as the Yankees rallied from a 6–0 deficit to tie the series at two games apiece before winning it in six. He was traded to the San Francisco Giants after the 1997 season. Hayes's son, Ke'Bryan, is the starting third baseman for the Pittsburgh Pirates.

FIRST DRAFT EXPERIENCE:

Hayes was selected by the San Francisco Giants in the fourth round of the 1983 MLB June Amateur Draft. He began his pro career in rookie ball at Great Falls of the Pioneer League.

"It was totally different than I thought by getting drafted and coming from a small town in Harrisburg, Mississippi. When I got drafted, I thought I was going to the major leagues. I went to Great Falls, Montana, which was unbelievable, a difficult place for me because it was the simple fact that here's a kid that's never anywhere in his life outside of the state of Mississippi and now, all of a sudden, I'm in Great Falls, Montana, without a mom, without a dad, without anything that's familiar and it took me a little while to adjust. More than anything, I know in my situation it was more self-doubt. You always had that support there for you when you were at home and basically for me, playing high school baseball, all my friends were there, but now, all of a sudden, I'm in a foreign place. You don't have that support around like you had before.

"One of things for me was I struck out four times my first four years of high school baseball. When I got to pro ball, I struck out [a lot] in the first season, so that in itself was a shock for me. It gave me self-doubt thinking I wasn't good enough. After a while you get used to it. I grew up a tough kid, never with any excuses. Everything I had to work for, even school clothes. We grew up without a lot, not only myself but mostly all the kids that were in my neighborhood. So going over to Great Falls, Montana, after a I finally realized what was going on, it was a choice."

FIRST MANAGER WHO HAD A REAL IMPACT ON HIS CAREER:

"The one guy who was very instrumental in my career was Wendell Kim [his A-ball manager at Fresno during his third professional season]. This guy used to be on me from the time I put my uniform on, to the time I take it off. I didn't understand it at the time [but] I use it now and I tell a lot of kids out here, 'If the coach ain't talking to you, he don't see nothing in you. If the coach ain't getting on you, he don't see nothing in you.' A lot of people don't understand that. They think, oh, this guy's picking on my kid or he's doing this or the kid is thinking that coach doesn't like him. The reason why the coach says something to you, he sees something in you. If he ain't saying nothing to you, he don't see nothing in you."

FIRST EXPERIENCE WITH YANKEES FANS:

"I remember an incident at Yankee Stadium. We were playing a Sunday day game. I never really
interacted with the fans when the game was going on. My first at-bat, I struck out. I went back out in the field, I made an error, then the inning was over. Then, I run back out to the field to play defense the next time and this guy told me, 'Hey, hey, you suck. You stealing money.' He knew down to the penny, you know? So I went back to the bench and I was like, 'Paul O'Neill, this guy's all over me.' Paul was like, 'What is he saying?' I said, man he knows exactly how much I make. So I said, 'Hey man, you gotta work tomorrow?' and he said, 'Yeah,' and I said, 'I don't, we got a day off and guess what?' I'm gonna make exactly what [you] told me that I was gonna make every day.' That's what I told him. After that, that guy was like my best friend at Yankee Stadium. All he wanted was me to say something to him, period. It didn't matter what I said. When I look back on the game, I wish I would've been more interactive with the fans. Remember when I got to the Phillies, I replaced [Hall of Famer] Mike Schmidt. Right then and there, I got the brunt of every joke and everything else and it put me in a shell."

FIRST TIME PLAYING FOR JOE TORRE:

"I remember one day coming in and Mr. Torre had told me that I was gonna play against lefties. We were playing the Angels. They had about four left-hand starters. We walk in there, I look at the board, I'm not in there. I'm mad, I'm mad, I'm mad. Why am I not playing? I never expressed it to anybody. I just went to the [batting] cage and hit a thousand balls. That's how I took my frustration out. I'm sitting on the bench during the game, I stood, down to my right I see Darryl Strawberry. I look down to my left, I see Tino Martinez. So I said to myself, these guys been did way more in this game than I've ever done. From that day forward, I never was mad again. I approach every day like it was my last day and I gave 'em my all. I hope the fans out there in the Yankee world and everywhere I played, I hope that's the way they look at me and they think of me approaching it that way because that's what I did. I gave 'em my all every day."

FIRST TIME HE MADE FOUR ERRORS IN ONE GAME:
July 15, 1989 as a member of the
Philadelphia Phillies vs. Houston Astros at Veterans Stadium
Hayes committed four of the Phillies' six errors in a 9–6 loss.

"I remember coming in after the game and all the guys were, like Darren Daulton and some of those guys were like, 'Hey man, you know you gotta stand up there and talk to the media.' I said, 'Hey dude, I don't got no problem with that.' I'll be the first one to admit that I played terrible. That's one thing, I know that playing on the East Coast, those people are so savvy when it comes to baseball that they can tell when you're not being honest. A-Rod [Alex Rodriguez] had a problem with that in New York when he first got there because it was never his fault. Now, when you come out and you stunk the place up and you tell everybody you stunk the place up and you willingly go out there and work hard and pay the price, man, the people in New York. That was one of the greatest places I ever played at.

"As far as my career, being on the Yankees. I don't think it helped because I was in the prime of my baseball playing career, but at the same time, I understood that if I wanted to win a World Series, I was
gonna have to make sacrifices just like a whole lot of the guys that were on that team did. I understood that right away and that's why it didn't affect me. I don't look back and say, 'Well, I wish I would've did this or I wish I would've did that. The only thing I said that I would look back on, I wish I would've did was interact more with the fans because there's a market out there for everybody. It's back to the old thing. Closed mouth won't get paid. A lot of people in Houston where I live, they have no idea who I am and I love it like that because I can go on and be a normal person like everybody else. I come to New York, I can walk down 125th on the West Side, people know who I am and that's okay too.

"My future is over with. All I can do is go out and reminisce on the good times. Reminisce on the bad times. You're not playing for yourself. You're playing for the love of the game and we all gotta approach it that way. I listen to a lot of people talking about they played the game the right way. You play the game the right way, there's a runner on second, you get him to third. I never played with anybody that played for money. Everybody played to win the game. You do whatever it takes to win the game and I hear this all the time, saying, 'I love this guy. He plays the right way.'

"I love the Yankees because the Yankees have always treated me with the utmost respect. They came and told me the truth. Hey, you can do it. You can't do it. I understand that. I know as a player I'm gonna give you everything I got. You gotta pull that uniform off of me. When they finally pulled it off of me, it was time for me to move on with stage two of my life and that's been a father as a parent, being a loving husband. Trying to give back to society, trying to help out in any way I can. That's what I represent."

Charlie Hayes by Eric Kittelberger

12
MIKE HEATH

Catcher Mike Heath played one season with the Yankees as a member of their World Series–winning team in 1978. As an 18-year old, Heath was selected by the Yankees in the second round of the 1973 June Amateur Draft out of Hillsborough High School in Tampa, Florida. He was part of a significant 10-player deal with the Texas Rangers that was consummated in November 1978 in which he and 1977 American League Cy Young Award winner Sparky Lyle were traded along with three other players to Texas for pitcher Dave Righetti and four other players.

FIRST BASEBALL IDOL:

"When I was young, there was no doubt that it was Harmon Killebrew. I think the reason was that we didn't watch much baseball, my dad and I or kids in the neighborhood. It just wasn't a thing we did. We were always outside, but I think when I saw him play several times, I loved his name and so I'd always play Harmon Killebrew up at bat."

FIRST TIME HE SPOKE TO LEGENDARY COLLEGE FOOTBALL COACH BEAR BRYANT:

While growing up in Florida, Heath played linebacker and received multiple scholarship offers, including one from Bear Bryant, the legendary football coach at Alabama.

"I was actually a strong safety or outside linebacker, a strong safety back in the day. He had called the house like a day after I signed. My parents had told me that he had called, that he wanted to offer me a scholarship to play football at Alabama. I'm like, okay, that's cool because I had already signed my baseball contract. I was in Johnson City, Tennessee, but the first time I actually spoke to Bear was in '78 when I got called up with the Yankees. We're in Yankee Stadium and taking BP [batting practice] and nobody's in the stands at that point. So I look over there and Dick Howser was talking to Bear Bryant. I'm like, 'That's Mr. Bear Bryant.' So Dick Howser yells at me, get over here, come here. So I come running over there. He goes, 'Do you know who this is?' I said, 'Yes sir. That's Mr. Paul Bear Bryant,' and Mr. Bryant's raspy voice he said, 'How you doing, son?' I said, 'Good, Mr. Bryant.' He's talking to Dick Howser, he says, 'You boys signed him before I had an opportunity to call him.' Then Dick looks at me and Dick goes, 'Did you play football?' I said, 'Yes sir.' Bear goes, 'Did he play football? He was 5-11, a hundred and fifty-five pounds in high school. Hit like he was 6-2, 220 [lbs].'"

FIRST DRAFT EXPERIENCE:

"We get a phone call. I say we, because [fellow Florida high school prospect] Manuel Seoane was there. We were at the news [Channel 8 News] headquarters in Tampa and we're sitting there or just walking around and we are watching the ticker tape. The tape that comes across the wire because there was no big hoopla back in the day. They're making a show out of it to make money. So we sat there and the names come across. Mine came across as number two by the Yankees so it was pretty exciting. [Simulates an announcement] 'The Yankees choose Mike Heath in the second round.'"

FIRST GAME AS A CATCHER:

"Spring training in '76, I felt I was having a good spring training with the Triple-A team. Bobby Cox was our manager, Floyd Boyer was one of our coaches. What I remember is that I'm taking ground balls at third base. I think they had Dennis Sherrill or Mickey Klutts at shortstop. Anyhow, taking ground balls at third base and Floyd comes over to me and he goes, 'Mike, come here. I gotta talk to you.' He said, 'We've been friends for a long time.' I said, 'Floyd, get down to it. Are you releasing me?' I mean, this is kind of swan song talk, you know you're outta here. He goes, 'No.' He says, 'We're thinking about moving you to a catcher. What do you think?' I said, 'Whatever it takes to get to the big leagues, I don't care. Whatever it is.' He says, 'Then you need to get off the field and go and see Bobby in his office, Bobby Cox. So I go there and walk in. Bobby was there and says, 'Mike, we think this is a good position for you,' you know, selling this to me and all that and he gave me a catcher's mitt and just said, 'I think this is a good position for you but the only bad things of it is you're gonna have to go back to A-ball.' I'm like, 'Hey, Bobby. Whatever it takes to get to the big leagues.' I remember going [back down] because I was in the Florida State League in '75, I went back [there in] '76. At that point, we had got Domingo Ramos and Damaso Garcia, two kids from the Dominican that were awesome. So I played, short, second, third, short, second, third, catch, short, second, third, third. I caught only [18] games that year."

FIRST TIME HE WAS CALLED UP:

"I gotta go back to '77. It was Jerry Narron and I platooning in West Haven. We all had great years, I mean the team was unbelievable. The West Haven Yankees the next year was a great team also, but they wanted me to go to [Triple-A] Tacoma, Washington, to split time with Jerry Narron. I had told 'em that I really didn't want to do that. I wanted to go where I could play every day. If this is my destiny, I'm gonna go play every day, so they sent me back to West Haven in '78 and I was playing every day. Rick Stenholm was there. Rick just passed away the other day, he was a good friend of mine and we were in the minor leagues together. We're sitting at a place in West Haven called the Ground Round having dinner and the Yankee game was on. Fran Healy got hurt, Cliff Johnson was catching. I love Cliff. Great guy, man. When I got up there, he treated me very, very good and he was just missing balls. Stenholm goes, 'Heath, they're gonna call you up, man.' I'm like, 'There's no way, they're gonna call up Jerry Narron, you know?' The guy hits 15 home runs, he had a great bat on him. I thought, the big leagues were looking more for that than what they were a defensive guy, you know. Sure enough, around 12:30, I get a phone call to my apartment and it was the general manager of the West Haven Yankees. He says, 'Hey, pack your bags. You're going up.' I said, 'Tell New York, just let me stay here. Tell the Yankees, just let me stay here, let 'em call up Narron. I don't want to go to Tacoma.' He goes, 'No, dude, you're going to the big leagues.'" He told me he'd pick me up [the next] morning. I think he picked me up about eight o'clock the next day. He drove me and my wife and dropped me off at the Stadium and walked in the Stadium and it was like, 'Wow!'"

FIRST TIME AT YANKEE STADIUM:

"I mean, there was no doubt. I was in awe. When I walk in, Pete Sheehy and Nick [Priore], our clubhouse guy, I think Pete was the one that came up to me and says, 'Welcome.' He says, 'Here's your locker.' I turn around and I look. It was right by the door and there's my name with my locker. I had my name already on the locker. So this is the funny part. I go sit at my locker and a couple guys come up, 'cause I knew some of 'em because of spring trainings. So I'm sitting at my locker just admiring this whole place. Then all of a sudden, I hear all this discussion in this room. Blah, blah, blah. We got a rookie catcher. We don't need no rookie catcher. We need pitching on this team right now. We're struggling. Like, that's [manager] Billy Martin. The reporters come walking out of his office and they all just said, 'Hey, how you doing? How do you like being here?' that kind of deal. We knew our place in the game when we were kids coming in. We knew our place and you just went about your business. All of a sudden Billy comes walking out of his office and comes walked directly to me after I'm hearing, 'We don't need no rookie catcher,' and he shakes my hand and he says, 'Hey, nice to see you, son.' He says, 'We could use you right now.'"

FIRST TIME PUTTING ON A YANKEES UNIFORM:

"Putting on a Yankee uniform? Absolutely [meant a lot to him]. Getting drafted by the Yankees, absolutely. Being a rookie, being called up with the Yankees, absolutely, but it was something that was like, I knew I was gonna be there one day. I felt that in my heart that I was gonna be there. I think a lot of kids have that goal, but I just felt that I was gonna be there. I didn't take it for granted, but I knew I was gonna be there. To be called up, be drafted by the Yankees, being called up by the Yankees and playing for the Yankees, even catching one inning in the World Series with the Yankees and being around the Yankee greats is priceless."

FIRST IMPRESSION OF BILLY MARTIN:

"First impression, he was a hard-nosed manager. Kind of had control. I felt and admired that. He would have a lot of fun with the players. He was always talking to 'em and they were talking to him and they were teasing him. He had teased them, it was awesome. Some guys might not like him, but that's their judgment, not mine."

FIRST MAJOR LEAGUE GAME: June 3, 1978 vs. Oakland A's at Oakland-Alameda County Coliseum.

Heath entered his first major league game as a defensive replacement for Thurman Munson.

"I was so, all right, it's my time. Let's get in there. Let's do your thing. Don't fuck up. You're gonna do this. You're good. You know you're good. You can do this. That's why you belong here. This is your opportunity. Let's go get it. I didn't even think about screwing up. I really didn't. I just knew I deserved being there and I worked my ass off to get there. Now it's time to show 'em that you need to stay here."

FIRST HIT: June 28, 1978 vs. Milwaukee Brewers at County Stadium.

In his second start at catcher, Heath singled off of Brewers lefty Jerry Augustine in the top of the third inning for his first major league hit. He also scored his first run.

"I think it was a base hit to right field, I do remember getting that. It was quite the excitement. I remember that. That was good. Quite exciting. I mean, you get the ball and all that and it's like, 'Okay, got my first hit, let's go.' All right, we still got a game to play."

FIRST TIME HE THREW OUT A RUNNER TRYING TO STEAL SECOND:

Heath threw out Paul Molitor trying to steal second in the bottom of the fifth inning for his first caught stealing.

"My defense overshadowed my offense and I wanted to throw everybody out defensively. So yeah, throwing guys out, blocking balls and working. That was my deal. I wanted to be the best defensive catcher. I was aggressive. I made errors when I probably shouldn't have, but that's why I was aggressive. I know that some other catchers, they'd pick and choose when they want to make throws, but I felt that I could make up the difference if a guy stole and stuff like that. I could make up the difference with my arm. I just played aggressively. I was never afraid to make a mistake."

FIRST REACTION TO BILLY MARTIN BEING FIRED:

In July 1978, the Yankees fired Billy Martin [it was announced that he resigned] and replaced him with Bob Lemon.

"I remember them talking about Bob Lemon coming over and taking over. I do remember a meeting that we had in the clubhouse. I think on that day, everybody was voicing their concern about [how] we need to pick it up as a team. You know, we're the best team money can buy and we should be doing better and it's our fault more than anything that we're fucking up and let's try to turn this around. I swear, I remember this and maybe not, but they asked Lou Piniella, 'Lou, you got anything to say?' He says, 'All I gotta say is, if this team is having a meeting, the best team in baseball is having a meeting. We must be really fucked up.'"

FIRST WORLD SERIES EXPERIENCE:

Heath was a member of the 1978 World Series champion Yankees. He got into Game 5 as a defensive replacement.

"You're a little nervous, but at the same time, you go out there. I just tried to look at it as another game, to be honest with you. Probably, if I had to start every game and being a rookie, that it would probably be a little nerve wracking the first game, but once the bell rings and you got that first pitch underneath your belt, you're ready to roll. It was a great feeling to be there and be able to catch an inning."

FIRST TIME HE WAS TOLD HE WAS BEING TRADED:

"I remember receiving a phone call from Thurman [Munson] and he goes, 'I heard you just got traded.' I'm like, 'I hadn't heard anything,' and he said, 'Diane [Thurman's wife], Mike got traded, right?' So Thurman Munson was the one that called me and said you got traded in this 10-player deal. He said, 'Hey, good luck, kid.' He says, 'I was ready to give up my job to you but I can't retire yet. Now I gotta keep working at it.' He was probably just joking but he said he was ready to give up his, you know, give it to me and let me start catching some, but he just wished me good luck."

FIRST EXPERIENCE PLAYING EVERY DEFENSIVE POSITION EXCEPT PITCHER:

Heath played every defensive position, except pitcher, at some point during his major league career.

"I'm a very versatile player. I loved it. In fact, whenever I got the start in center field, that was one of my happiest moments to start in center field because my best friend, Dwayne Murphy, he's a center fielder for Oakland all those years [that] I got the start at the position. He ruled for many years but being able to be so versatile, it made me feel good that I knew the manager could count on me and put me into any position. He knew I wasn't gonna hurt the team besides catching a thousand games in a career."

Mike Heath by James Kimball

13
TOMMY JOHN

Left-handed pitcher Tommy John played 8 of his 26 Major League seasons with the Yankees in two separate stints. John signed with the Yankees as a free agent following the 1978 season and was 21–9 with a 2.96 ERA in 1979 and finished second in the voting for the American League's Cy Young Award. The Yankees traded John to the California Angels in August 1982, but he returned to the Yankees in May 1986. In 1989, John became the oldest pitcher to start on Opening Day when he took the mound for the Yankees against the Twins in Minnesota. The 45-year-old went seven innings and picked up the win in a 4–2 Yankees victory.

FIRST VETERAN PLAYER WHO GAVE HIM GOOD ADVICE:

"There was a left-hander that did play pro basketball, played with the Minneapolis Lakers before they became the LA Lakers. His name was Steve Hamilton. Steve was from Morehead State and Steve started with Cleveland and he played for the Yankees for a period of time. He told me, one spring training, it was '62 or '63, 'You know, there's gonna be a lot of coaches that are gonna tell you things. This is what you've gotta do to be good. This is what you gotta do to be great,' and he said, 'It may not be able to fit your style of pitching. What you've gotta do is you've gotta look and assess what they're saying. Try it and if you can use it, use it. If not, then you gotta can it,' and I said, 'Yeah, but they'll get mad at me,' and he said, 'Absolutely, they probably will, but the thing is, they'll still have a job and you won't.' He said, 'That's the part that you've really gotta be tough on.' I know a lot of coaches thought I was stubborn, hardheaded. Yeah, but I wasn't dumb. I knew what I had to do and I just did what I had to do and that was to pitch away from guy's power. I tried to pitch the ball down and away, down and away, down and away to right-handed hitters. Left-handed hitters, I tried to throw the ball down and in, try to get 'em to swing over the top of the ball and they hit it on the ground, either second baseman or first baseman, but I knew that's where my bread and butter was and I stayed with it, rather than go to some part of the game or some part of the strike zone that I really wasn't very good at."

Steve Hamilton was known for throwing the "Folly Floater," an eephus pitch that he would tantalize hitters to keep them off balance.

"[Hamilton] drove one guy. He threw it to [Indians first baseman] Tony Horton and Tony Horton the next day had a nervous breakdown. Now I don't say that the Folly Floater drove him over the edge but he crawled back to the dugout on his hands and knees. He swung and missed and he asked him to throw it again, and he threw it again, and he swung and missed. Then, he crawled back to the dugout on his hands and knees. A day or two or three days later, he was in a hospital for a nervous breakdown. Everybody said it was the Folly Floater, but I think there were other issues."

FIRST MAJOR LEAGUE MANAGER:

Former major league catcher Birdie Tebbetts was John's first big league manager with the Cleveland Indians.

"He was very, very, very intelligent, baseball wise. I remember that he had a pitching school during spring training. He would talk to the pitchers once or twice a week and we'd just go over certain things. Now, you have to remember, I was just out of high school. This was my first spring training. His thing was, you should be able to pitch three, four pitches ahead. I just thought, My God, I'll never, you know, how do you pitch three or four pitches ahead? I can tell you in all the years that I played baseball, I never pitched three or four pitches ahead because the hitter will tell you what he's looking for by what he does to the last pitch. So, the thing is I want to get him out on a ball away, therefore, I've gotta throw two or three balls inside and he jerks a double down the left field line. Well, your plan kind of went awry. I remember that meeting and I remember saying to myself, My God, I'll never be able to do that. And you know what? I was right, I never was able to pitch three or four pitches ahead. You pitch, you throw the ball to the hitter. If he takes it, you throw it again. If he swings and misses, you throw it again and you keep throwing it until he does something with it. So the hitter will tell you basically what he is looking for, what he does to the pitch you threw last."

John played for some of the more notable managers in the history of baseball, including Hall of Famer Tommy Lasorda and Billy Martin.

"The best manager I played for, well, Dick Howser was very good. Bob Lemon was very good. [Walter] Alston was very good. Al Lopez was outstanding. Eddie Stanky was very good, but the guy that really got more out of his players, he wasn't a great manager, but he got more out of his players was Lasorda. He just made the game fun, he made the clubhouse fun. You have these guys that have the clubhouse tight and the players are tight. I know a couple of sportswriters in the Bridgeport area and they said [when John managed the independent league Bluefish] I should have been tougher on all this stuff. Tougher on what? You're in a second chance league. Guys are hanging on by their fingernails and the last thing they want to do is get some old guy like me to come in and yell at 'em and tell 'em that they gotta player harder. If you have to motivate these guys in the Atlantic League, their best shot is to get out is to play their butts off and get back in affiliated baseball. Lasorda was the best guy that I played for, but the best managers I ever played for, they didn't try to overmanage. They ran the game.

"I don't believe in bunting. I'm an American League manager like that. I would rather sit back and bunt in the last three innings of the game to try to get a run and tie the game up or win the game, but the first five or six innings, swing the bat. The guy may bunt the ball but a double may be in his bat that drives two runs in. The old saying is, if you play for one run, that's what you'll get, one run. Earl Weaver put it very distinctly when he was managing Baltimore. He said, 'The game of baseball is pitching, defense, and three-run homers,' and Earl was right on."

FIRST PREFERENCE FROM HIS CATCHER:

"I like to pitch to good thinking catchers. [Thurman] Munson, John Oates, Rick Cerone was very good. We had some good catchers with the White Sox. I like to go over and tell my catchers, 'Okay, let's go with my sinker, see how it's working. If it's doing okay, then we'll go sink or curveball. If it's not sinking, then we'll mix in more curveballs early. We just went over kind of a game plan and then I just relegated it to the catcher. Generally, I threw what he put down because I didn't want to stand out there going, 'No, no. God, is this the right pitch? Okay, I'll throw it,' because a lot of times when you do that, you second guess yourself. When you second guess yourself, the pitch won't be as good as what it should be. I just went with Thurman and Thurman would throw fingers down and I would throw 'em. In fact, one time in Boston, I was pitching a good game and he said, 'You think you got good stuff, don't you?' I said, 'Yeah,' and he says, 'Bull, next inning you throw whatever you want, I'm not gonna put a signal down. You throw that crap up to the plate and I'll catch it.' I did that for two innings. He never called a sign and Boston was looking. They thought I was calling the signs. I finally asked him, 'How could you do that?' He said, 'You gotta understand your fastball is gonna be tailing down and away. Your curveballs were gonna be breaking down and in. So I would just look for the ball down and then I would react to the spin off the ball. If it was a curveball spin, I would look for it down and in and catch it. If it was a fastball, it was going to be down and away.' He said, 'It's pretty easy to catch you,' and that deflated my balloon, I'll tell you, real quick."

FIRST GAME: September 6, 1963 as a member of the Cleveland Indians vs. Washington Senators at D.C. Stadium.

John pitched one inning in relief and gave up two hits and one unearned run and did not get a decision.

"I remember when they called me into the game, I couldn't get the gate to the bullpen open. I'd never seen a latch like that in my life. They didn't have latches like that in Terre Haute, Indiana. I can't get the gate open. I'm going to have to climb the fence and jump down. This is going to be so embarrassing. Finally, it had to be divine intervention but the gate popped open and I trotted out onto the field and the second hitter I faced got a base hit down the third base line. His name was Don Zimmer. This was about 150 pounds lighter than he was."

FIRST INJURY THAT LED TO "TOMMY JOHN SURGERY"

In July 1974, while pitching for the Dodgers, John hurt the elbow on his pitching arm. The left-hander underwent a brand-new technique that saved his career and became known as "Tommy John Surgery." Dr. Frank Jobe performed the revolutionary surgery in September 1974. Jobe took a tendon from John's right wrist and used it to replace a ligament in his left elbow. John returned in 1976 and pitched 14 more seasons and made three All-Star teams, including two with the Yankees.

"I thought I was the most unlucky person in the world. I've never played on a champion team and you had a chance and it looked like we were going to win and go to the World Series and all this. I thought, son of a gun, here we're gonna go to the World Series and I'm injured and I'm not going to be able to pitch. As much as I thought I was the most unlucky person in the world when things started to unfold, I found out I was the luckiest person in the world because I got to be around Frank Jobe and his team of surgeons. They put Humpty Dumpty back together again and Humpty had a pretty good career post-surgery.

"Dr. Jobe, I trusted him not only as a surgeon, but as a friend because that's what I felt he was. I didn't think that he would tell me anything that would not be good for me as a person or good for me as a ballplayer. He treated me as a person first and a patient second. I knew that what he was going to say was going to be in my best interest. He told me you don't need the surgery, but I can tell you if you do not have it, you will never, ever play baseball again as you know it now. He said, 'If you want to pitch again, we've gotta do this ligament replacement surgery. We've never done it before. The procedure is sound because they do it in the hand and wrist, but it's never been done on a pitcher that throws 125 pitches a game. That's what we can do.' He said, decide what you wanna do. I don't have it done, I'll never pitch again. If I have it done, he said, well, chances are you won't pitch again. I said, 'What, 50 percent or no?' He said, 'I have no idea, but I would say less than 10.' So, somewhere around five, less than that. [Dr.Jobe] said, 'I don't know. You may go out on your first time throwing, it comes unraveled and it's done.' 'Okay, let's get it done.' Because if I don't have it done, I'm never going to pitch again and I wanna play ball so the only chance I had of playing baseball again was to have the surgery. I didn't see that there was any downside risk."

"The fact they name it Tommy John Surgery was kind of a happenstance thing. Dr. Jobe kept talking about the ligament replacement surgery, the ulnar collateral ligament replacement surgery with the palmarus longus tendon and blah, blah, blah. He said, the surgery we did on Tommy John. Then it shortened it down to the Tommy John surgery and now it's just called, he's gotta go in and have Tommy John surgery. As soon as you say that, everybody knows what it is because they know Tommy John surgery is ligament replacement surgery in your elbow. The success rate is a little better than 90 percent, so when you go into rehab, there's a slight chance that you might not pitch again. I tell you, if you do your work and you do it diligently and you don't try to rush things and let nature heal at its own pace, you've got a very, very good chance at coming back and being even better."

FIRST WORLD SERIES EXPERIENCE:

While pitching for the Dodgers, John lost to the Yankees in the 1977 and 1978 World Series. John was with the Yankees when they lost to the Dodgers in six games in 1981.

"It would be nice to have a world championship ring, but if you look at my record in the playoffs and World Series, it's second to none. I think my ERA is in the twos (2.65) and my playoff record, World Series and all that is like 6–1 or 7–2 or something (6–3). I pitched well, it's just that we didn't play well as a team to win four games. We ended up losing four games and could never get on the right side."

Tommy John by John Pennisi

14
TONY KUBEK

Tony Kubek played his entire nine-year career with the Yankees. In 1957, Kubek became the third Yankee to be named American League Rookie of the Year. Kubek was a four-time All-Star and three- time World Series champion. After his playing career, Kubek went on to a successful career in the broadcast booth, first with NBC Sports and later on with the MSG Network, working Yankees games from 1990 to1994. In 2008, he was named the winner of the Ford C. Frick Award that honors baseball broadcasters.

FIRST BASEBALL IDOL:

"My father. My father played professional baseball in the 1930s. He played in the American Association, which was then the Milwaukee Brewers. So, he was a professional baseball player and did well until he helped my mother raise her brothers and sisters [who] were my aunts and uncles, so he couldn't make enough money playing baseball. So he quit and got a job in a factory. He had some good years. In fact, in 1931, one of the stories. My mother kept a scrapbook and some of the things. My dad was a Milwaukee boy and played for the Milwaukee Brewers then, which most people never heard of but it was a Triple-A ballclub with the American Association and my dad played against one of the greatest teams of all times.

"The 1931 New York Yankees played a day game in Yankee Stadium. They hopped the train, took the train to Milwaukee, played a day game, an exhibition game to help the Milwaukee Brewers franchise on their off day. Played the game and then went on to Comiskey Park in Chicago. That Yankee team in '31 had eight future Hall of Famers, [Babe] Ruth, [Lou] Gehrig, [Lefty] Gomez, [manager Joe] McCarthy and you could go on and on. My dad was on that team with the Brewers. It's something you would not obviously remember but my dad told the story many years later. I wasn't born until 1935. He said when they played, Gehrig played in the outfield, right field. They put Babe Ruth at first base so he could be closer to the fans. As the game went into the ninth inning, somebody hit a ground ball to Ruth at first base. He purposely let the ball go through his legs, ran off the field, doffed his cap to the fans and it was a packed house, standing room only, and said, 'We gotta go. Trains don't wait. We gotta catch a train. We got a game in Chicago at Comiskey Park tomorrow.' So after my dad quit professional baseball, he played in what they call industrial leagues around Milwaukee. I was the bat boy at times when I was very, very little.

"So, I had baseball. My mother's parents died very young. My mom and dad were not married at the time. So my dad came home after a day game one day and my mother was there. She was the oldest of six kids and my dad said, "What's going on?' She said, 'They're taking us all to an orphanage,' and my dad said, 'No, you're not,' and we went to his blind mother down on the south side of Milwaukee who was also Polish. My mother was born in Poland and his mother said to him, 'Are you kids gonna get

married? He said, 'Yes,' 'Go get married.' So they ended up keeping all the kids and my mother and

father raised, they were like my aunts and uncles but they were like my brothers and sisters. All four of those kids went into World War II. The oldest one, Johnny, he was wounded fighting [Erwin] Rommel. He was a catcher and played a lot of amateur baseball. Might have been a pretty good ballplayer but during the war, he got wounded in North Africa. My aunt was like my sister. She enlisted in the WACs. [Women's Army Corps]. She was stationed in New York. The third one was Uncle [sic] He signed a contract out of high school with the White Sox, played one year and then went to the military, got wounded, blown up in a truck in Berlin. He survived, but he was hurt. That was the end of his career. Then, the last one, Eddie, he was the fourth one who was in the military in World War II. They say he was one of the best. I played alongside him later on in sandlot baseball, but there was a lot of baseball influence in our family and the neighborhood, but my father was really the one who kinda led the pack. He was a left-handed hitter. My dad was in the American Association and Casey Stengel was the manager of the Toledo Mud Hens in the same league. When I came to the Yankees, Casey said to me one day, he said, 'You know, Dad was a hell of a ballplayer. Left-hand hitter, he could hit, he could run, throwing wasn't the best but he was a good player.' He said, 'I tried to trade for him but they wouldn't give him to me.' So that was Casey's story. He said, 'Your dad was a good line drive hitter.' He said they ruined him. They tried to make him a pull hitter. Said, 'I'd never do that to you,' so that's the old professor talking."

FIRST EXPERIENCE WITH THE YANKEES:

Kubek was signed by Yankees scout Lou Maguolo who was also credited with signing Elston Howard and Bill Skowron, among others.

"Lou Maguolo was out of St. Louis, he signed a lot of players. I was always around baseball my whole life. I spent more time on playgrounds, playing basketball, and in high school, running track and playing football and basketball. I did study but I lucked out. When I was in high school, I mean there were scouts and bird dogs, as they call them, all over the place on sandlots. They watched you play and they'd hit ground balls to you and they'd throw batting practice. So a lot of the teams were trying to sign me. I went through a couple of camps when I was probably 15, 16 years old, around the city of Milwaukee. They had camps for so many amateurs and scouts, they work you out. My dad, when scouts were looking at me, he said, 'You now, I'd like to see you sign with the Yankees. [Phil] Rizzuto's getting older at shortstop. That's a team that's had a lot of success.' He never mentioned to me that he was on that team that played against the great Yankees of early twenties and early thirties. Lou Maguolo arranged a trip for me and my dad. My day never wanted a car. A friend of ours who worked at a service station drove my dad and I to Chicago, Comiskey Park. I worked out with [the Yankees]. Casey was in the stands. Nobody was in the stadium during the day. Happened to be a night game that day. [Yankees coach] Jim Turner was there, Bill Dickey was one of the coaches and stuff. They were all in the stands watching. [Frank] Crosetti threw batting practice. Ironically, Jerry Coleman had just gotten out of the war. Jerry was a fighter pilot for the Marines and he had been shot down during the war. Jerry was in World War II and the Korean War and had just gotten out of the army. Great second baseman. Jerry probably weighed about a hundred thirty-five, forty pounds after he got shot down and being in the military. He hit, practiced double plays and stuff. It was maybe an hour workout. Then watched the ballgame and went back home. I was only 17 at the time so I wasn't legal to sign a contract. So my father ended up signing a contract with Lou Maguolo there, Casey was there. I was sitting on a trunk and my dad was signing my contract. I didn't go out and play that year in '53. I finished high school in the middle of June that year."

FIRST PROFESSIONAL MANAGER: Marvin Crater

Kubek began his professional career in 1954 with the Owensboro Oilers of the Class-D Kentucky-Illinois-Tennessee League.

"Marvin Crater, he played a little professional baseball actually. Then he was a cop, too, and he managed you as a catcher. I remember him catching a game, but we had a couple of other young catchers. Marv Crater was a disciplinarian, just a kind guy that understood young guys. We were probably still in our late teens. First time I'd been away from home, I didn't start very well. I remember that. It was really going poorly after the first 10 games or so. I think it was Mayfield, Kentucky. Marv Crater called me, he said, 'You're not swinging the bat. The bat is swinging you, you're lazy.' He said, 'I've seen you in batting practice. I've seen you hit before. I saw you hit in spring training.' He said, 'Just get the bat and dominate the bat.' Well, it was a little pep talk that he gave. I started hitting a little bit better and ended up hitting pretty well. I forgot what exactly, three-forty or something [.344] it was only D-ball but that was nice. Where we played, the lights weren't very good. Some of the teams we played against had a lot of hard throwers, usually wild and so forth.

"Some of the families, they were taking [in] some of the young ballplayers. We had five [in a room upstairs] and if somebody didn't do well, they didn't stick with 'em, after more than a couple of months, let 'em go."

FIRST MAJOR LEAGUE MANAGER: Casey Stengel

"I should say this. Casey, he was a great instructor of little things and fundamentals. He had, what he called, his acceleration camp. Now, I don't know what they call it now, if they even have it. Maybe its rookie league or something else. Before spring training even started my first year, 1954, I packed my suitcase. My dad and mom put me on a train in downtown Milwaukee, took it down to St. Petersburg. This was before the big team, the major league team even started spring training. It was two to three weeks before their spring training day. Casey would have the best prospects evaluated by scouts and so forth. He would have them come down early for three weeks and it was Miller Huggins Field. In 1954, I went to that camp. After that, I went off to spring training to Hattiesburg, Mississippi, for spring training with I don't know how many minor league teams are there, but there were probably three or four of the Yankee farm teams there and we all stayed in the house for spring training. Casey would actually do what he called an offensive and defensive routine and he would do it all by himself. He was such a great storyteller, he's gonna make it funny, but he would start his offensive routine in theclubhouse, 'Okay, you got a game today.' Now, this is a bunch of young guys, they had the minor league managers there, they had some of the scouts. Maguolo was there and some of the key scouts and stuff, who [would] kinda chaperone the guys and get 'em down there on time. 'Who [do] you play, who's pitching, who throws well, you know, who doesn't throw well?' Then he'd take you down to the batting circle. 'Now do you know the signs?' and then he'd let you know, 'Don't forget the signs.' He'd take you down to home plate and what you're supposed to be doing at home plate and knowing what everybody's doing. If you hit a ball to the outfield, if you take the extra base or not, how to cut bases its very sharpest. That was his offensive routine. He went from base to base, taking the lead, getting a good secondary lead, da, da, da, da. How to get a walking lead off third so you can score on a ground ball. I mean, on and on and on. Then he would take his defensive routine and take position to position. For me, it was shortstop. Man on first, ball is hit to right field, where do you go? Just thinking about what might happen in the possibility before they happened, that was ingrained enough.

"Interestingly enough, Whitey Herzog was in one of those camps. I don't know if it was '54 or '55. Whitey was older than I so he was a little more advanced. When he managed Kansas City and he managed the Cardinals, he had a friend that he played with, [outfielder] Dick Tettelbach. I think he made the big leagues [Tettelbach played two games for the Yankees in 1955 and also played for the Washington Senators.] Yale graduate so he was a really bright guy. Whitey would get Tettelbach, who could impersonate Casey for the George Bretts and Frank Whites and Ozzie Smiths. He'd have Tettelbach come down and imitating Casey's offensive and defensive routine. That was something that Whitey stuck with. There may have been other baseball people who did that but Casey's was so in depth and Billy Martin used a lot of Casey's stuff. That Deadball Era, there was a lot more bunting, more hit and running, stealing of home plate, stealing bases, etcetera, etcetera.

"So I went to that school three years in a row, '54, '55, and '56. After that acceleration camp, all the guys would go to their spring training level. I remember the first year I was there, the first big league pitcher I ever faced in 1954 was Bob Grim who I think he made Rookie of the Year and I'm 17 years old. He had a good fastball so I say, 'Oh man, this is the big leagues.' You played against guys that were more advanced than you and stuff. When the pitchers came through and it overlapped that acceleration camp, I batted against Whitey Ford. It was guys from the same organization. He wasn't throwing like he would in a regular season game or a World Series game or whatever but it was still [going] against Whitey Ford. Bill Dickey was around, Jim Turner was around, the pitching coach and so forth. So those guys could watch you and they could give you tips down there and everything else."

Hearst Newspapers sponsored the Hearst Sandlot Classic. It was a series of game throughout the country in which players would be selected to play for the US All-Stars in a game against the New York All-Stars in New York. In 1952, Kubek earned a spot on the US All-Star team.

"They would pick two guys that would go to New York and they would play the New York All-Stars. A writer from the [Milwaukee] Sentinel took us on the train. We stayed the Hotel New Yorker there for a week. We worked out at the Polo Grounds. We saw one game in Yankee Stadium and then we played one game against the New York All-Stars. So that was another learning experience for me. That was the first major league game I ever saw.

"Must have been '56. Casey kept me in spring training and I went with the team when they used to go north on a train and stop in various cities. For some reason he kept me before I went off to spring training and I played at Denver that year. He kept me with the team and we ended up going north through Florida and ended up in New Orleans and stopped to play a game there, the minor league ballpark there. He says, "Hey, Kubek, go out to center field.' Mickey [Mantle] is gonna go take a shower to get ready to catch a train when we head north. So I had never played center field, I was always [a] shortstop in the minor leagues. Somebody hit a ball to short center field. Apparently, I made a good catch and

Casey said, 'I'm going to take you to New York.' He said, 'I want you to see Ebbets Field.' So I sat in the bullpen, then he sent me out and I went to Denver for spring training. Casey wanted to know if late in the ballgame, if Mickey needed a rest, if I could play center field. Ironically, in '57, when we got to the World Series, I never played a game at shortstop. Mickey got hurt, I played center field some. I played left field, I played third base. I never played shortstop in the '57 year, I was Rookie of the Year. Casey had a plan. It wasn't the easiest thing to do to try and know where you're gonna play but he knew I could play center field and cover the ground in Yankee Stadium and other places and throw and everything else.

"The Yankees played the Dodgers one game in spring training in Miami. Casey started me at second base and in '56, which was Jackie's [Robinson] last year. Jackie got down to second base and I walked over to the bag. He said, 'Son.' I kind of looked at him and he said, 'I watched infield practice.' He said, 'You're gonna do okay, you're gonna be all right.' Ironically, I went on to do the Game of the Week. We were doing a game in Cincinnati [during the 1972 World Series] and Jackie had been a little upset. He should've been with baseball, the slow progress [employing a black manager] they were making. He was standing at field level of the new ballpark [Riverfront Stadium]. He was standing there and he was gonna make a talk and I came down with the sound man right near home plate. I was talking to the sound man and I didn't see him and this voice said, 'Tony,' and it was Jackie in a nice suit. I didn't even know he was gonna make a talk at home plate before the game started. Almost like a welcome back to baseball. I didn't know he was almost totally blind at the time, but he heard my voice and he said, 'I've been listening to you,' and so forth. It was a very brief conversation and then I had to go upstairs to start the game. We never did get an interview with him. I think Jackie died not too long after that."

FIRST MAJOR LEAGUE GAME: April 20, 1957 vs. Boston Red Sox at Fenway Park.

In the top of the eighth inning, Kubek was sent up a pinch-hitter and flied out in his first major league at-bat.

"I'd like to say that I was really thrilled but I can't. I'm sure there was some inward exhilaration but it was almost like this is a job. I'd been around. Some guys that were in Milwaukee that had made the major leagues, it was almost like it's more than just a job. You don't know if this is gonna be your lifetime career or whatever it's gonna be at the time. When you're very young, I guess you're kind of looking around at what's going on. It's a job that can overwhelm you. In my mind, going back to Casey, I'm thinking about the game. Who's playing, who's pitching as much as I am about who's across the room. The guys that welcome you, I'll never forget the first time I met Mickey. It was probably at the end of one of those acceleration camps. It was the transition for spring training where the big team was coming down, the major league team. The first thing Mickey did was he walked over to me and he said, 'Hey, welcome.' Next thing you know, Whitey's coming over to you and everything else. So it was like you're one of the boys immediately. It was like, 'Hey, we know of you. We've seen what you've been doing in the minor leagues and now you're here.' Guys like Jerry Coleman and Gil McDougald. My first roommate in the big leagues was Moose Skowron. I don't why, [maybe] because we were both infielders. Did [Casey] do it because we were both Polish? I don't know why. After that, it was Bobby Richardson. Casey I remember saying, 'Moose [is] gonna show you the ropes and he'll take care of you.' I always kidded Moose after that. I said, 'You really took care of me. We never saw the light of day. We get up in the morning and say let's have breakfast in the room.' Then, we'd have a hamburger steak for dinner on the road with a head of lettuce and whatever. We never left the room. He said, 'That's the way it's supposed to be. We're ballplayers now. We're supposed to be thinking the game all day.'

"First time I ever went to what was called the real famous place in the Bronx. [A] steakhouse on 161st and Grand Concourse, just up the hill from Yankee Stadium. That was the [Concourse Plaza] Hotel that a lot of the single players stayed at and the guys, before their wives got there. Charlie Keller was a coach. He said, 'Tony, let's go out, I wanna take you somewhere. We walked up the hill, went down the hill to the other side to this steakhouse, which was very famous. [Babe] Ruth hung out there with his buddies and drank beer. There was a nice Italian section there. It was the way guys treated you. Crosetti didn't go out much with the guys. He's kind of a private person. A great coach and a great guy. Do you know he took me out one time? It was really the Yankees. I guess 'cause they were a New York team and won so much. They were somehow construed by someone as being arrogant. You know people get jealous when you win a lot. [The owner of the restaurant] was a baseball fan and when you go there, he'd tell you stories. There was sawdust on the floor. They had two Dobermans there and he used to tell stories. He'd go over to a table and say, 'Well, the gas house guy was in town from the Polo Grounds, which is right across the river that you could see it from Yankee Stadium. He said, 'Pepper Martin and those guys started practicing their sliding on the sawdust and were knocking tables over and dishes.'

"I got recalled to the service right after the '61 World Series and Mickey says, 'Come on downtown, we'll take you [along with Tony's wife] out. Well, he took us to Danny's Hideaway [a Manhattan steakhouse] and Milton Berle came and sat with us at the table. Then we went to the Basin Street East [nightclub] and the lead act was Don Rickles. Nobody heard of him and then Don Rickles came over to the tables making fun of Mickey and me. Vic Damone came over and sang "Happy Birthday" to my wife, Margaret. Mickey was like a god, everybody knew him."

FIRST MAJOR LEAGUE HIT: April 28, 1957 vs. Boston Red Sox at Yankee Stadium

Kubek came off the bench to replace Mantle in center field. In the bottom of the fifth inning, Kubek got his first major league hit, an RBI single off Red Sox pitcher Frank Sullivan to give the Yankees a 2–0 lead.

"It wasn't sensational. I think it was a ground ball between first and second, I'm not sure. I remember it was a big right-hander, Frank Sullivan. He was more of a sinkerball, slider pitch. Probably did a lot better against right-hand hitters because he comes down from the side with those sweepy curve balls. I know that it wasn't hit that hard."

FIRST MAJOR LEAGUE HOME RUN: May 1, 1957 vs. Detroit Tigers at Briggs Stadium

Kubek's first major league home run came off Tigers right-hander Frank Lary, a noted "Yankee killer" in the top of the fourth inning. Lary was 28–13 against the Yankees in his career.

"Detroit was very comfortable. They always talk about Yankee Stadium, the short porch [in right field] but Detroit had that overhang where it actually was in fair territory. That upper deck there. I think it got in the upper deck. It was hard to hit one in the lower deck 'cause that thing hung over the warning track. It was a nice park to hit in if you didn't hit to center field. There's certain teams [you] hit better against, maybe it's 'cause I was left-handed, but Frank Lary was not an easy guy to hit. He threw fairly hard, his ball just moved all over the place. I wouldn't doubt one bit in retrospect that he wasn't doctoring the baseball like a lot of pitchers then just got away with it, where they said you can go to your mouth and you wipe it on your pants. You wipe your hands off but your fingers are soaking wet. I'd forgotten it was even against Frank Lary. They called him the Yankee killer. He had really good stuff that moved a lot, hard breaking stuff and his fastball did a lot of different things."

FIRST WORLD SERIES: 1957

Kubek played in six World Series with the Yankees, beginning with the 1957 Series against his hometown Milwaukee Braves. In Game 3, Kubek became only the second rookie to hit two home runs in a World Series game. The Yankees lost in seven games. Kubek committed a key error in Game 7 that led to Milwaukee's win.

"The irony of it was I got a few boos. That was my hometown (laughs), all the other guys who did this, they didn't do it in their hometown. When we got to Milwaukee on a train, Casey said we were going right to the ballpark for a workout. Casey said, 'Why don't you just stay?' Del Webb was one of the owners. He had a good friend who had a resort about 25, 30 miles out of town. I think it was Brown's Lake Resort and that's where we stayed. Casey said, 'You can stay at home, but stay with your folks,' and stuff like that. I stayed at home that first day and it was no fun. Folks had a little home, the south side of Milwaukee and there was garbage thrown on the lawn. It was pretty bad. My dad, the phone never stopped ringing. It wasn't like you had the secret phone number, like mobile, like cell phones but nobody could get your number. So it was like chaotic. I finally went and stayed out at Brown's Lake then hit two home runs. It was unlikely, but that was the scouting reports. Somebody said, 'Kubek hits the ball over the plate and not a spray hitter but he's a line drive hitter so we wanna bust him inside so he doesn't hit the ball to left and right center in the alley. I think [Braves pitcher Bob] Buhl and [Bob] Trowbridge both threw me a slider inside. One threw me a fastball inside and got around on it and that was it. You know, unlikely. Other guys, I think Charlie Keller had done it [hit two home runs in a Series game as a rookie]. I think he was only one who done it before that. Charlie probably got killed in Yankee Stadium because he was a straightaway hitter. He was way before me so it was a surprise.

"I remember Don Larsen. I talked to Don quite a bit. As Yogi would say, I talked to Don Larsen before he died. No kidding. Larsen, he had a friend taking care of him. Don's wife had some memory loss. Don showed me this picture with him, with Don, with Mickey, 'cause Mick had a homer in that thing too. Larsen pitched that game and he said, 'I was telling this attorney friend of mine, can you believe it? Kubek's hometown and they're booing him, they're not cheering him at all and then he is a Milwaukee boy.

"One of the plays in Game 7, that World Series, I was back at third base for the last game. Billy Bruton was on first base, he could run and Johnny Logan. There were no outs. Logan could have been up there bunting. They could have hit and run so Jerry Coleman's playing second base. He's gonna shade in case there's a bunt or trying to go the opposite way. He's moving farther away. Logan could swing away. I'm playing about even with the [third-base] bag and the runner could have tried to steal second base. So what happened is Logan hits like a one-hopper and I get the ball. Jerry Coleman's on the run trying to get to second base for the double play and I threw the ball a little high to him. He caught it, I don't think he even jumped, but when he came down, he didn't touch the bag. He missed the bag. They gave me an error and Jerry Coleman came to me and said, 'Tony, I thought I stepped on the bag but the umpire said I missed it.' They ended up scoring, I don't know, it's two or three runs which ended up being the ballgame. [Lew] Burdette beat us three times. Burdette, I don't think was supposed to pitch the seventh game. I think [Warren] Spahn was scheduled but Spahn [had] a flu or something. So Burdette came right back and it was spitball and spitball after spitball, but he beat us three times. Can you imagine someone from the south side of Milwaukee, between sandlot ball, having the baseball background. Now, I'm in front of the home fans.

"When we were in Yankee Stadium, it must have been the first time I went to the bathroom before the game and obviously I'm kind of nervous. I'm barely 20 years old, playing in my first World Series and my stomach was really rumbling. Well, in the closed door next to me, I hear this guy gagging. It was Mickey. Afterwards, he said, 'I was throwing up.' He'd already had a triple crown. I don't feel too badly now because Mickey's nervous and he's [won the] Triple Crown, he's hit a home run in the World Series, so things like that kinda loosen me up a little bit. That was kind of exciting in Milwaukee for me."

FIRST WORLD SERIES WIN:

Kubek was a member of the 1958 team that beat the Braves in a rematch from the previous season and became the second team to rally from a three-games- to-one deficit to win the Series.

"I remember I had a decent World Series in '57, decent, even though we lost, but in '58 we're down three to one. I remember we're at home and [coach] Ralph Houk comes in and said, 'Okay boys, we're not gonna take any prisoners.' He kind of got a chuckle and then Mickey came in late with his Neiman Marcus suit on and tie and he walked in the clubhouse. I don't know if Casey had him do this or whatever. He came in and we're playing the Braves obviously and he had a fake little hat or a little thing where like the arrow went in one side of his temple and came out the other side of the temple. He walked in and just starting laughing like we've been ambushed by the Braves. Everybody got a chuckle. Turned out, we packed our suitcases every day 'cause we thought we're going home. A lot of guys lived in New York but some of us were going home right after the series ended. There weren't any big fancy parades then, so we were ready to go home. The next thing, we're down three-two and it's [now] three to three. I didn't finish. Casey pinch-hit for me 'cause I was really going terribly."

FIRST EXPERIENCE HITTING SECOND IN FRONT OF ROGER MARIS DURING 1961 SEASON:

"I had probably the best seat in the house for that. I didn't even realize it at the time but I think I tied for the doubles lead with [Hall of Famer Al] Kaline. (Kubek finished tied for second with 38 doubles in 1961.) I was on second base looking right in when Roger was up a lot of times. So that was kind of a thrill. As I think back, I'm thinking, how many great players you were on the field with. [Hank] Aaron and [Eddie] Mathews and then [Willie] Mc-Covey and Frank Robinson and a lot of pitchers [Warren] Spahn and a lot of these guys were in the Hall of Fame and I'm on the same ball field [as] them. That's kind of a career thrill right there. I mean, aside from winning world championships, you have the down times too when you lose World Series, like in Pittsburgh."

(His thoughts when Maris hit #61)

"I'm always shocked when I read or hear that there [were] only like 21,000 people there. The pennant race is over, obviously, and people have said it's not true that the team was pulling for Mickey over Roger. I don't think it was that. People forget Roger was an MVP the year before, what did he have, 39 or 40 home runs? So it wasn't like he was a flash in the pan. He'd groomed his swing for Yankee Stadium. When Mickey went down, we're pulling for Roger because Mickey missed the last six, eight games, whatever it was, but Roger just had the perfect swing. I found out later that when Roger got traded to the Cardinals, I remember talking to Bill White, Dick Groat and Mike Shannon became a great friend of Rog. We read the box scores. This guy said, 'We thought all he could do is hit home runs.' Then, when Roger went to the Cardinals, he wasn't hitting home runs after he had that fracture in his wrist. Roger could run, he was a terrific baserunner. He could chase the ball down. He played center field (during 1961 Series against the Reds) in Cincinnati. Mickey hardly played in Cincinnati, so [Maris] was a center fielder if he had to be. Roger was stubborn as can be. He just was so determined. He had a routine and he pretty much stayed in the routine. He got his batting practice, he took his infield.

Unfortunately, he'd go to smoke a cigarette and then sit on that table and sign baseballs as we signed dozens and dozens before every game for the Yankee front office. Roger, I just don't think that his hair fell out or he got whatever that disease is. I don't think it was the pressure. I think it was just something that was gonna happen no matter what. He knew how to beat the pressure. He had Mickey, who took him under his wing, who had been through a lot. The great part of New York is the demands fans have. The winning traditions through Ruth and [Lou] Gehrig and everything else, they expect you to win, expect you to be great every day and that can spur a guy on. When Mickey went down, Roger just kept the same routine. He just kept doing his thing, knowing who's pitching, knowing what they might throw him and focusing until we won the pennant which was early in September when Detroit was right on our tail. Roger stayed in his routine. Mickey kept the pressure at bay, not during the game 'cause Roger was always focused, but I think getting him away from it. Going to some of the restaurants that Mickey knew where people wouldn't bother him. Traveling together, rooming together, out near the old Idlewild [now LaGuardia] Airport. Roger was determined, and the more people said that he couldn't do it or he shouldn't do it, the more determined or obsessive that he was gonna do it. He kept his swing. Very seldom that he got out of his groove. Couple of times during that year, he came to me and said, 'Tony, I just don't feel comfortable at batting practice. Are you standing in place?' I said, 'Yeah.' Roger used to stand in my footprint, so to speak, in the batter's box. Little concerns like that.

"There were no press conferences then, that was the hard part. Roger was so accommodating. I mean, guys would call him on the road and he'd go out to lunch with him before night games, dinner then afterwards on the road especially. I think a relief was when Roger got to Kansas City when his family was around. Roger and Whitey Herzog were good friends from the Kansas City area. We were going into Baltimore and Roger's going for 60. Whitey Herzog is now playing with the Orioles and they were buddies. Whitey said to Roger, 'You're getting bugged by writers and fans.' Fans could get your room number, they could bang on your door and say, hell, can you give me your autograph. That's just the way it was back then. So Whitey says, 'Stay with me.' So Roger stayed with him on that three game road trip to Baltimore. We get into a place where there's a hurricane on the coast and the wind shifted, started blowing into a left-handed hitter's face and one ball he [Maris] hit went foul, might have been pushed by the wind. Then, what was gonna be his last at-bat to get the Ruth record. Whitey's playing right field and all of a sudden, Luman Harris, the manager started to walk out and we look out and here's Hoyt Wilhelm warming up in the bullpen. Hoyt had pitched a no hitter when he was a starter in '58 against the Yankees. Roger wasn't there but Wilhelm was almost unhittable with the knuckleball. Whitey Herzog, you could always hear him in our dugout and stuff like that. He was throwing his glove up in the air and Whitey's yelling, 'No Luman, no,' but Luman Harris played the game the way it was supposed to be. The game didn't mean anything. There's a guy at bat, he's gonna bring his reliever. Roger, I think it was the first pitch, a check swing, a little nubber right back to Wilhelm. After a while it got a little bit of a laugh and Roger said, 'Oh, I hit him anyway.' There were a lot of guys pulling for Roger."

FIRST ROOKIE OF THE YEAR AWARD:

In 1957, Kubek was named the American League Rookie of the Year. He hit .297 and captured 23 of a possible 24 votes to beat out Boston Red Sox third baseman Frank Malzone. The Yankees finished the season against the Red Sox in Boston. Kubek was hitting .299 in the penultimate game of the season.

"We go up to Boston and I'm hitting, I think .299. Bob Fishel was our PR director. He said, 'Casey just called me in.' He said, 'Casey wants you to know, you get one hit, as soon as you get that hit, you're out 'cause you're hitting .300. The first time up. I think the kid's name was [Dave] Sisler. He had glasses on, he threw right-handed. Threw very hard and this right-hand pitcher threw a fastball. Hit me right in the kneecap and that was it. (At this point, Kubek grounded out in his next two times at bat before he was removed) Casey takes me out so I ended up [at] .297. I didn't get hit by many pitches but I did that time."

(How did he find out that he had won the award?)

"We had a bunch of guys right after the World Series where we did [get together] for years. One was a retired doctor, one was a retired dentist, one, they were still active at that time and I came home. I was unmarried in '57, came home to spend the day and we took a trip up to northwestern Wisconsin. We were duck hunting and goose hunting and we could fish on the lake. So, I was up there and we didn't have a telephone available there, so I didn't even know at the time. Finally, when I got back after about six days with this bunch of guys, somebody said nobody could reach me up there. So I didn't find out about it right away. I've been against Frank Malzone and [he] was a really good player for Boston. Chances are, if he hadn't spent some time [in the majors] the year before, he may have been the guy who deserved it more than I did, to be honest with you."

FIRST ALL-STAR GAME:

Kubek was named to his first All-Star Game in 1958.

"I didn't have a good year in '58, but I guess it was off the '57 year. [Hall of Famer Luis] Aparacio was so darn good. I mean to make that All-Star team, that made you proud enough. I remember Ted Williams was there and Casey was managing. Casey went down the bench and said, 'Williams, you're gonna pinch-hit.' Ted grabbed the bat and he was stalking up and down with the bat. He'd say, "Who's throwing? How did he throw?' I remember Ted Williams saying, 'I gotta get ready.' He was like a young 16-year-old kid. Just so enthusiastic. Well, he ended up striking out as a I recall, but he said, 'Oh man, that guy's got a great fastball. I'd like to hit against him again.'"

FIRST RECOLLECTIONS OF HITTING A HOME RUN IN HIS FINAL MAJOR LEAGUE AT-BAT:

On October 3, 1965, Kubek played what turned out to be his final major league game, although he didn't know it at the time. A neck injury forced the 29-year-old Kubek to retire in January 1966. In what was his final major league at-bat, Kubek hit a home run off Boston Red Sox pitcher Dick Radatz.

"I didn't know it was gonna be, it was meaningless. I didn't even know it until somebody brought it up. I don't know how long ago that was, but I know Peter Gammons told that. I got to be friendly, we talked quite a bit. He was in Boston. In spring training, I would talk to him and he said, 'You know, Radatz said you were the toughest guy he ever had to [face].' I said, 'Me?' 'Yeah, he said he loved to pitch to Mickey 'cause he could strike Mickey out.' He said, '[Radatz] said he couldn't get you out.' I know left-handed hitters, all of them in Fenway Park all did a lot better. I would guess that Ted [Williams] said he couldn't hit at Yankee Stadium. I don't know if it was the background or whatever else, but he said he had trouble, even with a short porch.

"[In] 1964, I was having trouble already from a neck injury I got in the military that was starting to act up later on. The Mayo Clinic suggested that I not play. I went in with my wife, and we had two boys at the time, went in to visit Ralph Houk and Dr. Sidney Gaynor. He said, 'Well, you know I've seen the X-rays. I think you're okay.' So I played [in] '65 and it was probably even worse. I said I gotta quit. Mayo Clinic said they weren't doing sophisticated cervical surgery at the time. They didn't wanna go in and maybe damage nerves or anything else. So I lived with it and eight years ago, I finally had the surgery."

FIRST TIME BEHIND THE MICROPHONE AS A PLAY-BY-PLAY BROADCASTER:

"First time I ever did play-by-play was in San Francisco. It was a Monday night game. This was before Monday night football. They put on Monday night baseball to see what would happen. After a weekend, people are home, da, da, da, da. So they had various guests but we had Satchel Paige up in Boston. I talked to [Joe] DiMaggio, he came on and we had Leo Durocher, we had Dizzy Dean twice. Chuck Connors, we had him on. I was doing it with [Curt] Gowdy, and Gowdy was sitting in the middle and Connors was to the left. I was to the right and Gowdy's doing the play-by-play. I think [Willie] Mays made a good catch. The producer said, 'Let Chuck do this replay.' Chuck came out, he said, 'Wasn't that a great, fuckin' catch by Willie.' I looked at him and Gowdy looked at him and Connors looked at us both and it dawned on him that this is live TV. Gowdy and Connors were laughing so they went to the back of the booth, which was like a couple of steps and I'm by myself. Producers were yelling in my ear, 'Tony, Tony, where is everybody? Who's doing play-by-play? Come on, somebody do play-by-play.' I said, 'They're in the back of the booth laughing.' 'Okay, so do play-by-play.' So I'm doing play-by-play to finish that inning. Later [Connors] said, 'Curt, did we say fuck on the air?' Curt said, 'Yes you did and this is live TV.'"

FIRST REACTION TO BEING NAMED THE WINNER OF THE FRICK AWARD:

In December 2008, Kubek was named the winner of the 2009 Ford C. Frick Award, presented annually to a member of the broadcast media for "major contributions to baseball."

"When I got the Frick Award [was] one of the best days. I got to be good friends with two guys, Maury Wills, who just passed away. When NBC signed him, they said, 'Put him under your wing.' We traveled together to spring training for information. They did the same thing with Sandy [Koufax]. So I got to know him fairly well. When I got in the Hall of Fame, first voice I heard after I was told by one of the writers that I had gotten the award, was Sandy saying, 'It's about time,' and he hung up on me. I did talk to him after that. You don't expect that kind of stuff. When you're around long enough, I think you just stick to the game as much as you can. That's what I tried to do. So the award was special, but doing the game of baseball, that was just something that's been in my blood all my life.

Tony Kubek by James Fiorentino

15
JIM LEYRITZ

Jim Leyritz was signed by the Yankees as an undrafted free agent in 1990. The charismatic utilityman played nine years with the Yankees in two separate stints. Leyritz played on two World Series champions and is known for hitting three of the most iconic postseason home runs in Yankees franchise history.

FIRST BASEBALL IDOL:

"Pete Rose. Being a batboy in spring training, watching his work ethic and not being the best athlete on those '70s Reds, but being the hardest worker. I just idolized him for that and that's why I kind of patterned my whole game after that."

FIRST BASEBALL GAME HE ATTENDED AS A KID:

"It was a Cincinnati Reds game and it was actually spring training. I just remember having the access because Tommy Brennaman was a good friend of mine. Of course, his dad [Marty], the announcer for the Reds, we had access. We stayed at the team hotel, so I got to see the players outside of the field and going to that first spring training game was pretty special."

FIRST EXPERIENCE WITH THE YANKEES:

Leyritz played on the University of Kentucky baseball team. After the 1985 season, Leyritz was signed by the Yankees as a free agent.

"Yeah, we had just completed a game in Wichita at the NBC Tournament. We got done with the game, I was actually catching and I believe it was Bill Livesey and Doug Melvin, they were the [Yankees'] scouts. Bill Livesey was the crosschecker and Melvin was the regional guy. They came up to me after the game and said, 'Hey, listen, what are you doing catching?' Because I had not been able to catch since high school after I broke my leg the four days before the draft. At Kentucky, I wanted to go back to catching but the coach's nephew was the starting catcher so there was no way I was catching there. I said, 'I can catch.' They said, 'Well, not according to what your college coach told us.' Long story short, 'We wanna sign you.' I said, 'Let me call my dad. I called and I had him fly in the next day. The next day, I got an offer also from the Kansas City Royals and this is 1985. If you remember, the Royals had just won the World Series. My dad flew in that morning. I told him. 'Hey, Dad, we got two offers. Now we have one from the Yankees and one from the Royals.' He said, 'Well, let's listen to 'em. Let's see what they have to offer.' We went back and forth with both of 'em. We got both of them up to $8,000 as far as a signing bonus. The one thing my dad said to me, this is typical of my mother and father, my dad said to me, 'Jimmy, right now the Kansas City Royals just won the World Series. Their farm system is rated in the top five. The Yankees think right now that they have a horrible farm system. You can move up a lot faster if we go with the Yankees.' Of course, we called my mother up and told her what was going on and she said, 'Well, I don't care who you sign with, I want them to pay for your senior year. So if you want to go back to college, if you don't make it, you'll be able to have an education.' We went back to both teams and said, can you pay for my senior year of college if I go back? The Royals wouldn't do it, but the Yankees would. The next day we signed with the New York Yankees."

FIRST MINOR LEAGUE EXPERIENCE:

Leyritz made his pro debut in 1986, splitting the season between the Oneonta Yankees of the New York-Pennsylvania League and the Fort Lauderdale Yankees of the Florida State League. At Oneonta, Leyritz's manager was Buck Showalter. Bucky Dent was his manager at Fort Lauderdale.

"In 1986, I reported to my first minor league camp. The first day I come in and Buck Showalter is the roving instructor in that camp. He comes up to me and he said, 'What position do you want me to put down for you?' I said, 'What do you mean?' He said, 'Well, Livesey just put on here he didn't have a position.' I said, 'I want to catch,' and he started working me out at catcher. The thing that really changed things for me, positively and negatively both, is that I grew up with Pete [Rose]. Like I said, I grew up with Pete Rose as my idol. As a batboy in spring training, he always told me, 'cause he was a switch-hitter, he said, 'Even if you don't switch-hit in the game, always work both sides. That way your body stays even and your eyes stay even, everything stays in balance.' So, from the age of 13 on, I took batting practice every single day. If I took a hundred cuts from the right side, I took a hundred cuts from left side.

"The one thing that Pete Rose always used to do in spring training is he would stay afterwards, after everybody else was done and left. He would stay after, hit the cage and do this drill where he'd hit 150 baseballs. He would hit 50 to right, 50 to center, and 50 to left. He would tell us whenever the ball hits the top of the cage or hits the ground first, it doesn't count. That's how disciplined of a hitter he was. I stayed after spring training [was over] the first couple days and I was hitting left-handed and Roy White was the roving instructor at the time. He comes walking by the cage and he sees me hitting and he said, 'What are you doing hitting left-handed?' I said, 'I've always worked on it. I've just really never done it much in a game. He said, 'We have no left-handed, I mean, switch-hitting catchers in the organization. If you can switch hit, you probably would have a quick ticket to the big leagues.' This is Roy White, so I wasn't gonna argue with him. So I started switch-hitting in that spring training. When the clubs broke [to go North], I went with Buck Showalter to extended spring training in Sarasota, which is where they send the guys that aren't quite ready, or in my case, working on switch-hitting. I was there, probably three or four weeks. Then, they called me up to Fort Lauderdale. That's when I played for Bucky Dent. At that time, their number one catching prospect in Single A was a big, tall, right-handed hitting catcher. I was gonna be starting on the left-handed side, you know, bat left-handed.

"I was 10-for-34 at one point. I don't know the exact stat from each side but I think I was like 10-for-20 right-handed and I was 0-for-14 left-handed. When I got called up to Single A, I started seeing a lot of breaking balls, things that I never really worked [on]. In the extended spring training, the pitchers that are in that league, they're just working on trying to get their fastballs down. So I was seeing mostly fastballs and and I could hit that pretty easily. When I started seeing changeups and breaking balls, little cutters and things like that. I was swinging at balls that were hitting me in my back leg and was truly embarrassing myself. I walked into Bucky Dent's office one day and I said, 'Bucky, I'm not switch-hitting anymore,' and he says, 'Well, you don't get to decide that.' I said, 'Yes, I do.' And we got into a big heated discussion about all this. At the time, I didn't really know who Bucky Dent was. I looked at the back of his baseball card and he was a .220 lifetime hitter. I was a kid that grew up in Cincinnati, Ohio. I didn't really know much about the Yankees. When he said to me, 'Kid, if you don't switch-hit, they you're outta here.' I said, 'Well, okay.' I think he expected me to say 'I'll keep doing it 'cause you tell me to do that.' I was like, 'I don't care, if you're not gonna let me hit right-handed, then, yeah, go ahead, ship me out.' And he's like, 'Son, you'll never make it. You don't listen to anybody.' I said, 'No, but I know what I can do right-handed and I'd rather hit right-handed.' Next day, I got sent out to Oneonta with Buck Showalter, which was like rookie ball. Rookie ball starts in June, so I got sent back to him and I finished the season with the Oneonta Yankees and Buck

Showalter and I hit .360 right-handed. That offseason, *Yankees Magazine* did a little article on me and I made a comment. I didn't use his name but I said, 'There's certain coaches in this organization that don't know talent,' 'cause they asked me why I quit switch-hitting. Of course, he knew that I was referencing him but not everybody else knew that. So I stopped switch-hitting and that was my experience my whole first year."

FIRST BIG LEAGUE CAMP:

Bucky Dent was the Yankees' manager when Leyritz attended his first big league camp in 1990.

"Well, as you can imagine, I use this story to tell kids all the time about you gotta be very, very careful on the people that you see as you're going upward and be respectful, because if you don't, it can come back to haunt you. Of course, it did come back to haunt me. Bucky was the manager in 1990, my first big league camp. I think I hit .357 or something like that in camp. Of course, back then we played that Governor's Cup game. I hit a home run to win that game and it was the last day of spring training. We were all getting ready to go to New York. I think we were down to 28 players. I was still on that list and I thought for sure, the year that I had, I had all my bags packed [and] ready to get on the plane. The game gets over with and all of a sudden I get called into Bucky's office. Of course, I know what's gonna happen. He says, 'Hey, you had a great spring, but unfortunately, you're gonna the start the season in Triple A. We want you to learn to play a couple of different positions. We want you to go back to third base, but just remember what happened in A-ball. The irony of that is Bucky gets fired, I think it was June fourth and by June sixth, I get called to the big leagues."

FIRST TIME HE PUT ON THE YANKEES UNIFORM:

"Well, you know it was really cool because [former Yankee pitcher] Alan Mills and I both got called up and we flew together into Baltimore. We didn't get to the stadium until around 4:30, five o' clock, so we missed batting practice. We came in, of course you go to your locker and it's not the pinstripes, it's the gray uniforms that you see. We both were like just sitting there because the guys were out in the field. We were walking in the locker room and it was just really, really cool to see, at that time, I was number 12, to see the jersey hanging up and the Leyritz [nameplate] on the locker. I said to Mills, 'Dude, this has been quite a day.' He goes, 'I don't know about you, but I hope I can stay up for this game.' We played a doubleheader in Toledo that night. When [Columbus manager] Rick Down told us we were going to the big leagues at 1:30 in the morning, we literally got in the car and drove from Toledo to Columbus, packed our bags and we had a ten o'clock flight to get out, so we didn't have a whole lot of sleep, a whole lot of rest."

FIRST MAJOR LEAGUE GAME/FIRST HIT/FIRST RBI: June 8, 1990 vs. Baltimore Orioles at Memorial Stadium.

Leyritz entered the game in the ninth as a pinch-hitter and singled in the tying run. The Yankees ended up losing the game, 5–4, in 10 innings.

"We're sitting there on the bench, taking it all in. Buck Showalter [a coach with the big club at the time] walks by, comes up to me and says, 'Hey, Stump has a knack for using people to pinch-hit with their first couple of days up here.' He said, 'Just be ready,' and this is about the fifth inning. So I went in the locker room and I started stretching and just getting ready. Put my bat and gloves on, started taking some swings off the tee. As the game progressed, we got into the ninth inning. Actually, it was the bottom of the eighth and I'm watching the game on TV and I see [closer] Gregg Olson warming up for the Orioles. On the telecast, I think it was Jim Palmer who was doing the game. He was saying, "Look at the bullpen, Gregg Olson's warming up. He's 13-for-13 in saves this year. One of the most dominant closers in the game.' I'm just saying to myself, Well, I guess I'm not gonna play tonight 'cause he's not gonna pinch hit me against the right- hander. I went back down to the bench. I still had my gloves on and my bat ready just in case.

Sure enough, Steve Sax is on deck and Buck comes up to me and goes, 'Hey, Stump wants you to get ready.' He goes, 'You're gonna pinch-hit for [Wayne] Tolleson.' I'm like, 'Oh crap.' So I walk up to the on-deck circle. Sax goes up to bat, there's two out and he hits a routine ground ball to Cal Ripken and Ripken short-hops, I think it was Randy Milligan at first base. and he misses it and Sax is on. Here we go. Here's my chance to go up against Gregg Olson. He throws the first pitch. Back then, Gregg Olson's signature pitch was a nasty curveball. Sure enough, he threw me first pitch curveball, it hit 57 feet and I swung at it 'cause I was so excited to swing. I swung at it, missed it, went to the backstop. Steve Sax goes to second base. At this point, we're down by one run. The next pitch, [Olson] throws another one. I swing at it in the dirt. Then, he throws a fastball up and away. I took it, then he throws me another curveball, but this time I at least hit it and I hit a line drive down the first-base line and it was just foul. I got a little bit of confidence by just making contact. I want to say he came back with another curveball and I hit a ground ball right through third base and shortstop for a hit. Steve Sax scores the run so I break his record [streak] or whatever he was doing. The tying run comes in. We don't score another run. Randy Milligan gets the ball for me. I have my first base hit in the big leagues off Gregg Olson in my first at-bat. Then, I go out to play defense at third base in the bottom half of the ninth. I think they loaded the bases and we had the infield in and they hit a ground ball to me. I made a great play. I probably could have stepped on the bag and maybe throw to first, but the right play was to try and throw home. I tried to throw home and I short-hopped [catcher] Matt Nokes and he couldn't handle the throw and we ended up losing the game. I had a bittersweet beginning."

FIRST GAME AT YANKEE STADIUM: June 13, 1990 vs. Boston Red Sox.

Leyritz entered the game as a pinch-hitter in the eighth inning and singled off Roger Clemens.

"Well, at the time, an agent from New York told me, 'When you get to New York, I'm gonna put you up in a hotel in the city. I want you to experience what New York City's all about because you never know how long you're gonna be in New York.' He said, 'I want you to take the subway, 4 train to the field and go in the back entrance.' I had no idea what he talked about. Here I am, a kid from Cincinnati, Ohio, and he's telling me to take the subway. All I've heard about the subway is, you know, people get shot on it. So I trusted him when I took it and I got off the back entrance. I went to walk in the back entrance and the security guy goes, 'Can I help you?' I'm like,' Yeah, I'm Jim Leyritz. I'm one of the new players. I was told to come in this way. I just got off the subway.' He's like, 'Oh yeah, come on in.' So when you go in the back entrance of the old stadium, you walk right into Monument Park. My agent wanted me to take that in and see, this is where you are. You're in part of history. You know, Joe DiMaggio, Babe Ruth, Lou Gehrig, and all those monuments that you see. That was such a cool moment for me. Then of course, I'm walking across the field. I get to the pitcher's mound and I'm looking around, just taking it all in. Of course, we didn't have cell phones back then, so I couldn't take a selfie, send it to my dad. I go into the locker room and I'm looking for my locker and sure enough, my locker's right next to Don Mattingly. I was so freaking excited that I went right to the telephone in the locker room and I called my dad. I said, 'Dad, thank you so much for your support, everything that you've done for me, but guess what? I made it.' Then he said, 'Son, I'm so proud of you.' He said, 'Let me ask you a question. What are you gonna do to stay there?' My dad was always one of those people that, when you reach a goal, you set a new set of goals because you need something else to reach forward to. I go back to my locker, I sit down and in comes Don Mattingly. He's like, 'Hey kid, you got a locker next to mine?' He goes, 'Just remember one thing. Don't be afraid to ask questions.' I said, 'What?' He goes, 'You don't stay in this league unless you have questions.' If you want to ask me anything, I'm here for you.' I thought that was the coolest experience that I had that particular day. A guy like that saying to me, 'Hey kid, if you need anything, don't be afraid to ask.'"

FIRST IMPRESSION OF YANKEES-RED SOX RIVALRY/FIRST FACE-TO-FACE MEETING WITH GEORGE STEINBRENNER:

"It was a heated rivalry. I was so pumped up. Of course, I went and [already] got my first at-bat, got my first hit, but then I come back to Yankee Stadium. I got the pinstripes on for the first time and I'm sitting there on the bench taking it all in. We're facing Roger Clemens and it's the Red Sox, so it was such a cool experience. I get a chance to pinch-hit. Stump [Merrill] calls on me to pinch-hit. I think it was the seventh inning [actually eighth] against Roger Clemens. My first at-bat in Yankee Stadium and I was able to get a base hit off him. Stadium was pretty cool too. What was even cooler is Mr. Steinbrenner, who I had met at the University of Florida in 1986 at a basketball game that he was at. My first time meeting him, I went down and introduced myself and he asked, because I had a Yankee outfit on, like a Yankee jacket, Yankee emblem on my necklace. He goes, 'Are you a Yankee fan?' I said, 'No, Mr. Steinbrenner, you signed my paycheck.' He said, 'Wait a minute. What's your name?' and he actually took out a piece of paper and he wrote my name down. In 1990, he was suspended, but my agent [Tom Reich] happened to be George's drinking buddy and they were really good friends. I didn't know this at the time, I didn't find this out until later, but my agent and George were sitting together watching the game. When I got to my locker after that game, there was a bottle of champagne and a message. It was a handwritten message from [Steinbrenner] that said, 'Congratulations, kid. You told me you'd be here one day.'"

FIRST HOME RUNS: June 30, 1990 vs. Chicago White Sox at Comiskey Park.

Leyritz' first two big league home runs occurred in the same game. His first was off White Sox pitcher Melido Perez in the third inning. The second one came off Ken Patterson in the ninth inning of a 10–7 Yankees win. Leyritz had three hits and four runs batted in.

"It was Comiskey Park, the old Comiskey and we were facing Melido Perez. At the time, we had on our team Pascual Perez, his brother. We had our team meeting before the game. Melido Perez had a fastball, a slider, and a forkball. Those were his three pitches. In our team meeting, they told us that he'd tip his pitches. What he would do, his finger was outside of the glove on his pitch. Whenever he threw a fastball, his finger didn't move. When he threw his slider or his forkball, his finger moved. So we had that and sure enough, he did it. So when I went up to bat, he did it on a slider that he threw to me and I hit my first home run off that. My second home run came off a guy named Ken Patterson, a lefty who had come in for relief. Ken Patterson was my teammate with the Yankees a few years earlier in the minor leagues. I took him deep for my second home run, my first two home runs in the major leagues. That night, the Yankee media, the *Post* and the *Daily News* and all these big papers come in and talk about what a great young player playing the game with enthusiasm. They had a lot of great things to say about me."

FIRST TIME PLAYING THE OUTFIELD: July 1, 1990 vs. Chicago White Sox at Comiskey Park.

"The next day, we play a day game at Comiskey Park and Stump Merrill calls me in the office and says, 'Hey, listen, you're swinging a good bat right now. I want you in the lineup,' and we're facing Greg Hibbard, who's a left-hander. He said, 'I wanna get your bat in the lineup, but I want [Mike] Blowers in the lineup too, to play third base. We're gonna put you in left field. Now, this was my first time ever playing left field in the big leagues and it was a windy, sunny day at Comiskey Park and Andy Hawkins was pitching. Andy Hawkins had the no-hitter lost because of me. This is after I hit my first two home runs the night before. Of course, I dropped [the ball] the no-hitter with the bases loaded. They scored three runs. Thank God, Jesse Barfield made an error on a fly ball that he lost in the wind and the sun and they scored another one. So, we end up losing that game 4–0 with three errors and four unearned runs, but Andy Hawkins still got the no hitter. (Hawkins' no-hitter was later removed from the record books because he only pitched eight innings.) This was my first time actually realizing what the media and what playing in New York would be like, because that night I got interviewed and I said, nonchalantly 'cause Andy Hawkins had already come up to me and said, 'Kid, don't worry. It won't be the last error you make in the big leagues. Shake it off, ' 'cause he knew it was my first game in left field. When the reporters came in, I said, 'Hey, listen, I feel bad for Andy. I already told him that but it won't be the last error that I make.' The next day in the paper was 'Leyritz is cavalier in his attitude of dropping Hawkins' no'hitter.' That was my first taste of the New York media. One day you're on top, the next day, you're the goat."

FIRST TIME HE SAW HIMSELF ON A BASEBALL CARD:

"The first one I saw was a Donruss card. It was funny because they had a picture of me in my catching gear with a ball coming into home plate, but on the card, it said third baseman. I thought that kind of ironic that they had me in catching gear. That was the first card I ever saw."

FIRST POSTSEASON HOME RUN: 1995 American League Division Series, Game 2 vs. Seattle Mariners at Yankee Stadium.

Leyritz hit a two-run, walk-off home run in the bottom of the 15th inning to give the Yankees a 7–5 win and a 2–0 lead in the best-of-five series that they eventually lost.

"I caught all 15 innings. In the 12th inning, I came up with Don Mattingly on second base and I hit a 3-1 pitch right back to Tim Belcher. I came in and I snapped my bat. I was breaking it up in the tunnel. As I was breaking it, David Cone was walking back down to the tunnel and he's watching me do this. He comes up to me and he goes, 'Hey, that was impressive.' I said, 'What?' He goes, that the fact that you have that much energy after catching 12 innings. He goes, 'Shake it off, you'll get another chance, don't worry.' Sure enough, the 15th inning comes and I go to the bat rack. Buck Showalter grabs me and goes, 'Hey, this is your last at-bat. [Mike] Stanley's gonna go into catch. You've caught 15 innings.' He says, 'Make this at-bat count.' Sure enough, Pat Kelly gets walked and then I come up and Belcher goes behind, 3-oh to 3-1. He grooves a 3-1 pitch and I hit the walk-off home run. The thing I remember most about that is as soon as I'm coming around we have the big pile on at home plate. We're all excited and I walked by Buck Showalter and I look at him. I go, 'Hey skip, did I make it count?'"

FIRST EXPERIENCE WITH THE "CORE FOUR" OF DEREK JETER, JORGE POSADA, ANDY PETTITE, AND MARIANO RIVERA:

"Mariano got sent down. We didn't know what they were gonna do with Posada because he was formerly a second baseman and he was just learning how to catch. Mariano started the season in '95 and was a horrible starting pitcher. They literally sent him back down to the minor leagues. Jeter was a different one. Jeter and I met each other in the offseason of '95 and '96. I was living in Clearwater, he was staying in Tampa. He came down early from Kalamazoo to work out at a minor league complex. We were working out together. He would come over to my house for dinner 'cause my wife would cook meals for him 'cause he was by himself. We used to work out every single day at the complex. I would watch him. He would go to the field and he would take a ton of ground balls. He would take a lot of extra hitting. I remember saying to him, 'Kid, easy 'cause you know this is only January. We got a couple of months before spring training starts. He goes, 'Nope, this is what I do. This is my routine.' You could tell that the kid wasn't your normal kid. He reminded me a lot of myself in that you're the first one in the park, you're the last one to leave and you put in the extra work. I could see that in Derek. The interesting thing is, I think [Joe] Torre and all those guys, they'll tell you [Jeter] would not have made that team in '96 had Tony Fernandez not broke his hand. Think about that. You think about how that started. Who knows how the Derek Jeter era would've started."

FIRST WORLD SERIES EXPERIENCE: 1996

"The World Series was something that I had never experienced, besides as a fan, 'cause I grew up [watching] the Reds. Of course, we had the '75 and '76 championships, the World Series. The first experience in '96 was delayed because we got rained out the first game. The next day we came to the ballpark was even more exciting. By getting rained out, it actually just added to even more tension and more like, let's get this thing started. I was starting Game 1 with Andy Pettitte pitching. To this day, it was one of the few times in a World Series that I was in the starting lineup [for the] opening game."

FIRST WORLD SERIES HOME RUN: Game 4, 1996 World Series vs. Atlanta Braves at Atlanta-Fulton County Stadium.

Leyritz hit a game-tying, three-run home run in the eighth inning off Braves closer Mark Wohlers. Leyritz's home run became one of the most iconic in franchise history as the Yankees rallied from a 6–0 deficit to win Game 4 and take the series in six games.

"I remember being by the bat rack and talking to [Darryl] Strawberry and saying, 'Hey, listen, I only have two bats left. I broke two during batting practice today.' He had a brand-new set of 12 bats and I said, 'Can I steal one of yours 'cause I don't wanna break my against this guy [Wohlers].' Straw said, 'Yeah, go ahead.' So I grabbed Darryl Strawberry's box, took one of his bats and started to walk up to the on-deck circle. I looked at [bench coach] Don Zimmer and I said, 'Hey, Zim, what's this guy got?' 'cause I had never faced Wohlers before and I really didn't pay much attention in the meeting about what he threw and what he had. He said, 'Leyritz, he throws a hundred miles an hour, just get it ready.' So I go up to the on-deck circle and I get a chance to see him and he throws two sliders to Mariano [Duncan, the Yankees' second baseman] so I got a chance to see what his slider was from the on deck circle. I didn't know he had a split. All I figured was fastball, slider. I go up to bat and sure enough, the first pitch he throws me is that 98-mile-an-hour fastball. I took a huge cut at it, I fouled it back. Usually if you see a hitter foul a ball straight back, that usually means he's on the ball. You know his timing's there. I look at the bat and the foul tip mark is right on the label. So I wasn't even close to getting the bat out it the zone. Then, he throws me two sliders, not good ones, both of them up. Then he comes back with a 99-mile-an-hour fastball that I fouled back again. Tim McCarver and Joe Buck were on the [television] call. The first 2-2 slider he throws me, I barely foul it off. McCarver says, I think the adrenaline gets going and Wohlers is gonna throw this one, you might reach a hundred miles an hour. He throws me another slider or he hangs it and I hit the home run. We tied the game up, the momentum swing was so big in our dugout, you could just feel this is our game. We're gonna win this thing. Of course, Wade Boggs gets the bases-loaded walk [to force in the go ahead run in the 10th inning] and Charlie Hayes hits a ball to Ryan Klesko, who loses the ball in the lights. We scored two runs and we end up winning, 8–6."

FIRST EXPERIENCE WITH BEING TRADED:

In December, 1996, Leyritz was traded to the Anaheim Angels.

Mr. Steinbrenner was really close with my agent, Tom Reich. Torre had told me when he took over as manager, he had told my agents and Mr. Steinbrenner that he could get me 400 at-bats because I could play so many different positions. Of course, I was gonna catch Andy Pettitte. In 1996, I only got 250 at-bats, so I wasn't very happy about that. After hitting the [World Series] home run, I told my agents, I said, 'You need to talk to Mr. Steinbrenner and let them know if I'm not playing every day, I would like an opportunity to go somewhere else. I was literally on the field in Tampa at the minor league complex like I did the year before, with Jeter working out. Back then, we didn't have cell phones. I was working out and one of the coaches said, 'Hey, you got a phone call.' I go into the locker room, I jump on the phone and it's my agent. 'Hey, good news, bad news.' I said, 'Gimme the bad news first.' He said, 'The bad news is you're no longer a Yankee. The good news is you're the starting catcher and you got a three-year contract from the Anaheim Angels. You're going to be their everyday catcher.' This was my seventh year in the big leagues and I only had a one-year contract every year. You can imagine the stress that it gives you in the offseason, not knowing if you've got a contract coming the next year. I finally had a three-year deal and an opportunity to go play every day. I start packing up my locker and I go into Mr. Steinbrenner's office. I said, 'Hey, Mr. Steinbrenner, I wanna thank you for giving me an opportunity to go play every day. You know, I'm gonna miss the Yankees, but thank you for this opportunity. He said, 'Sonny, you will always be a Yankee and you're more than welcome to be here. He looked at me and he said, 'What are you doing with your bag?' I said, 'Well, I'm no longer a Yankee. I can't work out here.' He said, 'I just told you, you will forever be a Yankee. Go put your bag back and you can work out here as long as you want.'"

FIRST TIME BACK AT YANKEE STADIUM FOR A WORLD SERIES GAME: 1998

Leyritz was a member of the San Diego Padres when they played the Yankees in the 1998 World Series. During player introductions before Game 1 at Yankee Stadium, Leyritz received a standing ovation from the fans.

"It was interesting because [former player] Steve Lyons was working for Fox at that time and he called me and said, 'Hey, are you gonna take the train up to the stadium like you did when you played?' I said, 'Absolutely.' He goes, 'Can we film you going up to the stadium, 'cause we wanna do an episode on it.' So, he literally rode with me from the Grand Hyatt on the 4 train, up to the stadium. I remember coming in and we did this whole thing and I made a joke, 'Oh, shoot, I can't turn to the right, I gotta go to the left 'cause I'm on the visiting team.' I'm not going to my normal locker room. We're doing the starting lineups and they introduce Quilvio Veras leading off and then it was Tony Gwynn. Of course, [the fans are] booing everybody. Then, they get Ken Caminiti, they boo him. Then, they introduce me and of course, everybody is applauding. Standing ovation was so cool and so neat to have that moment that the Yankee fans were giving me that moment. All of a sudden, Wally Joyner gets announced and they start booing again. He comes up and he walks by me and goes, 'Thanks, Leyritz, you made me look really good now.'"

FIRST WORLD SERIES HOME RUN IN HIS SECOND STINT AS A YANKEE:

In July 1999, Leyritz was traded back to the Yankees in a deal with the San Diego Padres. Leyritz hit a home run in Game 4 of the 1999 World Series sweep against the Atlanta Braves. Leyritz' home run came in the eighth inning off Braves pitcher Terry Mulholland and was the final home run that was hit in the twentieth century.

"That year, I was on the Padres and I got hit by a pitch by Chan Ho Park. That '98 team got the approval for Petco Park because in October they were getting ready to have the vote. Before we started our playoff run, things didn't look very good as far as them getting approval. Of course, we went on that great run and in November they had to vote and the vote went through and they got approval to build Petco Park. As soon as they got the approval, they traded everybody. They traded Caminiti, they traded [Steve] Finley, they traded Kevin Brown. I remember talking to [Padres GM] Kevin Towers and saying, 'Hey, why am I still here? Why aren't you trading me?' He goes, 'Well, 'cause I need you to work with our young pitchers and help us, we have a lot of young pitchers, but I'm telling you, I'm going to trade you before the deadline. Don't worry.' I think this is June twenty-first, I get hit by a pitch by Chan Ho Park and I break my left hand and I'm like, crap, I'm not gonna be able to get traded. I have a cast on, I continue to throw batting practice every day to our team, just to stay in shape. Got the cast off on July eighteenth and started resuming swinging a little bit and getting ready. I got sent to the minor leagues for rehab assignment. On July twenty-fourth, I played my first two games for the [advanced A- Ball] Rancho Cucamonga minor league team. I think I had six at-bats (actually four) but I was able to swing the bat pretty good. Then I got sent to Las Vegas for the Triple-A [Stars] for eight more at-bats. I think I struck out five times, but I hit a couple of really good shots. On July twenty-ninth, I get a phone call from Kevin Towers [who] says, 'Hey, we got a deal for you. You're going back to the Red Sox,' and I was like, No, please. (Leyritz was traded from the Texas Rangers to the Red Sox for the 1999 season,) My experience in '98 with [Red Sox pitching coach] Joe Kerrigan and [general manager] Dan Duquette was horrible. 'Kevin, please give me 24 hours,' and he goes, 'For what?' I go, 'Just trust me,' and he goes, 'Okay, I'll wait.' So I picked up the phone. Back then, there was none of these tampering rules and all that stuff they have nowadays. So I picked up the phone and I called George's secretary, at the time was Debbie Nicolosi. Her and I were very, very close when I was playing for the Yankees. I called her up and said, 'Debbie, you need to get a message to George that they're trading me to the Red Sox.' She went and told George, 'Leyritz just called me and said [the Padres are] trading him back to the Red Sox.' Within 24 hours, I got traded back to the New York Yankees. The crazy thing when I get there, Torre calls me into his office and says, 'I didn't even know you were coming.'

"The greatest part about that home run happened in July, when I got sent back to the Yankees. I was taking batting practice. In the old days, when Strawberry and I were together, we would have home run contests 'cause we weren't in the starting lineups. So we would take home run contests and I used to hit the ball pretty much just as far as he could. So I get called back and I can't even hit the ball out of the ballpark in batting practice and Jeter and [Chuck] Knoblauch and all these guys are giving me a hard time. I said to them, 'Guys, don't worry. I'll hit one when it counts.' For the rest of the season, they gave me a hard time and I did not hit a home run, all my at-bats that I had, until that World Series home run. When I hit that home run, as you see me rounding the bases, as you see me coming into the dugout, you can see Jeter and Knoblauch, they're greeting me. They both said, 'You have to be kidding me,' 'cause they both remembered me saying I was gonna hit a home run when it counted."

FIRST TIME HE WAS REFERRED TO AS "THE KING":

"That happened in 1995. We were playing in Baltimore and I was hitting in the lineup behind Don Mattingly that whole week. We had played in Toronto earlier and I had a couple home runs and I was telling Don Mattingly, I can hit a home run anytime I want or with anybody's bat. That's what I said. We were in Baltimore and I said, 'Hey, Cap.' We were standing by the bat rack. I said, 'Pick out anybody's bat, I'll hit a home run.' So he picked out Danny Tartabull's bat and it was a big 36-ounce bat. I went up to face Rick Sutcliffe and sure enough, the first time I'm up with that bat, I struck out and the whole team knew what I was doing and they were all giving me a hard time, especially Sterling Hitchcock. At the time, I was his personal catcher. He was giving me a hard time. He's like, 'Leyritz, I thought you said you could hit a home run with anybody's bat. You didn't do that.' I looked at him and I said, and the whole bunch, I said, 'Screw you guys. Next time I go up there, I'm taking my bat and I'm hitting the first pitch out.' The next time around the order, there's two guys on base. I go up with my own bat and Sutcliffe throws me a first-pitch fastball and I hit a three-run home run. I come 'round the bases, I come back in the dugout. Sterling Hitchcock's on his knees and he's bowing to me going, 'You are the King! You are the King!' and Don Mattingly goes, 'Yep, Leyritz, you are the King' and that's where it started."

FIRST ACTING ROLES:

Leyritz had a small role in a 2013 horror movie titled, *Grave Digger*. He also appeared in the TV series, *Arli$$* about the world of professional sports.

"*Grave Digger*, I don't remember much about 'cause it was just a short, little thing, but the *Arli$$* thing was really kind of cool because I actually watched that show a lot and I really liked it. They come to me in Anaheim and they say, 'Hey, listen, will you do this show,' and I said, 'Absolutely.' We shot the segment and it aired. It was pretty cool. I remember Robert Wuhl coming and him telling me he was a big fan. He is a New Yorker and a big fan, so we shot the segment and it was pretty cool. It wasn't just one line, it was a couple lines and it was pretty cool to be a part of that."

Jim Leyritz by Maz Adams

16
JACK MCDOWELL

Jack McDowell played one notable season for the Yankees. McDowell was acquired in a trade with the Chicago White Sox to be their ace pitcher in 1995 and he helped them get into the playoffs for the first time in 14 years. McDowell began his career with the White Sox and won a Cy Young Award in Chicago. The right-hander made 30 starts for the Yankees in 1995 and was 15–10 with a 3.93 ERA.

FIRST BASEBALL IDOL:

"I grew up in Los Angeles. I was California born, so grew up a Dodgers lover. Steve Garvey and all those guys at that time were the guys that I was checking out. When I was in Little League, I wore number 6 'cause I loved Steve Garvey."

FIRST GAME HE ATTENDED AS A KID:

"I think it was a Dodgers game. I think it was the one where students had good A's and B's got to go to games and I think that was the first one I got to go to."

FIRST TIME PLAYING FOR HIS BROTHER IN HIGH SCHOOL:

"Well it was very cool because growing up my father had me from T-ball, Little League, Pony league, all the way till high school. I was a pitcher and an infielder, that's just what I did. I was made just as an infielder 'cause both my brothers were infielders at Notre Dame [high school in California]. Seven or eight years before that, the McDowells are infielders, they aren't pitchers. My freshman year, I didn't even get allowed to pitch. So, my brother came in sophomore year and took over the sophomore JVs. Then, I became a two-way dude and got to pitching again so it was really good. And for him [his brother], playing with the people that he played for, playing for Rod Dedeaux [at the University of Southern California], who was a great, great coach and taught just amazing baseball things. Not just controlling the game but teaching really good stuff."

FIRST DRAFT EXPERIENCE:

McDowell was drafted by the Boston Red Sox in the 20th round of the 1984 MLB June Amateur Draft out of Notre Dame High School in Sherman Oaks, California, but did not sign. Three years later, the Chicago White Sox chose McDowell as the fifth overall pick in the first round out of Stanford University.

"You get the phone call and yeah, found out that I was drafted, but it was 20th round and it like, you know, don't wanna do that. Think about back in the day what the money was that you were gonna get. You know, here's a five-dollar bill, you can go get a hamburger. Okay, I'm going to Stanford but the one thing that I kept in mind is that summer I played for the 18U [under] USA Team and had a crazy good summer and great tournament as well. Just dominated as a pitcher and I was wondering if [the Red Sox are] gonna up the ante a little bit because they saw where I'm actually standing now with older dudes and all that. It didn't really happen, so I kept going to school.

"The draft's crazy when it's right in the middle of the college World Series. So [the White Sox] drafted me, now they're watching me. It's funny because the day I was drafted was the one game I lost in the College World Series over my whole career. [White Sox teammate] Ozzie Guillen talked to me about that that. He just goes, 'We drafted you first round and then we watched the game and you got hit pretty good and gave up like five or six runs. We were going, what did they draft him for?' I'm like, 'Well, I hope that didn't bring you guys down pregame.'"

FIRST COLLEGE EXPERIENCE:

"You never really know moving up levels, how it's gonna work. You just keep going and keep playing hard and kind of make the adjustments. That's the thing about baseball. That's the one weird thing about baseball now that I don't understand is how they're taking away a lot of the minor league programs. The cool thing about it was playing at Stanford and the Pac-10 back then. Unbelievable how many dudes were in the big leagues already. By the time I was drafted after my freshman year that I played against or with, I played against those guys already and I'm kind of in the same pattern, so I think I got a chance to move forward in professional baseball. That was the one positive thing mentally for me. Hey, I knew so many guys that have already made it to the big leagues that I played against in college. Within three years, they had like eight or nine dudes already up in there. So that helped the mentality of being, 'Okay, I think I can do this.'"

FIRST COLLEGE WORLD SERIES CHAMPIONSHIP:

McDowell led Stanford to the College World Series championship in 1987.

"It was awesome. It was just one of those things and it's one of the things that I tell whenever I'm coaching anybody in this sport is, you know how you can celebrate all the individual stuff you want, but nothing individual in baseball can't be better than it was. I tell all the hitters and the pitchers. Tell me, all of the Hall of Fame hitters, what's their average, what's their batting average? You know, in the .300s. That means they get out seven out of ten times.

This is a tough, weird sport. That way you can do everything correctly and still not win or not do it good. You can make a perfect pitch and the guy throws his bat out there and flips it over the infield for a hit. Wait a minute, I did everything I was supposed to do. That's the thing about baseball, it's just end results. The thing that's cool is the only thing you can't get better at. I didn't get to win a World Series in pro sports and that was frustrating. Your individual play in baseball can always be better, no matter what kind of awards they give you and all that, but when you win the World Series, what else could you have won as a team? When else could you have done? Nothing. That is the one thing, winning championships is the one thing. You've reached the top level and can't do anything else. That was the top thing that you can possibly do, so that's what's so cool about it."

FIRST TIME CALLED UP TO THE MAJOR LEAGUES:

After pitching only six minor league games, McDowell was called up by the White Sox in September 1987.

"The thing that wasn't really let out was that was part of my signing bonus. Instead of giving me the money, they gave me a number of money and said, we'll call you up in September so you'll get paid big league money for September. I assumed, and I think they assumed too at the time, that I was just gonna get called up to hang out and probably not even pitch at all, but we had the one injury and took those last starts for him, so I was lucky."

FIRST MAJOR LEAGUE MANAGER: Jim Fregosi

"Well, he liked me there. The following year, my rookie year, if I'd get frustrated of not having a good start, he would tell me, 'Hey, listen, you there's a possibility you might not even belong up here, so don't be so frustrated about it.' I was like, 'Well, don't say that to me.' That was the one thing he told me. I know that I'm young and I haven't played a lot of minor league ball, but still want to do well."

FIRST GAME/FIRST START: September 15, 1987 as a member of the Chicago White Sox vs. Minnesota Twins at Comiskey Park.

In his major league debut, McDowell tossed seven scoreless innings and earned the win as the White Sox beat the Twins, 6-2.

"The funny thing, I was so visually locked into the catcher's glove and the strike zone and just trying to, 'Hey, I gotta make every pitch,' and it really just mentally had me locked in. I was so mentally locked into what I was doing, one inning when I ran off the field, I ran into the pole of the dugout instead of walking through the open area. I bumped into the pole. Just think about the game, you gotta walk out sometimes and not run over something."

FIRST TIME HE SAW HIMSELF ON A BASEBALL CARD:

"Oh yeah. I remember taking the pictures of 'em first. Was kind of looking at and going, wait a minute, they're taking a picture of me. This is gonna be a baseball card. Am I supposed to smile? Am I supposed to look strong? What am I doing? It's very interesting. Yeah, seeing those young pictures. The first rookie pictures were the only ones where I didn't have my goatee. Rookie year was the year I didn't have my beard on, but then we went to the black uniforms with White Sox. Everyone joked about that. Oh, let's start getting mean and scary with beards and stuff. So, I did the goatee thing. I remember [teammate] Steve Lyons at the end of that year. We went to the uniforms late in the season of '91. We switched it up and he was like, 'Well, I doubt you're gonna come back with that.' I said, 'No, now that you just said that, I'm gonna do it. I'm gonna come back with it.'"

FIRST ALL-STAR EXPERIENCE: 1991 All-Star Game at Toronto SkyDome

McDowell was named to the American League All-Star team for the first time in 1991 and pitched two scoreless innings.

"If you look at the list of that '91 All-Star Game, it's crazy how many Hall of Famers are on that. Heck of a game to be in. It was cool. It was cool going in and getting to personally met a lot of the guys that you played against but you really haven't talked with, that was kinda cool. That was fun to get in there. The most interesting part about it was when I went out there to pitch [in the 1992 game] and all of a sudden, it was [Texas Rangers catcher] Pudge Rodriguez. I can't tell 'em what our pitching signs are because they can steal 'em from second base. We do different things with our pitching signs to try and stay away from that. That was just part of the game. If you're gonna do that, if your third base coach is giving signs that you can tell which one's which, yeah, throw the pitch out and get the guy out stealing. That's the way baseball used to be. You used to come out, have to be smart about changing up certain things about your signs and what you did. I don't even remember what I told him. I think it was like, five is a fastball. I mean a fist down is a curveball."

FIRST EXPERIENCE WITH HIS BAND AS THE OPENING ACT FOR THE SMITHEREENS:

McDowell played guitar for a band known as "V.I.E.W." In 1992, they performed as the opening act for the Smithereens.

"That was cool. That wasn't just our first opening act, that was our first on the stage act that we did as a band. It was very cool. The first one was at a college, so that was kind of neat. A bunch of younger kids really liking the stuff. They liked the songs and [were] cheering the music. They enjoyed what we were doing and we had a lot of fun doing it. Yeah, it was cool. Not as much pressure either as you can make mistakes. I can make mistakes on the lyrics real quick and get back to it and well, it's gone. It wasn't like a home run so that's the good thing about it. That's the other thing about music and making movies and all that. Those guys are so famous, make so much money. I always laughed and said, 'Okay, it would be great if you were a pitcher and they could go, now, let's redo that pitch. You know, that one that went over the fence. No, that's supposed to be a strikeout, let's redo that one."

FIRST CY YOUNG AWARD:

While with the White Sox, McDowell was the American League's Cy Young Award winner in 1993 when he led the AL and was tied for the major league lead with 22 wins.

"It was cool. Couple years prior, I had a chance to be in 'em and didn't get at it. That last year we got it and I was like, 'Okay, that's cool.' You wanna just win championships, that's the most important thing. I think if I didn't win a Cy Young and won a championship, I'd be happier with the championship."

FIRST TIME HE WAS CALLED BY HIS NICKNAME, "BLACK JACK":

Minnesota Twins Hall of Famer Kirby Puckett is credited with coining McDowell's nickname, "Black Jack."

"The first time I ever head it was when Kirby was walking off the field after BP and we were walking on. He says, 'Hey, Black Jack, what's going on, man?' I was like, 'Hey, what's up man? What's going on?' 'cause we always used to talk and get along together. When he was a free agent, he called me and wanted to come to Chicago 'cause that's where he grew up. He said, 'You guys have a fun team, you guys have a good club.' I said, 'Yeah, we have a solid club, we're good, we're fine. We're getting better every year. You should come, come check it out.' [The Twins] ended up re-signing him. I remember that following year that they re-signed him, he led off the game against me. First pitch, right center bomb. One of the loudest crowd things I've ever heard. When I was with the Yankees and Seattle when they beat us in that series, that was real loud. The [indoor] domes gets so loud when the crowd starts going loud and gave up that home run on the first pitch of the year. That was their Opening Day there and he goes deep with it after they had just talked about re-signing him and being happy for that. So, I'm like, 'Oh, well, I gave you some cheers, dude.'"

FIRST POSTSEASON EXPERIENCE:

McDowell made his first postseason appearance with the White Sox in the 1993 American League Championship Series against the Toronto Blue Jays, going 0–2 with a 10.00 ERA.

"It wasn't much different. I mean, it was tough if you go back and look. I won the Cy Young and the 10 losses that I had, three or four of 'em were [to] the Blue Jays. They beat me every single game they played against me, which is interesting because I think part of what they knew is I was tipping pitches with something here and there. They would hit me from top to bottom, but they had a lot of dudes, players that had been around forever and they had a really good lineup and they did good against me all during the year and during the playoffs."

FIRST REACTION TO BEING TRADED TO THE YANKEES:

McDowell was traded to the Yankees for a player to be named later and a minor leaguer in December, 1994.

"Well, I find out when someone came knocking on our door in Chicago. It was during the lockout thing, well, they call it the strike but it was kinda caused by them. So yeah, someone knocks on the door and they have the camera there for the TV and they're like, 'Hey, you just got traded.' Like, wait, what are you talking about? I got traded? 'Yeah, you just got traded,' and I'm going, 'Well I'm supposed to be a free agent but they didn't give any of the days back. I had 15 more days I had to play in the big leagues to be a free agent, so it was crazy. I didn't know anything about it, but then it happened and I didn't know whether that was actually going to stay or not because it wasn't supposed to be legal to do that during lockouts and all that.

"You're not supposed to be able to trade or do any of that stuff or sign guys or any of that stuff. They don't do it. So, I didn't know whether or not that was actually gonna work and the [players'] association didn't know whether it was actually gonna be real or not either. Two days before the new spring training started, I just got called by the Yankees and [they] said, 'Hey, you know, you're with us now. You need to be out here in Florida in two days.' That was the craziest, toughest preseason get going at all for anybody because it was a short spring training. There wasn't a lot of pre-time that you knew to be getting your work done, ready to go into games and stuff like that, which is what you do every year.

"That was a very strange year. I was out in California at the time as we just had our first baby and he was out there. Introducing him to all the California family out there and I get that call and I'm like, 'Okay, I gotta fly back, leave you guys here. I gotta get to Chicago, get my stuff and go to Florida,' but then, when the season starts, I don't know where we're gonna live, what am I gonna do? I'm not set up yet. I don't know where to go. My wife, my ex-wife had to go over there and find a place for us to live and figure all that kind of stuff out."

FIRST YANKEES MANAGER: Buck Showalter

"I had a great time, loved him. Thought he was really good and one of the reasons why I didn't, wasn't able to sign back with the Yankees is 'cause when he was fired. He was one of the people that was behind me there. They had not offered me anything yet and there were only two offers out there. I better take this quick or they're gonna get somebody else and I don't know what I'm gonna do. So, I ended up signing with Cleveland."

FIRST TIME HE PUT ON A YANKEES UNIFORM:

"Oh yeah, it was cool looking through all that. My locker was right next to [Don] Mattingly's locker and that was kind of cool because I got to watch him play a lot before I got there. It was cool getting there and doing all that."

FIRST IMPRESSION OF THE YANKEES-RED SOX RIVALRY:

McDowell faced the Red Sox in his second start as a Yankee. He gave up three runs in eight innings as he beat Boston, 4–3.

"You just tried to go out and win a game. Didn't matter who you were playing against, you just went out there and worked hard and tried to win. So, it didn't really change anything up that it was the Red Sox for me. I still knew I had to go try to get some guys out and do some stuff and be better than that. So that's what you do."

FIRST INTERACTION WITH THE "CORE FOUR"

The Yankees had a group of successful players that came out of their farm system that were known as the "Core Four." The group included Hall of Famers Derek Jeter and Mariano Rivera, along with pitcher Andy Pettitte and catcher Jorge Posada, who were also All-Stars. All four made their major league debuts in 1995 when McDowell was with the Yankees.

"All those dudes, they just popped up and popped out. We had a lot of injuries that year, so we had a lot of guys filling in so we got to see a little bit of it all, but not really what they ended up being. The first day that Jeter got there, he was taking his ground balls during BP [batting practice] and he wasn't doing his shuffling throw and so his throws weren't as strong. I know Donnie [Mattingly] went over there and started talking to him about it. I actually went over and started talking to him because I was a shortstop growing up so that's what I kind of knew all about. Let's try to shuffle and get towards it and get more strength going to that and we talked to him about that."

FIRST TIME HE "SALUTED" THE FANS AT YANKEE STADIUM:

On July 18, 1995, in the second game of a doubleheader against the Chicago White Sox, McDowell was hammered for nine runs and 13 hits in 4 2/3 innings pitched. When he was removed from the game in the fifth, McDowell was greeted with a chorus of boos. He responded by "giving the finger" to the fans.

"It was against the White Sox who traded me. I wasn't super happy that they did that to me. I mean, think about it, the White Sox never even offered me a single-year contract ever. It was first year, second year and then it was arbitration, arbitration, arbitration. No contract offers at all so they were just on me from day one. Didn't know if they were gonna offer me anything for free agents or not. Then, when they traded me, I'm like, well, whatever, they traded me. Then to get booed by your home crowd, that was just embarrassing for me 'cause [the White Sox are] beating me up and then my home crowd's booing me. I'm like, somebody support me. I'm busting my butt for all you people up there in the crowd. Getting booed in that situation, that's not the correct thing to do. Som it just added a lot of embarrassment to me on top of the frustration of not pitching good."

FIRST POSTSEASON WITH THE YANKEES: 1995 American League Division Series vs. Seattle Mariners

"[The Yankees] hadn't been to the playoffs about as long as the White Sox hadn't been either. To get there, we were the first wild-card team ever in the history of baseball. They started the wild card that year and we got it. Had they had the wild card when I was with the White Sox, we would've been there a few times. If you go back and look, we were playing in the American League West with the A's when the A's had those crazy good teams in the late eighties, early nineties. We would win games in the nineties. We didn't win a hundred games but we 90-something a couple of times. Probably would've been a wild-card team then and got a chance to play and get in there. It was one of the funny things looking back on that. How we won the wild-card [clinching game at Toronto] and knew we got to the playoffs. There wasn't a celebration, we didn't on-field celebrate, like jump around and be all excited. We were just like we won a game. Normal, high five everybody. It wasn't like when you make the playoffs, everyone goes crazy. I guess 'cause it was a wild card and we didn't even know if that was cool or not."

You Never Forget Your First: A Collection of New York Yankees Firsts

Jack McDowell by Mark Springer

17
GEORGE "DOC" MEDICH

George "Doc" Medich was chosen by the Yankees in the 30th round of the 1970 MLB June Amateur Draft and pitched four seasons in New York. Medich got the nickname "Doc" because he was in medical school while he was also pursuing a career in baseball. Medich's best season with the Yankees was 1974 when he won 19 games. He is best known for being the trade chip for the deal with the Pittsburgh Pirates in December 1975 that brought back Willie Randolph, who went on to be one of the best second basemen in franchise history.

FIRST BASEBALL IDOL:

"Probably, Dick Groat. He was one of the best players on the Pirates and I grew up near Pittsburgh so of course we were all Pirate fans. He was a shortstop and was a good hitter. Just seemed like a really good guy. Him and Vernon Law. Law was a pitcher with the Pirates back in the late fifties and early sixties. I liked him too. Seemed like a good guy so those were probably two of my favorites. I always like Mickey Mantle and Whitey Ford. New York seemed like another country when I was a little kid so didn't get much exposure to them."

FIRST BASEBALL GAME THAT HE ATTENDED AS A KID:

"The first thing I remember is how beautiful the grass was. It was a luscious green. It just looked so pristine and the other thing I always remembered about that was the smell, the hot dogs and the beer. A lot of these new stadiums have lost that but the one that used to have it when I was played was Tiger Stadium. It still had that old ballpark smell to it and that always brought back a lot of memories. Tiger Stadium and County Stadium in Milwaukee still had that old ballpark smell to them.

"I don't even remember when I saw the first major league game. I do remember, it was 1959 or something. Our little league team took a trip to Cleveland and we watched the Indians and the Yankees play. I remember that because Roger Maris was still playing for Cleveland then. The Yankees won 10–4 and Yogi [Berra] hit a home run."

FIRST DRAFT EXPERIENCE:

Medich was drafted by the Yankees in the 30th round of the 1970 MLB June Amateur Draft from the University of Pittsburgh.

He was accepted to medical school and was torn between that opportunity and playing for the Yankees. Bobby Brown was a former Yankee who went on to become a doctor. Medich wrote Brown a letter to ask him about his experience.

"I was honest with the scouts when they came to Washington. I said, 'Look, I've applied and been accepted to medical school.' I said, 'I plan to go and also planned I could play baseball in the summer when I wasn't attending classes for the first two years. Then I could do my last two years of medical school part time, rather than go full time. Don't know whether the Yankees had an experience with Bobby Brown or not. The other thing was Lee MacPhail's brother-in-law was a guy named Walsh McDermott, who is an internal medicine professor at NYU, who wrote one of the more popular internal medicine textbooks. Maybe Lee talked to him about it, I don't know, but I wrote a letter to Bobby Brown. I called the Yankees. I said, I need this guy's address because I might get drafted and he's a doctor and I wanted to know how he did it. So I wrote a letter to Bobby and he answered me. He wrote me back and he said, don't do it (laughs). I grew up my whole life wanting to be a major league baseball player. I said, I'm at least gonna try. Our first trip [with the Yankees] to Texas in 1973, I'm up in bed, about seven o'clock and the phone rings and he says, 'It's Bobby Brown. I'm down in the lobby, get dressed, we're gonna go make rounds.' So he came and picked me up and we went over to Fort Worth and made rounds, cardiac rounds with him on his patients. I felt honored. We went to his country club, Colonial, and had lunch. So he was really a classy guy. He was the best.

"On draft day, I didn't even know I was drafted 'til about the third day. I thought maybe I didn't get drafted and then, my father-in-law, who worked for United Airlines and was on some of the [Baltimore] Oriole charters. [He] lived near Baltimore and has been with United for like 30 years, so I guess he knew somebody over with the Orioles and he called 'em. He said, 'Can you check to see if this kid's been drafted?' So he found out I'd been drafted by the Yankees and that's how I found out through him. About two days later, I got a call from [Yankees scout] Randy Gumpert saying you've been drafted. I want to come over and meet with you and talk to you about signing. So that's what happened. He drove over to Pittsburgh where I was living at the time and sat down with us and said, 'We'll give you a $5,000 signing bonus plus an incentive. If you make the big leagues, you'll get so much more.' My girlfriend, who's my wife now, we were sitting there. We planned on getting married in August and I said, 'Okay, let me talk this over with everybody?' I asked my wife, I said, 'Donna, do you wanna get married now and then we'll go to play baseball, or do you want to wait until the season's over?' She said, 'Let's go ahead and do it now.' We've known each other for seven years. We met in junior high school, so we got married and I went up to Oneonta [New York] and played A-ball, so that's how I got started."

FIRST PROFESSIONAL EXPERIENCE:

Medich began his professional career with the Oneonta Yankees of the short season Single-A New York-Penn League. George Case was his first manager.

"You know, Oneonta was a small college town up in the Adirondack mountains. That's the first place I ever ran into cable TV (laughs) because this town is up in these mountains. They can't get a TV signal up there. So they had cable in 1970, which I didn't even know about it. They had to tell me what it was. So we actually got Yankee games on cable up there. I remember just showing up with all these other guys that were kind of in the same boat. I knew one of them, Tommy O'Connor, he was a guy from Pittsburgh who I'd run into up at Pitt. He'd come work out with us once in a while, but he was on that team. It was a short season. We didn't begin 'til almost the middle of June. We had about a week to get together and work out and then we started playing. I think I pitched four games and they sent me to Double A, which was really a mistake. They should never have done that. I was there maybe three or four weeks and they moved me up to Double-A ball, which was a really big jump for where I was in my development as a pitcher. I was a little bit over my head." (Medich was 0–5 with a 4.93 ERA in eight starts at Double-A Manchester of the Eastern League.)

FIRST GAME AT YANKEE STADIUM: August 24, 1972 vs. New York Mets in the Mayor's Trophy Game

Medich was called up from Double A, West Haven of the Eastern League to make the start against the Mets in the annual exhibition game. Medich pitched a four-hit complete game in beating the Mets, 2–1 in the final Mayor's Trophy Game at the original Yankee Stadium before a crowd of more than 52,000.

"I didn't even know [the fans] were there. I mean, I was so focused and concentrated. Stands could have been empty, I mean I was that focused on doing what I was doing. The thing I remember about that day it was so damn hot. I think it was like 95 degrees there. It was really hot and humid and sticky. I didn't know any of these guys I was playing with but I did realize that at this point in the season, the last thing a major league team wants to do is to have to play an exhibition game. So we went ahead and played and I did pretty good, I guess, but also realizing that, I'm sure [the Mets] didn't bring their A game to this either. I had never been to spring training. I had never been there. The major league people had no idea who I was, so I guess they figured they'd shoot me up there and see what I got. Charlie Spikes and I both went up there and played. I remember Charlie, he came to bat and Charlie's this big strong kid. I mean he could hit the ball a mile. He hit one about 460 feet to left center field and somebody ran it down. He comes back to the dugout and he's like, 'Man, it's hard to hit a home run up here.'"

FIRST TIME IN YANKEES CLUBHOUSE:

"The only guy I knew in that whole clubhouse was Thurman Munson. He and I had played against each other in college. He went to Kent [State] and I was a Pitt. I actually went up there, we played at Kent one day. I happened to be pitching and Thurman was playing for Kent that day. He was the only guy that I kind of even had an acquaintance with. They were all kind of strangers to me. I was probably a stranger to them too but they're all really nice, very professional. I went and pitched and we got in my old Malibu and we drove back to West Haven after the game."

FIRST MAJOR LEAGUE START: September 5, 1972 vs. Baltimore Orioles at Memorial Stadium

In his first start, Medich faced four batters and gave up two runs on two hits with two walks.

"I knew there was something up there because nobody pitches a guy that's never been above Double A in a pennant stretch. Ralph [Houk] is too smart for that. I think he anticipated that I might have trouble initially and he had Wade Blasingame warming up in the first inning, a left-hander. So he turned their lineup over as soon as I came out of the game, he had a lefty pitching against him and I think that was all planned but it was kind of a nightmare. I forgot to cover first base on the first hitter and then I think I hit a guy and walked a guy and then the next guy got a hit and that was it for me. It was a tough winter, you know, I'm thinking, Jesus, you know maybe I can't do this. I had to live with that all winter. It was kind of tough. I tried not to think about it too much. I was going to school and working out, staying as busy as I could. I had a fairly good spring training [in 1973] and made the team.

FIRST MAJOR LEAGUE MANAGER: Ralph Houk

"Man's man. He was the kind of guy you'd get in the foxhole with. He had the leadership qualities that you wanted in a manager. He was a player's manager. He treated everybody as a mature adult, didn't put up with baloney. It was all business. I'll tell you another funny story. My first major league game in 1973 was the first time a designated hitter was ever used in the major leagues. It was Ron Blomberg and [Luis] Tiant's pitching for Boston. There's these two little guys in suits in the dugout from the Hall of Fame that want the bat, okay? Now, Ralph did not like anybody who was not supposed to be there in the dugout, so he grudgingly put up with these two guys. So Bloomy comes up to bat. I read other accounts of his but I was there that day and I know what happened. Luis hits Bloomy about two inches above his knuckles and the bat explodes. I mean, there's pieces of mountain ash all over the infield. This looks like somebody put a grenade in his bat and these two little guys in the dugout are thinking, oh no. Oh no. What are we going to do? Ralph never missed a beat. He turned around the bat rack, looked at a couple of bats, found one with Blomberg's name on hit, handed it to these two guys. He said, 'Here's Blomberg's bat, now get the fuck outta here.'

"I was sorry when he left. I pitched the next to last day in old Yankee Stadium. That was my last start before I had to go back to school. He called me in the office after the game. He said, 'Don't tell anybody this, but I'm not coming back next year.' He hadn't told the team yet. I said, 'I won't say anything, but why?' I said, 'Jeez, you've been a Yankee your whole life.' He said, 'I can't stand that motherfucker.' That's what he told me. He said, 'He comes in my office and puts his feet up on my desk and he's trying to tell me what to do. He's got no idea about what he's doing.' I guess they're two very similar personalities, were bound to clash, so George [Steinbrenner] did it his way and Ralph did it his way."

FIRST SPRING TRAINING: 1973

"I thought it was great. I mean, I was out of the cold, it was February and March. I was in sunshine, I was playing baseball, I thought it was terrific. I really enjoyed it. Spring training's a lot of fun when you're a pitcher because you know you can do your work. When the games start, in the days you're not pitching, you can go fishing or go play golf or go to the beach with your wife. It was almost like vacation. Of course, you had to work hard while you were there but we were all young then, in pretty good shape."

FIRST FULL SEASON: 1973

Medich finished 14–9 with a 2.95 ERA in his rookie season. Medich made 32 starts and had 11 complete games and he finished tied for third for the AL Rookie of the Year award with Kansas City Royals pitcher Steve Busby.

"That was a big confidence boost for me, 'cause I had enough talent to play with these guys. Up until then, I really didn't know. Nobody knows, so the first year was pretty important. I convinced myself I was good enough to play in the big leagues, so that was personally reassuring to me that I had enough ability to do that. I had to be very disciplined about my life and what I was doing. I was either playing ball, going to school and studying, or exercising to stay in shape to play. It was a pretty disciplined life up to that point. We had our first child that year too, so now I became a father."

FIRST TIME HE FLIRTED WITH A NO-HITTER:
July 20, 1974 vs. Kansas City Royals at Shea Stadium

Medich no-hit the Royals for the first eight innings but Fran Healy led off the ninth inning with a single to spoil the bid. It was the closest that Medich ever came to throwing a no-hitter.

"It was a nothing fastball right down the middle and I'm thinking, 'Did I just have a brain fart?' You know what I mean. I was three outs away from a no-no and I threw a nothing fastball right down the middle, but that's the way it is. A lot of guys pitched their whole career and never have a no-hitter. I don't think Fergie [Jenkins] ever had one. He and I were teammates for a long time. He's one of the best pitchers I ever saw and I don't think he ever had one. So there's an element of luck there. I got no complaints. I had a good year, we had a good pennant stretch there. We were in the thing right 'til the last couple of days. Every starting pitcher knows that they haven't given up a hit yet and that's baloney (laughs), they'll tell you they don't realize it, but that's baloney. They know they haven't given up a hit yet and unless they're totally schizophrenic, every starting pitcher knows that they haven't given up a hit yet. I'm positive of that. I came close another time in Texas. I went seven and then I gave up a questionable infield hit in the eighth inning. Then, in the ninth inning, I gave up another infield single. That was the other time I came close."

FIRST PENNANT RACE: 1974

In 1974, the Yankees played their home games at Shea Stadium and made a run at the American League East Division title. On September 4, the Yankees and Boston Red Sox were tied for first place with identical 72–63 records after Medich tossed a five-hit, complete game shutout to beat the Milwaukee Brewers.

"It wasn't fun playing at Shea Stadium. We never felt like we were home. We knew we were on somebody else's field and we were using the Jets clubhouse. It was a tiny little thing. I don't know how they put football players in there. It wasn't a very big room. One of the things that sticks out in that season in my mind was Elliott Maddox. Elliott Maddox took over in center field at some point in the season. He was the best center fielder in the American League. Then, he got hurt. I mean, it was a shame. He could hit, he could run, he could track down fly balls. It was a shame 'cause Elliott's a really, really good guy. He was the kick that we needed. Him and Thurman [Munson] and Bobby Murcer and Graig Nettles and [Ron] Blomberg, we had a fairly good offensive lineup. Roy White, everybody forgets about Roy White, you know the dignified Yankee. He was always steady. He had 25 home runs, hit .260, and drive in 80 runs every year. Sandy Alomar came over and started playing second base for us. That kind of filled a hole that we'd had for years. Sandy came over and replaced Horace Clarke. Then, Sparky [Lyle] was Sparky. He was at the top of his game. You bring him in, the game's over. It was thrilling. Finally, September baseball was significant, it really meant something. That seems to make the season a little shorter. I played on enough teams where you're 20 games out when September starts and it really gets to be drudgery. That year, all the irons were still in the fire. The important games were still there for us so we really kept our interest more than if we were battling to stay out of the cellar."

FIRST OPENING DAY START: April 8, 1975 vs. Cleveland Indians at Cleveland Stadium

Medich gave up five earned runs and took the loss on an historic day in Major League Baseball. Hall of Famer Frank Robinson became the first Black manager in baseball history. Robinson was in the lineup as the DH and he hit a home run off of Medich in his first at-bat as a player-manager in the first inning.

"It was cold. It was 35 degrees and the mound was frozen. It was really, really cold. You know we came right outta spring training, out of 80, 85 degrees and we get to Cleveland and you know, it's in the thirties. I'm not surprised. I grew up near Cleveland in Pittsburgh. I'm not surprised at the weather but that pitch that Frank Robinson hit out, I'd throw to him again. It was a good fastball. Low and away, right on the corner. He just went down and got it. Hats off to him. I always respected Frank a lot. I thought he was a very, very dignified, great ballplayer. Hats off to him, good for him. He hit it off me, he would've hit it off somebody else, what's the difference? I'm actually kind of glad, happy for him 'cause I knew he was in a tough spot. He's the first Black manager in the big leagues and he's got eyes on him that most of us didn't have. I thought he responded really well, so I have a lot of respect for Frank Robinson."

FIRST EXPERIENCE WITH BILLY MARTIN:

In August 1975, Yankees owner George Steinbrenner fired manager Bill Virdon and replaced him with Billy Martin.

"I was surprised [Steinbrenner] did it on Old-Timer's Day. None of us had an inkling that this was coming. We figured Bill's job was safe 'cause we almost won it all the year before, but I think George had this thing for Billy or ex-Yankees or something and he pulled the trigger on it. I remember being around Billy, he was really smart. I mean, he knew baseball inside and out. He was almost a baseball savant. He knew that much about the game and he was really good with baseball. Unfortunately, you don't spend your entire life at the baseball field and that's where the problems start. I just kind of wandered through those last six weeks of the season and went home wondering what it was gonna be like playing for him for a full year, because I knew he could be very temperamental. I was just wondering what it was going to be like. I got traded that winter and I missed the whole 'Bronx Zoo' thing, so I was kind of happy about that. I'd talked to the Yankees guys were my old teammates, about what was going on. They said, 'This is crazy around here,' with George and Reggie [Jackson] fighting and Thurman."

FIRST TIME HE HEARD HE WAS TRADED:

"I was in the hospital. I was going to clerkship in internal medicine and my pager goes off. I think it's about 10:30 in the morning and it's [Yankees GM] Gabe Paul. He says, 'We've traded your contract to the Pittsburgh Pirates.' I said, 'Who did you get?' He told me, I said, 'Well, that's a steal for the Yankees.' So I hung up. I had to call him back. I didn't know what to do, you know? I said Gabe, 'Let me get to a private phone, I need to call you back,' so I did. He said, 'Well, contact the Pirates and we will send all of your equipment over and all that.' I said, 'Okay, fine. Thank you, best of luck to you. It's been great being a Yankee.' There I was in this hospital in Pittsburgh and I couldn't tell anybody. I called my wife and my mom told them. I said, 'You can't tell anybody until you hear it on the news.' It was a pretty long day for me 'cause I think I was on call that night too and I had to stay there the whole day.

"So it was, you know, I was sitting on this secret and I couldn't tell anybody, so it was a lot of anxiety with that. I was really happy 'cause I knew most of the Pirate players because in the winter time, we'd work out together up at the Pitt field house. I knew Sangi [Manny Sanguillen] and Dave Giusti. I didn't know Willie [Stargell] that well or Dave Parker, but they had a very mature, veteran team. I felt right at home right away, like I'd been there a long time, so that was good. Then, I didn't have to move. 25 minutes from the stadium. I could just drive home."

FIRST TIME HE PERFORMED CPR ON A FAN: April 11, 1976 at Philadelphia's Veterans Stadium

Medich's medical training came in handy when he noticed a 73-year-old fan in the lower stands was having a heart attack. Medich went into the stands and performed CPR but unfortunately, the gentleman died. A little over two years later, in July 1978, Medich was with the Texas Rangers and again performed CPR on a 61-year-old fan in the stands at Baltimore's Memorial Stadium who was having a heart attack. Medich administered a heart massage until medical help arrived and saved the fan's life.

"In Philadelphia, I remember walking off the field with Willie Stargell and we're walking into our dugout and there's some guy in the third row, blue, blue as he can be, he could be cyanotic (occurs when there is not enough oxygen in the blood) he's just blue. Willie looked at me and he said, 'You gotta do something [laugh]. So you talking to me [laugh]? I hadn't even completed medical school at that point. So I went up, I knew basic CPR and we just started basic CPR on this guy until the paramedics got there. We had an ambu bag, something to breathe for him and we were doing chest compressions. Then, the paramedics came in and took him to the hospital. The poor guy eventually died.

"A couple of years later, we were in Baltimore during batting practice and the stadium's basically empty at that point when the visiting team takes batting practice when you're on the road. I'm standing in the outfield with Fergie and we're talking and chasing down fly balls and stuff. The guy comes on the PA and says, 'Paging any physician in attendance to behind the Oriole dugout.' I'm looking around, I don't see any physicians in attendance but me. So, they kind of pushed me. I really didn't want to get into that again but, like I said, I was the only one there. So I jumped into the stands and we started the same thing, CPR. This guy, I managed to get an IV into him and gave him a bowl of lidocaine. I think he had an arrhythmia. I don't think he had a heart attack. I think he was having an arrhythmia and he eventually made it. The paramedics came and the nurse at the ballpark was there. They took him to the hospital and he made it, which made me feel good. I was just wishing this stuff would stop happening but I realized, once I was given this medical education, that I had some responsibility to use it when I could. A couple of days was old news so it didn't really matter. One thing that came out of that though was I talked to the American Heart Association down in Texas and they put on a two-day CPR course for the baseball team. So all the Rangers learned CPR from that."

FIRST TIME PITCHING IN HIS HOMETOWN: April 16, 1976 vs. New York Mets at Three Rivers Stadium

In his debut game at Three Rivers Stadium, Medich went the distance in a 3–1 win over the Mets.

"That felt really good. I realized the Pirates gave up a lot get get me. I was really happy about that. That was also the year we had shortened spring training. We got locked out for about two weeks, so I was a little bit behind on where I should have been pitching wise. I was probably a couple of weeks behind. I was relieved a little bit 'cause the thing was to finish the game. That was a big thing with us back then. Any starting pitcher, when they gave you the ball, they expected you to finish the game and that's the way we felt about it. I was really happy about that I could pitch nine innings and fulfill my obligation to the team."

FIRST MAJOR LEAGUE HIT: April 26, 1976 vs. Los Angeles Dodgers at Dodger Stadium

Medich got his first major league hit off Tommy John when he singled in the top of the second inning. Medich would have five hits in his career, all of them coming in the 1976 season.

"It was a bleeder. Yeah, it was like a two-hopper right past second base. So I turned to [Pirates coach] Jose Pagan, I said, 'Jose, get the ball. It's my first hit.' I don't think he heard me. I never got the ball. Growing up, I was a pretty good hitter throughout my career. I hadn't hit for three years and I had never hit against major league pitching. So I was really in over my head at home plate. I was kind of lost, you know? I really didn't know what to do. That was something that going to spring training that year, I was bound and determined to work on that a little bit so that maybe I wouldn't get pinch-hit for so much if I'd become a little bit of an offensive threat. Not that I was going to be hitting home runs or driving in runs or anything but at least I'd like to think that I wasn't an easy out, which I wasn't."

FIRST WORLD SERIES: 1982

"One of the things that kind of modified that entire year for me was I got hepatitis in spring training. I was pretty sick for about a month in spring training. So when I started the season, I was behind my conditioning and I don't know if you've ever had hepatitis but it's the kind of thing where all of a sudden you get really tired. That happened to me throughout the whole year. I'd be going along and then all of a sudden, boom, I'd be hit with this tremendous fatigue. Maybe even right in the middle of a ballgame. It's like one inning I was fine. The next thing you know I was really tired so I fought with that all year. Towards the end of '82, I realized I wasn't gonna come back for another year so I'd like to play in a World Series once and this was my last shot at it. Pat Dobson was the pitching coach with the Brewers then and they came into Texas I think it was towards the beginning of August. I went up to him, I said, 'Hey, Pat, I'd like to play in a World Series one year, if you guys need any pitching, I'd be happy to come over and join with you guys just to get a shot at playing in the World Series.' You know, two weeks later, boom, I was there on waivers, so that's how it happened.

"I hadn't pitched in a World Series game. I hadn't pitched for 17 days and then I went out there and it started raining and then the wind started to blow. I was a little bit wild that first inning. I felt really, really strong 'cause I hadn't pitched so long. Things just went ot hell in the hand basket that inning. So I went out and pitched one more. I think the next thing I did a little bit better and got 'em all out but that was the end. At that point, I realized I'd played enough. I was very content with that being my last season, even though it wasn't a great one."

FIRST EXPERIENCE WITH MEETING A FAMOUS COMEDIAN:

"There was always people hanging around. I remember one time I was with the Yankees and I was in the training room out in Anaheim. I'm [lying] on the training table and then walks in Jonathan Winters. He says, 'I've always wanted a Yankee hat,' then he goes through this little dialogue, this pantomime throwing and catching a ball. So, we gave him a hat and then another time it was also in California. Here comes [Angels owner] Gene Autry walking through the training room just as lost as he could be. By then, he had full blown dementia. So I went up and said, 'Mr. Autry, are you lost?' He said, 'Yeah, I need some help finding out where I am?' So I took him over to the Angels clubhouse."

You Never Forget Your First: A Collection of New York Yankees Firsts

George "Doc"Medich by Jared Kelly

18
MIKE PAGLIARULO

Massachusetts-born Mike Pagliarulo began his 11-year manjor league career with the Yankees and spent parts of six seasons in New York. Pagliarulo was a solid fielding third baseman who provided the Yankees with some left-handed power. "Pags" hit 105 of his 134 career home runs with the Yankees. He had his biggest-Yankee moment on May 8, 1987 when he hit a walk-off, grand slam home run in the bottom of the ninth off of Minnesota Twins closer Jeff Reardon to finish off an 11–7 win.

FIRST BASEBALL IDOL:

"Growing up just outside of Boston, Medford, Massachussetts, they didn't have the exposure that they have today. The internet wasn't as big, so the Red Sox were the team. Red Sox, Bruins, Celtics. Carl Yastrzemski, when I was seven, eight years old, he was a Triple Crown winner and all that. I had my Yaz jacket and all that stuff. So, he was probably the first guy that I thought was the greatest. I went to my first ballgame [when] I was eight years old. My father took me to a game with my brother and we went and saw the Washington Senators and Ted Williams was managing the other team. The Red Sox lost that game, that was the first team that I saw that loved. I went to Fenway Park, it was beautiful. For me, it was beautiful. I mean it was a wonderful experience. Then, I went to college [University of Miami], I ended up playing against Yastrzemski's son, Michael Yastrzemski, who passed away too soon. He went to Florida State and our teams would kind of get together after games sometimes and he kind of gravitated to me 'cause he knew I was from Boston. We were talking, he goes, 'My dad's crazy, man. He's down in that basement, you know, a hundred swings with this lead bat he takes every day.' He said, 'That's crazy.' I said, yeah, I know and I'm thinking, that's why I do it, because he did it. I never really talked to [Yastrzemski] but he was the first guy, I guess, idolized."

FIRST GAME THAT HE ATTENDED AS A KID:

"What I remember, my father played in the minors with the Cubs, actually. So, he knew baseball and he's really the other guy I've ever listened to. He said, 'Now watch the infielders. Watch what they do,' and he's, 'Tell me what you see.' It was amazing. All the infielders were positioned and just when the ball was delivered to the home plate, I said, they went and did this little hop. I said, they looked like a bunch of frogs, you know what I mean? It was a little hop. He says, 'Yeah, they're on their toes.' At the time, the Red Sox had Louie [Luis] Aparicio playing shortstop. Eddie Brinkman was playing shortstop for the Senators, so I was playing shortstop and second base and I played in the infield. So I watched him, that's the thing I remember most.

"The other thing I remember is, I think it was Eddie Brinkman, he was on first base and someone hit a ball off the wall at Fenway and Billy Conigliaro was playing left field. The ball comes off the wall, so Brinkman goes around second base. Just before it happened, my father said, 'Watch this,' and he goes around he kinda like half falls or slides or whatever. Conigliaro threw the ball to second base and Brinkman walked in at third. It was a bad play, you could throw ahead of the runner and I was like, 'Wow.' I remember that when I was in college and I remember doing that in college. Funny how that played out 'cause I did that. We had a guy in college that liked to throw behind runners and I did it against him when we played against each other in the minors. So, I got to the big leagues and first time I'm at Fenway and Dwight Evans was playing right field. This is a good story. So I get a base hit, so I run to first base real hard and I'm gonna decoy him, you know what I mean? I'm gonna take a big turn and he's gonna throw behind me. So, I take a big old turn and he picks up the ball and [Evans made a gesture as if to say, 'Don't try it, rook.']. I go back, I said, 'How the heck did he see that?'

FIRST COLLEGE WORLD SERIES EXPERIENCE:

In 1979, Pagliarulo played in the College World Series for the first time.

"I think playing at Miami helped 'cause we played in front of big crowds all the time. We had at least 3,500 people at every game and we held the regionals, so there was always big games, I guess pressure games. This was a little different, though. I mean, you're playing against the best in the country. We played against good teams all the time and we were ranked really high every year, but it was good for us. It kind of taught you how to play in that situation. You learn things when you play in that kind of environment. That experience really helps because you can't get too tight. You gotta think about the game and one thing at a time. You gotta keep your thoughts together or you can really get messed up. A lot of guys don't play good in situations like that. It was a little bit nerve-wracking at first. I never really get nervous. I get butterflies but I mean, this was different. Everybody in the world's gonna see this. I thought being on television is a little different that playing in front of five thousand, but it was interesting. It was a good. It was a great experience regardless of what happened.

"What I remember most about that my first year, I played against Terry Francona. He played for Arizona, Jimmy Key played for Clemson. I got a base hit, right-handed off of Jimmy Key. I was a switch-hitter in college. There was a lot of good players that you played against and you later see 'em in the big leagues. Second year, I went to Cape Cod and played. That was a great experience too. On every team was like you didn't know it then but it was a former major leaguer that played on each team, one or two guys. So that was fun too."

(On playing in the prestigious Cape Cod League)

"I knew the Cape, but for me, it was like, you're playing in this high intensity College World Series and then you go down to Cape Cod and it's like, phew, you kinda need a breather, you know? Everyone else is all hyped up and I'm like, 'What's all the hype?' What I remember is when I got there, I got there later because we were in the College World Series and everybody else was already there practicing and everything. I got a job working for the city where I was on the highway with the weed wacker doing that stuff. I mean, it was a tough job. I mean, I love taking batting practice, but I'd go back to the place we lived. The family that we lived with, they had a giant hammock in the front yard and I just laid in that hammock and I missed batting practice. I was exhausted and then played a game. I didn't play that great and then the last two weeks, I said, all right we gotta get serious here 'cause we're getting close to winning this thing. So, the last two weeks, I quit the job and then I played really good for the last few weeks and got a couple home runs. My teammates [included] Glenn Davis and Scott Bradley, two guys who played in the big leagues. There was always Ron Darling, Timmy Teufel, they played. So, it was good competition."

FIRST DRAFT EXPERIENCE:

The Yankees drafted Pagliarulo in the sixth round of the 1981 MLB June Amateur Draft.

"At Miami, the scouts [are] at the games every day. The Detroit scout, I was supposed to get drafted by Detroit [said], 'We're gonna take you in the top three rounds.' [Their] GM, at the time, came down to see a game. We had a doubleheader and he was at the first game of the doubleheader, which I didn't play good. The second game of the doubleheader, I hit a home run right-handed over center field, made some diving plays but the first game, I didn't play good. He left after the first game and I went back to Miami and he goes, 'What happened?' I said, 'What do you mean what happened?' He does, 'You didn't play good.' I said, 'Must have saw the first game, not the second one.' So, I didn't get drafted by them, but I was drafted by the Yankees. It was like two days, I didn't hear it until the third day and the draft was already done, but I didn't see anything. It wasn't published. You couldn't see it anywhere. You didn't know whether you were drafted or not. You're just waiting by the phone so I went on a ride. Then I came back and someone said, 'Hey, you got a phone call from New York so call this number.' I called him up, they came to my house. Fred Ferreira, he drafted a ton of major league guys, Vladimir Guerrero and a bunch of other guys, [Pedro] Martinez and all that. So, he came by the house and it wasn't much of a negotiation. You really wanna play, he said, you play for the best organization. So, I signed, but it was good. I'm really glad that it was the Yankees. I'm really happy that I signed with that organization. I'm really lucky and fortunate that the organization was built the way it was. It was like, you get in that organization, they're like, look, play good and win, then we'll talk about a contract for next year, he said, but you're not moving anywhere. You're staying right here. This is what we do with the guys. This is how we develop 'em and they were right. We had more guys in the major leagues in the eighties than anybody else. So, they did something right about how they scouted guys, how they developed guys. Bill Livesey was probably a guy that was in charge of all of that stuff and Jack Butterfield. George [Steinbrenner] of course was running everything. He wanted results so that's how he did it. I didn't mind any of that. I liked that at least they cared enough to win."

FIRST PRO MANAGER: Art Mazmanian

Pagliarulo made his pro debut with the 1981 Oneonta Yankees of the short-season A-level, New York-Penn League.

"Art was a good guy. He was a college coach. I think he was at the highest level that he could be, but he was a good guy. He had to play certain guys and we had a good team. We won the league and everything there. I didn't play that great. For most guys, it was an adjustment for the bats. You had skinny aluminum bats, now you had to use these wood bats and I cracked all these bats and everything. What we did have there, you know, it was during the time when there was a lockout or a strike in '81. I don't know what it was but Joe Pepitone, Mike Ferraro, Yogi Berra, a lot of guys that came there from the Yankees, from the major league side. I learned a lot from Joe Pepitone. After that season, I didn't play that great but I ended up pretty good. I go to spring training the next year and I was down in the batting cage one day and Joe Pepitone says, 'What are you doing down here?' We had a good relationship. I said, 'Hey, Pepi, let me ask you something? How do I jump over all these guys in front of me?' Every third baseman we have in our organization is an All-Star or MVP of the league. I said, 'What the heck am I doing?' He goes, 'Did you ever see Yankee Stadium?' I said, no. He said, 'Stop switching, stay left-handed. I'll show you how to pull the ball the right way and you show power. Jump over everybody 'cause they're all right-handed hitters.' I went, 'Really?' So that's exactly what I did that day. Spring training, I stayed left-handed. We faced a lefty, got a couple of hits. [I] went to Greensboro that next year and and led the team in homers there. Nashville, led the team in homers there, then up to the big leagues. So Pepi helped out a lot. I didn't switch-hit anymore and it was the right thing to do. It helped my pull stroke and helped my power numbers. So that was good.

"As far as Oneonta goes, that's where I was introduced to a lot of these guys and you know, they're funny guys. They're fun to hang with but they knew so much about baseball too. As I went to college, we played the Orioles every year, once a year [during spring training]. You know, [Miami coach] Ron Fraser was one of the greatest college coaches ever. He said, 'Pags, come here. You have a little trouble with that bunt play. Go talk to that guy over there.' So I went over there. 'Mr. Robinson,' Brooks Robinson, 'Mr. Robinson, how you doing?' He taught me in one minute how to make the bunt play and how to practice it and I became really good at it. Then nobody bunted on me. I'm like, come on, I want some bunts. I would decoy guys to pretend I was asleep. So, they bunt, but [Robinson] told me how to make that play. It was so easy after he told me that. When you talk to guys that have that kind of experience and knowledge, it happens quick. Pepi taught me some things. Just think about doing this and you don't have to think about pulling off the ball. Just stay down and stay square and all this other stuff. I had never heard that stuff before, so that instruction really helped out. The Yankees always had the best coaches, I thought."

FIRST SPRING TRAINING:

"They gave me the number 44 and Reggie Jackson was there for spring training before and I was like, 'Oh my God.' So, I'm walking outta the clubhouse and Dave Winfield's in there and he goes, 'Hey, there's a lot of guts to wear that number.' I said, 'I didn't request it, they just put it in my locker.' I don't know what the heck happened but it was really great because I got to talk to [Graig] Nettles a bunch and he's the top guy. You're coming in, you're in the organization, you set your sights on where you want to be and that's where I wanna be. I never knew I would get that. I never doubt that I could, but you don't what's gonna happen, but I talked to [Nettles] about a few things. We talked about playing defense and stuff and our styles were a little different, but it was really cool to talk to him because you learned so much from a guy like that. I said, 'Hey, Graig, I thought you were a pull hitter. You hit everything the other way in spring training. What the hell's going on?' He goes, 'Look, I can't go over there unless I go there first,' and I'm like, okay. That's what they do. They practice hitting the ball the other way, they get the start of their swing shorter to see the ball longer and it's just a practice. In the game, he's looking to get out there. Curtis Granderson, same thing. All his batting practices, the other way, but that's just a thing that I never knew before.

"We talked about playing defense and working with certain pitchers. When [Ron] Guidry's pitching, don't worry about taking the bunt away, he said. [Yankees manager] Billy [Martin] is gonna tell you to take the bunt away. Don't worry about it. He'll tell you to back up. Meeting those guys was great. I didn't talk a whole lot. All I did was kinda listen. My first spring there, it was 1983. [In] '84 I played good again, but didn't make the team. I think, 'Who's playing third base then? Oh [Roy] Smalley and Toby Harrah, but I said, I can play with these guys."

FIRST TIME HE WAS CALLED UP: July 1984

"Rex Hudler and I were roommates in Triple A. There was talk about him getting called up because somebody was either sick or hurt or something like that, but they needed another infielder. At the time I was in Triple A, I think [manager Stump Merrill] was playing someone else at third base. I wasn't even playing for about four or five days in a row and all of a sudden, I found myself in the lineup in clean up. I said, 'Hey, Stump, what's going on,' and he said, and we were playing against the Mets too. He said, 'I just thought you should play now,' and I go, 'I heard Clyde King and Billy Martin were coming down to the game today.' We had a doubleheader and I had a great doubleheader. Then, we take a road trip after the game to Tidewater. The talk is about Hud, all of a sudden, we get to the room about one, two in the morning and the phone rings. I go, 'There it is.' He goes, 'Yep, that's it.' So, he picks up the phone, he goes, 'Pags, it's for you.' That's when I found out at two in the morning. Then I had a flight like six in the morning after that. I don't know why I took all day to get to Minnesota, but it took all day."

"I finally get there. I walk in and nobody's in the locker room. They were outside getting ready for batting practice. I don't have any bats or anything, so I get out there and I get all my stuff and the next thing you know, I'm in the lineup. I'm like, what the heck? So, we take infield and everything. I remember running out to the field and Rick Cerone [was] behind the plate. He goes, 'Can you spit yet?' I'm mountain dry a little, a little anxious or whatever, but it was good. It was a great experience in the Metrodome. That was when, you know Puck [Hall of Famer Kirby Puckett] and all those other guys, they had a good young team."

FIRST GAME: July 7, 1984 vs. Minnesota Twins at Hubert H. Humphrey Metrodome

In his first game, Pagliarulo had three hits and an RBI in the Yankees' 11-4 win over the Twins.

"John Butcher was the first guy I faced. First at-bat, I got a base hit. Next at-bat, I got a double. I ended up getting three hits the first game so that was good. Then a week later I kept playing pretty good. We went home, played Kansas City and I did well at home. They traded Roy Smalley after that so I knew I was gonna be given a chance for the rest of the year. It was great 'cause we had good coaches too. Lou Piniella was by far the best. He was the greatest. He helped out me and Donnie [Mattingly] a lot. We had a good team. We always had good players, but the difference when I get called up is they hit the ball a lot harder in the big leagues. We had Don Baylor and Dave Winfield. I said, everybody's bigger around here. I mean, these guys are giant men, so it was pretty interesting. They give you good tips, they talk about good tips, like, 'Hey, they're gonna challenge you right away with a fastball.' It was a good day. My wife came out, my parents flew out. They didn't even know I was playing so to have a really good game that weekend, it was fun."

FIRST MAJOR LEAGUE MANAGER: Yogi Berra

"Yogi was pretty quiet, subdued. He didn't talk a whole lot, he wasn't yelling a whole lot, but he knew, he could anticipate, good managers anticipate, they know what's gonna happen before it happens. Billy was great at that. I played for five managers that managed World Series champions. You kind of pick up some of the similar traits. They knew what was gonna happen before it happened. Yogi kind of knew stuff was going on. We needed another pitcher, they were struggling with that a little bit. When I got called up, we were like 20-something games out of first or something like that. We played really good in the second half so that was promising. Yogi, he was good. He would just be, 'How you doing, everything all right?' He'd give you the heads up. You're gonna be playing here, you can be playing this time, you ready to pitch here? It was very, very simple. It was very clear. He was funny, but he didn't joke around too much during the game. I was lucky to play for him and I was lucky to know him. He was a fabulous human being. I bet he had so many stories. I wanted to pick his brain so much. My first year I didn't ask too many questions. I just listened a lot."

FIRST HOME GAME AS A YANKEE: July 12, 1984 vs. Kansas City Royals at Yankee Stadium

Pagliarulo had an RBI single in his first home game as a Yankee.

"I'd never seen Yankee Stadium. We had an off day after we get back so I went out there. I took a cab out there and went right to the Stadium and walked in and looked at it and I couldn't believe how big it was. I'm like, 'Oh my God.' Compared to Fenway Park, I'm like this place is gigantic. It was just tremendous. I get chills thinking about it. I love the old Yankee Stadium. The next day I went in there. I got in there early and got my pinstripes on. I mean, really cool to have all that stuff. They [his teammates] kind of like knew that I was like, new, so they kind of supported [us]. The coaching staff and some of the other players. Don Baylor was a great, great teammate but also Dave Winfield. I mean, everyone, they treated me good. They were very supportive so we went out and played the first game and it was really cool."

FIRST MAJOR LEAGUE HOME RUN: July 13, 1984 vs. Kansas City Royals at Yankee Stadium

Pagliarulo hit his first major league home run, a two-run shot in the fourth inning of an 8–1 win.

"I think it was Bret Saberhagen that I had a home run off of. What I couldn't believe was, I was rounding first base and the crowd, [the stadium] wasn't that packed, but it was such a roar. It was loud and I felt like I would be lifted around the bases. It was really amazing for me. I'm like, 'Geez, this is unbelievable, special.' There were some other games that it was. I still remember the end of the season with playing Toronto, Guidry's pitching and he strikes out the first six guys in a row. I was sprinting on and off the field. It was great but it was a special feeling. Just being able to experience that once is a great thing. To play there for that long, it was great. I enjoyed my time there and I miss it, but I was very lucky to be drafted by them. I'm glad I didn't play good when the Detroit GM came down (laughs) when I was in college."

FIRST GRAND SLAM HOME RUN: September 18, 1984 vs. Baltimore Orioles at Yankee Stadium

Pagliarulo cleared the bases in the second inning with his first grand slam home run off f Orioles pitcher Dennis Martinez.

"That was good. It was a big thing. That was after I had been working with Lou Piniella and we talked about some hitting techniques and how I'm changing 'em. I was actually swinging pretty good. Dennis Martinez, for some reason I always hit him pretty good. He was a good pitcher too. I don't know how I did it, but I just did. It was just one of those things. I mean, we won the game. I was all right with all of that. You can't really sit back and think about it, although the first home run was tough to forget. I'm trying to think if I remember facing Dennis Martinez when I was in college."

FIRST TIME HE WAS TRADED:

In July 1989, the Yankees traded Pagliarulo to the San Diego Padres for pitcher Walt Terrell and a player to be named later.

"I remember Dallas Green was a manager. I don't think he liked me too much. I don't know why, but he got rid of everybody that was there in the past. He couldn't get rid of me until I was playing bad. I wasn't playing very well. I was still getting over some surgery. I shouldn't even started the year. I had Tommy John surgery actually in December, so I tried to play the year. Had trouble getting it across the diamond. My swing was not good. It was weak and all that stuff so I wasn't playing very well. I guess I should have been traded but I was kind of sad about it 'cause I love playing in New York. I mean, I'm from the Northeast. I feel very at home there but I understood what happened. We go up to San Diego and that was my first time being out there. What a beautiful place that is, but there's a big difference in organizations. What I found, [with the] Yankees, they're on top of stuff and you get these scouting reports every day and you're ready for the other team. Over there, I'm like 'Where are the scouting reports?' They said, 'Well, how do you wanna play this guy today?' I said, 'I don't know, I've never played here before.' 'Go ask this guy over here.' We had good players, it's just the organization wasn't as tight or structured as the Yankees were.

"In San Diego, I didn't know anything. I didn't know anybody else, didn't know the other teams or anything like that. So, it was tough to adjust but made the best of it. The guys on the team were great too. We had good players. We had a lot of talent. I mean, Robbie Alomar, Tony Gwynn. Jack Clark, Benito Santiago. Playing with those guys was fun. We came close to winning in '89 but I guess we would've made the playoffs if this system [was in place]. Heck, we would've made the playoffs every year in New York."

FIRST WORLD SERIES EXPERIENCE:

In January 1991, Pagliarulo signed with the Minnesota Twins as a free agent and was a member of their 1991 World Series–winning team.

"Before the season started, I went to the winter meetings all by myself. My wife said, 'What are you doing?' I said, I just want to get good baseball people around me. I need to be challenged and pushed every day. I need that structure. They're on you. Some guys don't like it but I liked to be challenged. I met with guys like Tony La Russa, Tom Kelly, and Lou Piniella and some other guys. [Twins manager] Tom Kelly asked, 'What are you doing out here?' I said, 'I just wanna get the right people around me, 'cause I know

I got a lot of game left. So, I wanna play in the right situation.' Two weeks after they traded [Gary] Gaetti to the Angels, I got a call from [GM] Andy MacPhail and we did the [free agent] deal. So I went there and playing in the playoffs, first time for me, it was easier. I think because the team had already won in '87. So, I was picking their brain and they told me some things that really helped me in the playoffs. They don't throw inside as much, they're not trying to hit you. If you get on base, one run might make the difference. Well, I'll get right on top of the dish then. I did well in the playoffs and that was a lot of fun.

"The World Series was so fun. It was a great experience playing against the Braves. They had a really, really good team. That year, we didn't have the most talent, but we had the best team. I learned that you need to play together. I know that today there's a lot of analytics in moving guys around but defenses played as a group. It's not played individually. Guys looking at cards like this. I gotta know where he is at. I gotta know where his first step is gonna be. I gotta know where the left fielder's first step is gonna be. Communication out there looking at a card doesn't [mean] communication to me. The teamwork was really good, the communication with the staff was good. Tom Kelly could really anticipate. He knew how to match up guys at the end of the games. Everybody had confidence in each other and it was really good. I think everybody played to their potential and that's why we won. We played as a group, which was really great. There were good people on the team too that helped."

FIRST EXPERIENCE PLAYING PRO BALL IN JAPAN:

In 1994, Pagliarulo played for the Seibu Lions of the Japanese Pacific League.

"I played good in Baltimore [1993 season] when I was traded there from Minnesota and they were gonna sign me back. [GM] Roland Hemond call me on the phone and said, 'We're gonna sign you back, we'll give you a two-year deal.' I said, 'Great, I'll sign it.' 'You don't even know how much it's for,' [said Hemond]. That stalled because [Orioles owner Peter] Angelos took over the team, they changed ownership. So, this Japanese team came in and I went there because I was gonna put my kids through college, so I ended up doing that deal. It was a bunch of other major leaguers over [there]. Danny Gladden, Rob Deer, and some other guys that played over there, so it was a good experience. It was unique because you were in a different world completely. There are two types of guys that go to play in Japan. One guy goes over there and says, 'Oh, it's not like [the] major leagues for this and that. The other guy kind of accepts where they're at.

"I was telling someone, the owner of our team was the richest guy in the world before Bill Gates. [Yoshiaki] Tsutsumi, they called him God and he had all these hotels. He owned trains and all this other stuff. We had spring [training], February first, we were in Maui for a month working out. Every morning, they'd go down and they'd have this big circle. 60, 70 players, coaches in sweatsuits. Every day, three different guys would come out and they would stand there and they would yell. It's like the formal way of saying, I proclaimed this, I'm gonna be this for the year. I'm gonna do this and be healthy and be a productive player and all this other stuff. They did it every day, for like a week. So I asked the interpreter, 'Look, do I need to do that.' He goes, 'What?' I said, 'I need to do that. Tell me what they're saying and then you write it down in Japanese. I'll remember it and I'll go out and I'll do it, but don't tell anybody yet.' He goes, 'Well, I have to tell the manager.' So, two weeks go by, I got it memorized. So, he said, 'All right, I'll tell the manager.' So, we went out there and it was for me, this was my way of saying, 'I'm here with you guys. This is your world, your league, I'll do whatever you want.' So, I went out there, I wish it was a camera. My God, would've been great to film it. I stopped yelling and I said what I said pretty good. Nobody claps or anything when you do it. Then we went off and we're going to have breakfast and all of a sudden, the interpreter says, 'Hey, [the] boys wanna know what you're doing tonight. You wanna go have a beer or something like that?' So they took me out afterwards. It was kinda like I was accepted in that regard. You gotta have an open mind when you're playing on the other side of the world.

"There's good baseball there, there's good players there and they're serious about it. They put their whole heart and soul in it, just like we do. I said, well, why don't I do the same thing. Everything that that culture has to offer and be open minded about it. Didn't try to show anybody up or anything like that, but that's how I got along. I got hurt halfway through and I would've went back 'cause I liked the game and I liked how they played but it's not the big leagues, but it was good baseball. A lot of players could've played here. For me, it was a good experience. Ended up being in the Japan series playing against Danny Gladden and Henry Cotto. They were with the [Tokyo] Giants. They end up winning that. I played against [Hideki] Matsui over there. He was a rookie I think and Ichiro [Suzuki]. I told Ichiro, 'Hey, you remember '94, your first year?' He goes, 'I remember you, Seibu Lions.' He was a really good player over there, then I was coaching him in Miami."

FIRST REACTION TO BEING ELECTED TO THE NEW YORK STATE BASEBALL HALL OF FAME IN 2021:

"I was very humbled and grateful. I mean, I'm just doing what I love to do and I can do it every day. To be honored for that is a great thrill. There's so many people I think that deserve to be honored. Ballplayers back then, they fought in a war. I mean, Yogi fought in war and he came back and played baseball. That's a hero. I just played. You find out later that I was in a position where I can help some people with some charity organizations and raise some money for some people in need and make some other people happy. You make other people happy and that's a great thrill. It was pretty gratifying; I was certainly humbled that I didn't expect it but it was a great thrill. I'm very proud that I could help so many people. At the end of the day, what you did for a short period of time and you can help some people, make some people laugh and have a good time and make 'em cheer, that's even better. That's what makes me feel good."

Mike Pagliarulo by Jared Kelly

19
FRITZ PETERSON

Left-handed pitcher Fritz Peterson pitched in parts of nine seasons with the Yankees. Peterson's tenure coincided with a down period of Yankees history where they weren't winning. He had 18 shutouts for the Yankees and was a 20-game winner in 1970. Peterson is known for swapping wives with teammate Mike Kekich in March 1973. Peterson, who was an amateur hockey player, was a color analyst (alongside John Sterling) for the radio broadcasts of the New York Raiders of the World Hockey Association during the 1972–73 season.

FIRST CONTRACT WITH THE YANKEES:

Peterson signed with the Yankees as an amateur free agent in 1963.

"I don't know how heavily other teams scouted me, but I did have an opportunity to sign with the Kansas City Athletics as they were [known] at the time. They became the Oakland A's later, but they actually flew me down to Kansas City and I had a decent workout down there. They really wanted me, but the Yankee scouts did such a great job that they convinced me that if I would ever play with the Yankees, being a left-handed pitcher, that I would always be independent and get a World Series share, so I bought their line and never got there [Kansas City]. I would rather have been with the Yankees on a losing team than anywhere else on a winning team. Not that I don't like to win, I really love to win. The Yankees are baseball to me."

FIRST PROFESSIONAL MANAGER: Gary Blaylock

Peterson made his pro debut for the 1963 Harlan (Kentucky) Yankees of the rookie-level Appalachian League.

"I flew on one of my first airplane flights, other than the one to Kansas City, and we went to Bluefield, West Virginia, and it was a puddle jumper. One of those flights that feels like a knuckleball. I got to the airport and took a cab over, like they told me to the hotel and I called my manager, which was Gary Blaylock. I said, 'Mr. Blaylock, I'm here. He said, 'What's your name?' I said, 'Fritz Peterson,' and he said, 'What position do you play?' I said, 'Well, I'm a pitcher,' and at the time I came off a really, really good college year [at Northern Illinois] where I was all-everything. Now I'm back to nothing in the rookie league and I'm nothing again. It wasn't a great feeling, but I found that there were some tremendous ballplayers from around the country that were number ones, wherever they came from. So it was really different and I was like, starting over again, but I'll never forget it.

"I remember [Browning-Leonard Park] was right next to the hospital, which was the only safe place to eat in the whole town, but we stayed in the [local] hotel, which my parents came down to visit me and they paid more money so I could move out of it, but it was a great experience. It was a coal mining town. The coach, Blaylock said, 'You guys don't go out alone in town 'cause they had a lot of coal miners there who didn't like their daughters dating baseball players.' Now I know why."

FIRST TIME IN THE YANKEES CLUBHOUSE:

"To show you what kind of guy somebody like [Mickey] Mantle was, he would actually come up to us in spring training. When the time was right, he'd come over and shake our hand and say, 'Hi Fritz, I'm Mickey Mantle.' Like we didn't know, right? He would break the ice for us and the other guys were the same way. They were real pros because they were used to winning so much. They almost took winning for granted, but at that time, it became a tough thing to do. It was awesome being out there in that field. I really couldn't believe I was out there."

FIRST GAME: April 15, 1966 vs. Baltimore Orioles at Memorial Stadium

Peterson pitched a complete game and defeated the Orioles, 3–2 in his major league debut. The left-hander gave up two runs with three strikeouts and did not walk a batter against a team that had three Hall of Famers in their lineup (Luis Aparicio, Frank Robinson, and Brooks Robinson).

"I remember everything about that game including the fact when I walked out there, I had 44,000 enemies against me. It was the fourth game and it was the [home opener] for the Orioles and we had lost three games in a row. It was awesome going out there, I mean it was different. I never looked into the stands 'cause I kinda learned that even in the minors. The only time I looked in the stands was when I was coming out of the game at the end. One way or the other if the manager took me out or if I finished the game. I remember my first hitter ever faced in my life was Luis Aparicio, who was an idol of mine. He got a hit and he scored, but it didn't bother me. We went all the way in. In fact, I got a first hit the first time up against the guy [Orioles pitcher Wally Bunker]. We were in the ninth inning. We were leading 3–1 and I had the three big boys, Brooks and Frank and Boog Powell to face in the last inning. I remember, I got Brooks out. Frank hit a home run to left center, which I did not mind at all because I didn't wanna walk him, so it was 3–2. Then I got Boog for the last out, a ground ball to first and we won. The part I really remember is I thought I'd be carried off the field like some movie but nobody even cared. They're so used to winning from the old days that it was no big deal for them, but it was for me. I could not sleep. I called everybody I knew in the world that night. It was just amazing. First of all, because the first pitch I threw put me in the record books, which I never even dreamed of as a kid. Then, to get through the whole game and win. It was amazing."

FIRST THOUGHTS OF THE WAY PITCHERS ARE HANDLED IN TODAY'S GAME:

"I think it's gonna extend people's careers because it's obviously gonna save the wear and tear [on] their arms, but I think each ballgame is different. I think the pitch count has really actually hurt teams in winning efforts, because you get a pitcher going and he's on a roll and it's the seventh inning and he's got 102 pitches or whatever their account thing is you're pulling 'em for a set-up man for your closer. You don't know how that set-up man's gonna do 'cause nobody's perfect. Instead of letting this kid go into the inning and get an out, get two outs, get three outs, maybe three pitches. Now he's into the ninth inning so a modern-day manager that would pull pitchers on pitch counts. I would let them go into innings and get an out because they may never not get an out, you know what I mean? They may get three outs in the ninth inning. You don't even need your closer, so I'm different. I'm a little old-fashioned in that stuff."

FIRST THOUGHTS OF SEEING WHITEY FORD AND MICKEY MANTLE AT THE END OF THEIR CAREERS:

Peterson was Ford's teammate in 1966 and 1967, and Mantle's teammate from 1966 to 1968.

"It was sad. I appreciated being able to get to know them a little bit and watching them. They weren't even really as good as the regular players at that time. Especially with Mickey. I never knew Whitey's arm was hurting so bad. Mickey did tell me one time that his knees were like two toothaches that never went away. You could just see him when he took swings, just kind of cave in and that hurt. I said in my book that I was actually happy when he said he was gonna retire after '68. I felt good for him because I knew how much pain he was in. It was just sad to see them not be the people I was in the early sixties on TV on Saturdays."

FIRST IMPRESSIONS OF MEL STOTTLEMYRE, BOBBY MURCER, AND THURMAN MUNSON:

"Mel was there before me, right? Mel was already good. Murcer was my shortstop in Greensboro, North Carolina (in 1965) and he was decent. He was a good country boy, just a nice kid. Thurman I didn't know until 1969 when he came up but he was the new breed already. He was cocky and he could back it up, but he always wanted to be included with us, the older guys. I had a group of guys we called "the nursery" that would go out and do things on off days, on the road trips, and stuff and Thurman wanted to be part of that and we let 'em in so it was really fun. Murcer, the same thing. Just a good team ballplayer. Those were old-fashioned Yankees. Munson and Murcer. They would knock a second baseman into left field to break up a double play. They'd run over a catcher. A lot of guys didn't do that, but those two did and it was really fun playing with those guys and most of the other guys as well."

FIRST THOUGHTS ABOUT BEING PART OF A YANKEES ERA WHEN THEY WERE NOT WINNERS:

"Mel and I were both a little bit disgusted that we could see that we weren't getting the kind of players that Baltimore, at the time, had and we weren't going to. It was a little bit frustrating and the work we had to do out there to win a ballgame was tough. I felt sorry for Mel. I think if Mel would've been on the earlier Yankees or the Yankees of now, I think he would've won 30 games a couple of times. I think he would've been a Hall of Famer but he was stuck in the middle and he was a nice guy. Still glad to be a Yankee, no matter what. It was still bad and it was still fun and I was making decent money, although my highest year there was, I made $75,000 and I was the second-highest paid player. Mel was the first. Again, that was good money in those days. I mean, looking at it today, I think we'd be getting a little bit more per inning."

FIRST TIME WIFE SWAP:

In March 1973, Peterson and Mike Kekich announced an arrangement to swap their wives. Peterson's wife, Marilyn, became Mrs. Kekich. The former Suzanne Kekich became Peterson's wife.

"It was more a husband swap, rather than a wife swap because the wives got the kids, which we felt was the right thing to do at the time, and they kept the animals. We were the ones that traded houses. The way it started was, Mike and I were best of friends at the time and we did everything together on the road, in spring training and during homestands we would get together, the families would. Our kids were both the same age as we had five- and two-year-old kids, each one of us. So, everything was kind of nice to just get together and just sing and have barbecues out. One night at a party at Maury Allen's, the writer. We were very close. We were at the party and we were having fun with a lot of other people. Ron Swoboda was there. At the end of the party, we were walking out to our car and I'm the one who said it. I said to my wife at the time, Marilyn, I said, 'Hey, why don't you ride with Mike back to Fort Lee? We're gonna go to a diner there and just have a cup of coffee and then go home.' I said, I'll take Susan, which was Mike's wife at the time and we'll meet you there. I really couldn't believe my ex-wife Marilyn would go for that 'cause she was from the conservative Midwest area, and yet she did. So, we went back there to Fort Lee, we had a good time. They stayed in the car and talked. I ate as usual at the diner and that was really fun. The next day, we were at the ballpark, Mike and I and we said, hey, that was really neat. Want to do that again tomorrow night, like Friday night and he said, yes. So, we talked to the wives and they wanted to do that too. We met at a steakhouse in Fort Lee. We met there and Mike and Marilyn went off in the car and Susan and I were there eating and having a few drinks. Then, we drove back and met them somewhere close to where we lived. We all went back to our houses with our wives at the time. We did it again the next weekend and it started to be fun and all of a sudden it started to get serious. We didn't see any harm in hit since we weren't i.e. cheating because the other knew we were doing it. I guess you might [call] it a habit or just a really fun thing until it got to the point where we didn't wanna stop doing that. We realized that we thought we all wanted to be with the other one. Actually, we thought the kids would not be harmed because they knew each one of us and we were all gonna help each other. I was gonna help them out financially. As it turned out, of course it didn't work out for all of us.

"I'm sure the kids were hurt in the process, which was not our intent at all. By that time, I just wanted to be with Susan more and Mike wanted to be with Marilyn more than the other. We just went ahead with during that 1972 season. Then it was announced in March of 1973 when [George Steinbrenner] had just taken over the Yankees, which was something that I'm sure he didn't plan on. Nobody did. In fact, when I was holding out that spring for a raise and when I got to spring training, the players said, 'Uh, what's new?' I said, everything 'cause they didn't know how to handle it at the time either. Nobody knew what to say but it happened and it's something that I don't advocate but it sure was a lot of fun."

Fritz Peterson by John Pennisi

20
DENNIS RASMUSSEN

Dennis Rasmussen pitched in parts of four seasons with the Yankees. The 6'7" left-hander was initially acquired by the Yankees from the California Angels in November 1982 and pitched a year in the minors before being traded to the San Diego Padres in September 1983. The Yankees re-acquired Rasmussen before the 1984 season in a trade for third baseman Graig Nettles. He was 39–24 with a 4.28 ERA in New York. In August, 1987, the Yankees traded Rasmussen to the Cincinnati Reds for right-handed pitcher Bill Gullickson.

FIRST BASEBALL GAME HE ATTENDED AS A KID:

"It was Anaheim, California, California Angels. It was probably a bat day or cap day or something like that. Growing up as an Angel fan, living just south of the stadium. I don't remember if it was that time or another time. I got my very first autograph when the guys signed a heck of a lot more often than they do now, due to security and all that. I understand all that. Even when I was playing, you could still get face to face with the fans and sign. I know there's a lot of people out there that got my autograph for sure, 'cause I was only pitching once every five days. Les Moss, he was a coach at that time with the Angels way back in the day. That was my first autograph."

FIRST BASEBALL IDOL:

"First one was Jim Fregosi. I didn't play shortstop, I wasn't right-handed but he was just having a heck of a career there with the California Angels and he was kind of the leader of their team. He was always the one in the papers, you know, we read the papers more than anything. I used to keep stats. It started out on graph paper. I had stats and I haven't found 'em in a while 'cause my stepson would love to see those. I still have stuff I haven't gone through, but I used to keep stats on graph paper of the hitters and pitchers of the Angels. Then I started doing it with the Dodgers. So that captivated [me], I didn't play video games. I didn't do that. That's what I did. I kept every game, just boom, boom, boom. I'm sure I missed some. Reading the box scores was fascinating to me. To this day, I still enjoy reading the box scores 'cause they tell you a little bit about the game. Now they do play by play, especially when runs score and there's scoring involved. I still follow some of my guys I had [coached] that are pitching in college now the last couple of years and I follow 'em and I text 'em and ask how they're doing after I look up their stats and the box score and try to read into it, but it doesn't tell the whole story, so I give 'em a call. 'Hey, how you doing?' I let them know that I'm following so they know at least a little bit about what's going on or if they're injured."

FIRST EXPERIENCE WITH PLAYING COLLEGE BASKETBALL AT CREIGHTON:

"I always grew up playing all sports. Never football, played some flag football. My dad didn't let me play football 'cause I would have got broke. I would've got snapped in half. I was tall, skinny, and a beanpole. Six-four, 170 as a sophomore in high school so I was just awkward. Played tennis growing up, but playing all sports was just what I did. One from the other every year, except one year I had a bicycle accident. It was one year I didn't play basketball, I didn't play baseball, then played the last couple of games of my freshman year in basketball. My dream, I grew up watching, I was a huge [UCLA basketball coach] John Wooden fan, UCLA basketball fan. We still stay in contact with a guy that was a high school classmate that went on to write for the LA Times Orange County edition, who covered my first start in Anaheim with the Yankees. He retired from the LA *Times*. It's kind of funny. When he came int the clubhouse to interview, here's a kid I grew up with and he used to be the one that would announce us at recess in elementary school. As, you know, Lew Alcindor, Sidney Wicks, Curtis Rowe, Gail Goodrich, all these guys. My dream was to play. I couldn't play at UCLA. That's a whole 'nother level basketball at the time. My goal was to play D-1 basketball and I was fortunate enough to do that. Played against a lot of great players, including Larry Bird for a couple of years."

FIRST DRAFT EXPERIENCE:

In June 1977, Rasmussen was chosen by the Pittsburgh Pirates in the 18th round of the MLB Amateur Draft but he did not sign. In June 1980, the Angels chose Rasmussen with the 17th overall pick of the 1980 MLB Amateur Draft.

"I think [the Angels] may have called my parents and they're the ones that told me. I don't think it was a telegram when you got that which was kind of funny. I'm sure it was my parents [who told him he got drafted] and I came home and then kind of had to do a 180. Right around the same time, I was elected to play in a USA-Japan series, collegiate. It was a college All-Star team that played against Japan here in the states. We toured, we played in Omaha, which was kind of cool. We had a kid, Tim Burke [a future major league pitcher] that was at Nebraska. He and I were both representing Creighton and Nebraska so that was a lot of fun. We worked out in LA. Worked out there and played like a week's worth of games. I signed and reported July 4th.

"When I reported, the first-round pick in the January phase when they had two phases of the draft was Bill Mooneyham [who played one season with the Oakland A's] and we reported the same day or within a day of each other. We were waiting or told to wait for the great left-hander Warren Spahn, who was the pitching coordinator. He was on his way from the golf course at Pebble Beach, 'cause we were just over the mountain from there in Salinas. We had to wait to throw for him on the side our first time on the sidelines. The next greatest story is I had no breaking ball or what I thought was a breaking ball and was wild as heck. Honestly, didn't know why I got drafted, but I was a good enough athlete. I asked Mooneyham, he had a nasty breaking ball. [It had] 11 to 5 break, I mean it was unbelievable. I asked him how he held it and he's a right-hander. I'm on the left side of the mound, he's on the right side of the mound. I saw his stuff and man, he's throwing strikes. I'm not even throwing strikes and how do you hold that breaking ball. He showed me, I worked on it and that's how I held it all my career. The crazy thing is I never deviated from that and ended up being one of my best pitches and kept me in the big leagues a few extra years 'cause I could still throw it for strikes as my velocity went down."

FIRST PROFESSIONAL MANAGER: Tom Zimmer

Rasmussen made his pro debut with Salinas of the California League (A-ball).

"His dad was Don Zimmer. It was kind of cool to have baseball blood that was managing you. We crossed paths over the years during my career and then after my career which was also cool. Salinas was a great start. I'm not sure if we even had a pitching coach that first year. I think we had a hitting coach in Tom Zimmer."

FIRST TIME HE WAS TRADED:

In November, 1982, the Yankees acquired Rasmussen from the Angels as the player to be named later in the trade from August that sent Tommy John to California. Rasmussen played for the Yankees Triple-A affiliate at Columbus of the International League in 1983 but was traded to the San Diego Padres in September. Rasmussen went right to the big club to make his major league debut.

"I went to winter ball in Caracas, Venezuela, and was playing for Caracas Leones. It was Thanksgiving Day and all the Americans, all the gringos were having Thanksgiving dinner with our wives at the Hilton where we stayed in Caracas. It was an off day, we were having our Thanksgiving dinner together as a group and somebody went downstairs to the lobby and picked up the American newspaper that came out about four o'clock in the afternoon every day. So they brought up a bunch of copies and we opened up the sports section and it was kind of written like the *Post* or *Newsday* or whatever. It says, 'Leones Rasmussen' in the headlines. 'Leones Rasmussen traded to Yankees.' That's how I found out. Three days later, the Yankees called and said 'We want you to come home, rest during the winter, come to spring training. I was like, 'Thank you.' I was ready to go and I really hadn't pitched that much there, just a month and a half. I probably got there in mid-October. So that's how I found out. Then went to spring training with the Yankees in Fort Lauderdale in '83.

"We played in the Governor's Cup [awarded to the winner of the International League playoffs], I think we played Tidewater, the Mets' [Triple-A affiliate], Yankees, Mets. We battle each other. [Dwight] Gooden, [Ron] Darling, [Darryl] Strawberry. It was [Don] Mattingly, [Mike] Pagliarulo, [Bobby] Meacham. Both the Yankees and Mets had great Triple-A teams. We finished and won the playoffs. Johnny Oates, manager, brought Edwin Rodriguez and I in the manager's office after we celebrated not too soon after that. He said, 'Hey, want to congratulate you, you're going to the big leagues.' Don't even remember. It was obviously a blur. We look at each other, 'Oh man. Awesome.' So we get on a flight the next day. We fly from Columbus, Ohio to Denver and make a connection in Denver to San Diego and the connection and layover in Denver. We see this tiny little guy that we all recognize coming up through the minor leagues by the name of Ted Giannoulas, who was the 'San Diego Chicken.' All the minor league guys knew him because he asked us to do skits with him. He was in the clubhouse getting dressed in the minor leagues, throughout the minor leagues. He goes, 'Hey, how are you doing?' I said, 'We just got called up.'

'Congratulations, is somebody picking you up at the airport in San Diego?' He was on his way to the same flight. We said, 'No.' He goes, 'All right, you guys come with me. I've got a car waiting for us.' Well, we pull up, we get our bags and we walk outside and it's a big, stretch limousine, never been in a limousine. We jumped in the back, he dropped us off at our hotel and that was our first ride to the hotel in San Diego, with the San Diego Chicken."

FIRST MAJOR LEAGUE MANAGER: Dick Williams

"He was kind of iconic. He was older at that time, but successful and knew that he had won World Series with the A's. He just gave me an opportunity to pitch and said, 'Go out there and show us what you can do.' Basically, that's all they said. So, I was in the bullpen early on for my first appearance. I got a spot start against the Braves, late in September. It was Tony Gwynn's rookie year, Kevin McReynolds [also]. We had a lot of good young players. Eventually, I was asked to go play winter ball with the Padres and Harry Dunlop, who was a coach and he took us down there, kept an eye on us, so we didn't get abused, throwing too many pitches. We went down there, there was like six of us. Greg Booker, Tony Gwynn, McReynolds, we were all down there honing our skills in winter ball in San Juan, Puerto Rico, for the Senadores. Love Puerto Rico and have a lot of friends and teammates that live there and that I've played with, coached with and stay in touch over the years. That's kind of how it happened.

On March 30, 1984, Rasmussen was traded back to the Yankees for All-Star third baseman Graig Nettles.

"I go to spring training in '84 with the Padres and I'm the very last cut. Wasn't gonna make the team, I was the sixth starter on a five-man staff. The very last day, I got traded back to the Yankees for Graig Nettles. Went to Columbus for a month. Yankees were struggling and I got called up with [Mike Pagliarulo] Pags and Meacham and we were all called up about the same time the Yankees were struggling. Yogi's [Berra] the manager, went to Seattle and got my first start in the middle of May 1984. The timing was great because the Yankees were struggling and Mr. [George] Steinbrenner wanted to make a point. I think a lot of high-priced guys weren't producing. Here he brought up a bunch of guys, I mean, it was amazing. A lot of guys were just hoping to get traded and get out of there because you were really playing for the other teams, but we were fortunate, the guys that got called up. Mike P had a long career, Bobby Meacham had a long career. It was great. Obviously, Mattingly did what he did. He got called up the year before."

FIRST IMPRESSION OF GEORGE STEINBRENNER:

"I did my first spring training with Mr. Steinbrenner and then years later living in Tampa and going to the games and him inviting me up to his box. He did a lot of things that people didn't know about and with a huge heart in that. He got a lot of controversial comments about some the things he did and all that. Bottom line, he just wanted to win, but he welcomes me to the team in spring training in '83 when I got there. Kind of tapped me on the shoulder and put his hand out and shook my hand and welcome to the Yankees. So that was pretty iconic.

"I met Yogi first, but Yogi was just like a father figure and a big teddy bear. Even when I got called up he goes, 'Welcome to the club. Go out and show us what you can do.' Very supportive. My pitching coach, Mark Connor. joined the next year and the big leagues. There was a comfort level that you had when you were there and you weren't making any money, there was no pressure on us. The only pressure is what you put on yourself playing in New York. I think it prepared me, not only playing Division I basketball and playing in front of, you know, ten, twelve thousand people at the time at Creighton in different venues against Notre Dame, DePaul, Marquette that had all these guys that went on to play in the NBA. Indiana State with Larry Bird. It wasn't fifty-five thousand people in Yankee Stadium, but I think that helped prepare me, along with Ron Guidry, Phil Niekro, Joe Niekro when he got there. [Dave] Righetti was still a younger player at the time, but had been there and thrown a no-hitter before I got there so he had started his career and had success. There was a lot of guys [stuck together quite a bit and had a lot of great mentors. Played with Tommy John there which was kind of cool having been traded for him. The best advice that they could give you was, give the media equal time. It's easy to talk about a good start. It's tough to talk about a bad start, but if you give 'em equal time, they have a job to do, respect that and they'll respect you. That was a hundred percent my experience throughout my whole career. To this day, the Bob Klapisches, Moss Kleins, In San Diego, Bill Plaschke, Bob Nightengale, Scott Miller, Kevin Kernan. All the guys I still stay in touch with and see that I seek out in spring training to say hello or if I go to a big league game and they're covering that certain team, I'll go out there and specifically say hello."

FIRST TIME WALKING INTO YANKEE STADIUM ON GAME DAY:

"Well, parking in the gated lot, coming through, having all the people out there waiting for you. It's not like anywhere else in the major leagues. It wasn't for many, many years. I don't know if it's different now, but it was crazy. They knew who you were, Yankee fans. They know their baseball, they know their sports in general. Even 10, 15 years later, I would be in town for an event and we were staying away from wherever this event was, but people would see you walking down. I'm six-seven, I look like I'm athletic. Some was, 'Hey Ras, how you doing? Loved watching you pitch,' which is pretty cool That didn't happen in other places that I played in, other cities. That's why it's arguably the greatest sports town there is. It was a privilege to play there. When I walked through the gate coming through the old stadium. I had to be careful hitting my head 'cause there was areas you had to walk through the tunnel. You walked down stairs immediately and find your way to the clubhouse. There's really no directions or signs. I think I probably followed somebody or asked somebody. Probably got lost the first time and had to ask direction at the elevator or something, that press elevator. I remember you just keep going. Keep following the tunnel. It was dark and low ceilings and wires and metal things. Right above my head. I felt like I was going to knock myself out on the way to the clubhouse.

Then, I get to the clubhouse door and the gentleman, rest in peace. Charlie Zabransky was the doorman at Yankee Stadium, going to the clubhouse for a hundred years. I mean, forever. I would seek him out when I played there afterward as a visiting player with the Royals. For four straight years, I mean he was the guy. His daughter reached out to me right after he passed away [in 2018] 'cause I stayed in touch with him for a while and then lost touch with him. His daughter reached out because he collected autographs and pictures of guys that befriended him. I was one of those guys and she said, I'd like to send you a picture. Charlie passed away. He lived till his nineties and always spoke highly of you. I've heard many stories. We exchanged Christmas cards every year now and ever since that time she sent me a picture of Charlie and I from the Yankee clubhouse. That's just priceless to me. Those are the memories that I had. He was really the first person I saw. Then I go in and meet the old, crochety Nick Priore, clubhouse guy and Pete Sheehy, who never said a word, but everybody listened as soon as he spoke, which was funny. Got all your uniform and all that and showed where your locker was. It definitely was a whirlwind, but you're young and dumb and you didn't know what happened. I didn't get called up with anybody. I think everybody kind of came up at different times, but all within a few days of each other. Brian Dayett, Bobby Meacham, Pags, all of us from that first month in Columbus."

FIRST TIME PUTTING ON THE YANKEES UNIFORM:

"I had got called up, like many times and many other players with the Yankees. Got called up just in case they decided to make a roster move and put somebody on the disabled list at the time. Now, it's the injured list. So I was there just hanging out during BP, got dressed, showered 'cause I wasn't activated for a couple of days. Then I went back to Columbus and then it was a week later, but the first time I got called up I didn't get activated so I went back down. I guess that prepared you for the big stage, although it would've been great to be able to [get in a game]. They had the uniform ready and all that and I couldn't put it on. My first Yankee uniform in spring training, I'll never forget it was number 63 because I still have the first glove that I used. All I had on it was 63, just around the thumb, number 63 that reminded me. I used that as my gamer for probably half my career because I only used it when I started. I didn't blow through it, I had to restring it later on, years later, but I still have it. Very proud of it, brings back a lot of great memories."

FIRST TIME HEARING LEGENDARY YANKEE STADIUM PA ANNOUNCER BOB SHEPPARD:

"I remember hearing him announcing the first game I saw there in uniform in the dugout. Obviously, when I got called up early and then got sent back down, I was at the games but it wasn't in uniform. I do remember he announced the lineup and it was just magical. Then, to hear 'New York, New York,' Frank Sinatra's "New York, New York.' I stop in my place when I hear that song anywhere. If it hear it on the radio, I'm turning it up and it just all floods back and all the great memories of playing at the old Yankee Stadium."

FIRST FULL SEASON UNDER LOU PINIELLA AS MANAGER:

In 1986, Piniella was named Yankees manager. Rasmussen became the Yankees' ace as he set career bests with 18 wins and a career high 131 strikeouts.

"It started in spring training because I struggled. I pitched okay my rookie year in '84. Think I was 9–6. I was 3–5 my second year and struggled and hadn't figured it out yet. Went to spring training, probably wasn't one of the five starters and was pitching on the same day as Tommy John. I was scheduled, my second to last start, I pitched in Pompano Beach in spring training. Gave up a run and then gave up a three-run homer to Curtis Wilkerson, the second baseman for the Rangers and Mr. Steinbrenner was in the stands. It was rickety old Pompano Stadium and the wives were sitting right there. It wasn't a lot of seats right behind the screen and he stood up and [said], 'I've seen enough,' 'cause I heard about it later. 'I've seen enough, you're on your way to Columbus,' about me after that happened. The reason I found out is [from the] 25, 30 writers. After that, I got taken out and the inning was over and I walked down to the clubhouse, down the left field corner, and they brought me into interview me to tell me what Mr. Steinbrenner had said. All I could say is, 'Wow, I just hope you saw the conditions. I mean, it was howling wind, blowing out to left, it was a pop up to left. It happened with two outs. If the wind wasn't blowing, it might have been a fly ball to straightaway left or whatever. Bottom line is I gave up runs and didn't do my job and I hope I get another opportunity.

"Five days later, I'm scheduled to start again in a minor league game. Tommy John's pitching in the major league game. Well I know that's the kiss of death. There' no good that comes outta pitching in a minor league game, trying to make a major league roster as a rookie or young pitcher. The day before, Tommy John comes up sore, tweaks his back and [pitching coach] Sammy Ellis calls me at 10:30 at night and said, 'Ras, you're pitching tomorrow in the big league game against the Royals. You gotta be on the bus, the early bus to Haines City to pitch against the Royals.' I said, perfect, this is my opportunity. Through seven innings, gave up one run. Lou named me the fifth starter and I went on and won 18 games and he loves to tell that story. Also who loved to tell that story anytime I saw him was Gene Michael, 'Stick.' Any time I went to Tampa and Yankee spring training or whatever and we were around people, he goes, 'One of my greatest memories about Ras, I was pulling for him to make the club and then he goes out, makes the team and Lou names him fifth starter and goes on and has a big year for us even though we didn't win in New York.' I ended up credit for 18 wins but [Dave] Righetti had a phenomenal year. At the time, a record 46 saves."

FIRST TIME HE TOSSED A COMPLETE GAME ONE-

HITTER: September 29, 1992 as a member of the Kansas City Royals vs. California Angels at Anaheim Stadium

"I was never really close [to a no-hitter]. I wasn't close as two outs in the eighth inning or taking one to into the ninth inning. The longest I did as a Yankee was six and two thirds. I was at County Stadium in Milwaukee and I gave up a swinging bunt and I can't remember who that was [referring to a game from June 1987, Milwaukee's Jim Paciorek got the first hit in the seventh inning]. It was a swinging bunt that rolled down the third base line and Pags let it go, hoping it went foul. It hit the bag. The game in '92, which was an incredible and memorable year in general, 'cause I actually pitched pretty well the year before. Didn't get a contract with the Padres, had to scramble.

"Johnny Oates [who was now with the Orioles] signed me. He was my manager at Columbus. He signed me in '92. Come to camp, didn't make the team with the Orioles, got an out in my contract. June first, got my release, wasn't pitching well. On my way back, drove [Highway] 80 back to Chicago. Got there in the morning. The Cubs were playing the Padres in a getaway day at Wrigley Field. I went to the hotel, I know they always eat breakfast before the game at 7 a.m. I saw the Padre manager, Greg Riddick, told him, 'Hey, I can still pitch. I just didn't get the opportunity.' He says, 'We're good. We got a lot of pitchers, sorry.' I saw Syd Thrift , the Cubs' GM, in the corner talking to an agent. Went over, interrupted his breakfast, he said yes. Apparently, they were getting ready to put Frank Castillo on the disabled list and he wanted me to meet him at the ballpark. I went to the ballpark with my bag where everyone enters. All the home players, [Ryne] Sandberg, [Andre] Dawson. Everybody's coming through, [Greg] Maddux, all the guys coming through and I've got my bag and sitting in the lobby and they're going, 'What the hell is Ras doing here?' They bring me downstairs, I throw for Billy Connors. They call my agent, they wanna sign me. They send me to Des Moines. Two starts after that second start, they called me up. I was there for six weeks, got released. Kept driving to Omaha where I was living, thought I was done, called the Royals, got a job with Omaha, pitched in Omaha the day the season was over in September, our last game. I went home and the next day, Jeff Cox, our manager, calls me and said, 'Hey, the Royals need a starting pitcher and I recommended you. You need to be in Kansas City for tonight's game.' I said, 'Perfect.' So I got called up from my offseason of one day and drove the three hours to Kansas City.

"Ended up pitching, ended up being 4–1. That last start of the season was against Anaheim, against Bert Blyleven, which I originally thought was his last career start, but it was second to last. Three up, three down the first three innings. Lead off the fourth, Damion Easley got a base hit to left. Couple of pitches later I picked him off and retired everybody else, so I retired all 27. I know it's been done, 10 plus times, maybe more by now. The thing I'm most proud of, it was the day of our team party. Game was in an hour and 44 minutes and all the guys, that's what they remember. They don't remember that it was a one-hitter and all that. Lynn Jones, our first base coach who used to write out the lineup card, gave it to me the next day. Said, 'Hey, you might wanna keep this and that.' I said, 'Oh no.' Maybe really didn't think much of it, the magnitude [of what] I did. Wasn't something that happens every day so I got it signed and I've got it up on my wall in the den, which is cool with a picture and it's all autographed. George Brett signed it. Didn't play in my game, his back was sore. He played the next day and went 4-for-4 [and] got his 3000th hit."

FIRST TIME HE SAW HIMSELF ON A BASEBALL CARD:

"That's pretty cool. It still is pretty cool. I literally could go out and check my mail today and there's probably one or two envelopes with cards in it with self-addressed stamped envelopes and a cool letter saying something, we met or whatever. I save all of those. My stepson, who's 21, graduating from Central Michigan, [a] hockey player. I call him my agent. I save those for him. He opens them up, reads a letter and if they bring up a story or they bring up something in the letter, he asks me to expand on it and tell him about that and there's probably a story that comes from that.

He collects cards and he likes going through the cards of eras that guys I played with or against. We go through anywhere from '83 to '95 or really from '75 to '05 'cause I crossed over with so many guys when he goes through all those cards. We go through the letter. He goes, I think we should send a picture to this one. Let's sign this one here. You gotta read this letter and answer some of the questions that they ask you. So I would say, eight, ten, twelve pieces of mail a week still and I sign everything. It might not be right away, but I sign everything 'cause I wait for him now that he's in college and he's two and half hours away so now I gotta wait and that's what we do on his spring break.

"Renee, his mom, my wife, gets to hear some of these stories of either the autograph stuff or when we go through baseball cards, he gets to hear some of these different stories and then he's gotten to meet some of the guys that I played with or against if we go to the ballparks. That's also fun, reaching out to those guys. I remember one of my favorite ones. We went to Cleveland and I played with Terry Francona. I think he left us tickets. I called him, whatever. I've got the commissioner's office gold card that gets two tickets to every game. Any game other than playoffs. So I use that if I need to, but a lot of times I'll call so I can sit in the family section with guys and I'll know the coaches' wives or whatever. We get there and Michael Brantley's playing for the Indians at the time, and I saw Mickey [Brantley] sitting in the stands I recognized him, his dad who played in the big leagues with Seattle. Had a shorter career but immediately, I said, I'm pretty sure I faced him. Baseball Reference [Baseball-Reference.com] sees that I gave up of the two home runs that he hit in his career. It was a smaller number [32] but he got two off me. We go up and I introduce Hayden [his stepson] to him. [Hayden] goes, tell me about what you were looking for when my dad was pitching to you. Just so you know, I know you hit two home runs off him. Mickey smiled from ear to ear hearing a story on that."

).

Dennis Rasmussen by James Kimball

21
BOBBY RICHARDSON

Bobby Richardson was one of the best second baseman in Yankees history. He played his entire 12-year career with the Yankees and was an eight-time All-Star, five-time Gold Glove winner and three-time World Series champion. Richardson was named the 1960 World Series Most Valuable Player, the only time in baseball history that the Series MVP came from the losing team. The Sumter, South Carolina, native is one of four players to have 11 or more hits in two different World Series (1960, 1964).

FIRST BASEBALL IDOL:

"I think, really Stan Musial. My dad took me over to the Cincinnati farm club and Cincinnati played the Cardinals in an exhibition game when I was 12 years old. I remember after the game, the name I knew was Stan Musial at that time and my dad saw him walking towards the bus. They'd already dressed. We had hung around a little while and he said, 'Why don't you ask him for an autograph?' I said, 'Oh, he wouldn't want to sign.' He said, 'Well, just ask him. If he doesn't, that's no problem.' I went over and he was very nice and gave me a very legible autograph, said a few kind words to me, and then got on the bus. I think because he had been so nice and because he was a name player, the name player-perhaps at the time, he was my first idol."

FIRST CONTACT WITH THE YANKEES:

"I'd gotten cut from the high school team and my dad said, 'Well, you know Legion [American Legion baseball] starts a little later and anybody could go out. You're 14 years old, you're certainly eligible to play and I did go out for that and I made the team. We won the state championship, the regional championship, and we were playing in Charlotte, North Carolina, against Richmond, Virginia, and the winner of that game would go on to the American Legion World Series in Omaha, Nebraska. Before that game, they took us out to see the film, Pride of the Yankees, the story of Lou Gehrig. I thought, what a great organization. I'd like to be a part of that team. We played the game that night and there was a Yankee scout there. The Yankee scout had asked coach to hit some balls [in] the hole at shortstop and he had watched me play the game. After the game, he came up to me, still 14, and said 'I can promise you that when you graduate from high school, you'll have a chance to sign with the Yankees.'

"Those next three years until I graduated, a lot of correspondence from the Yankees. I remember that I signed exactly on the day that I graduated from high school with the Yankees. At that time, there were eight teams in the American, eight in the National [League]. I had the same offer from 12 of the 16 teams. If you got over $4,000, you had to go up and spend two years on the parent roster and that'd be a waste of time for a 17 year old. I didn't think the Dodgers had courted me pretty heavily and they had given me a few things. It was a no brainer. Signed with the Yankees, three-day quick trip to New York to work out with the Yankees and then to come back and start out in Norfolk, Virginia."

FIRST PROFESSIONAL MANAGER: Mickey Owen

"I did take that bus from Sumter [South Carolina] to Norfolk, Virginia. It was a late bus, I left here in late afternoon so I didn't get there until the wee hours of the morning. The only thing I knew was the name of the hotel. I went to the hotel, I remember I checked in. They did have a reservation for me. The next morning,

I got a call from Mickey Owen, he said, "I know you probably don't know the way, I'll pick you up. We'll go out to the ballpark together.' I knew he was a former major leaguer. I was impressed with him and how much attention he gave to me as I got out there, introduced me around and so forth. They had a shortstop by the name of Dick Sanders and he was their best player, doing well, home runs, everything and he was going on a three-week military commitment. So, I was put in at shortstop to take his place. To be honest, it was a little too fast for me. I didn't do well. There was a lot of pressure. After three weeks when he came back, I wanted to quit and come back home. I just felt like I was over my head and my dad came up and got together with the general manager, J. P. Dawson, and they both said, we just think you started a little bit too high. We wanna send you to the rookie league, let you finish the season out in Olean, New York, and it was agreed that we do that. I did go and I do remember that I did very well. I hit over .400 [.412] in maybe, 30, 35 games [32], something like that. So, the next year [1954], I skipped over Norfolk and went to Binghamton, New York, a Class-A [team] and I did well in that league. I think I was second in the league in hitting [batted.310, fourth in the Eastern League] and I think, maybe MVP of the league. I'm not sure about that, but I do know we played the Yankees in exhibition games. Casey Stengel came over to me afterwards and said, 'I want you to come down. We're having an instructional school for younger players. I want you to come down before spring training next year, a week early and to go through that instructional school. I do remember [Mickey] Mantle hit a home run and I thought, 'Man, what a great ballclub,' but we did beat 'em, 5–2 or 5–3 or something like that. I enjoyed very much my time in Binghamton."

FIRST CALLUP: August 1955

"Well, Ralph Houk [Richardson's manager at Denver, the Yankees' Triple-A affiliate], first of all, was my manager and he was the one that alerted me that the Yankees had an injury. Gil McDougald had been hit by a line drive or something. I'm not sure what the injury was, but couldn't play for a couple of weeks and wanted me to come up and fill in for him. The thing I remember that Johnny Pesky was our coach in Denver, and his wife was going up on the same plane and we arranged that the two of us would sit together. So all the way from Denver to New York, I talked to her about how it was in the baseball world and in the Big Apple. Her husband had been at Boston all those years. The Pesky Pole [at Fenway Park] was named after him. He was a wonderful coach. He had taken [Tony] Kubek and I under his wing, spent a lot of time with us in the infield out there."

FIRST REACTION TO BEING IN THE YANKEES CLUBHOUSE:

"The thing I remember the most is how attentive two people were to me. One, Frank Crosetti. His locker happened to be next to the one they assigned to me. Kubek and I were both on the left side when you walk in, the left side of the door. That's where Frank Crosetti had the corner. That's where he kept all the baseballs and all and he was an infielder. I remember he looked over at me and he saw my spikes and it was the ones I wore in high school and so forth. He said to me, 'What size do you wear?' and I told him, he said, 'I've got a new pair here I'd like to give to you.' I tried on those but I didn't put 'em on. He said, 'Why aren't you putting them on?' I said, 'Well, you put 'em on, on this rug here?' and he said, 'Yeah, you do.' So I put 'em on and went out and I was to field some ground balls from Crosetti. Then I was to walk up to the batting cage and take some swings for the regulars and shower, then watch the game. They were playing the St. Louis Browns. I did field ground balls and I came up and stood around the cage, but I wasn't about to step in front of Yogi Berra [or] Hank Bauer and Mickey Mantle came over behind and said, 'Come on kid, step in here and take some swings.' I remember that so well and how he encouraged me. I remember we were sitting there in the dugout for the first time and he said, 'Hey kid, come over here and I'm gonna make like I'm showing you around Yankee Stadium. The photographers will be over here in just a minute. You'll be in all the New York papers tomorrow morning. Sure enough, click, click after a minute and the next morning, the *Times*, the *Daily News* had my picture with him showing me around Yankee Stadium for my first trip up and we became buddies after that and just wonderful teammates. He was there my whole career. He was there when I got there and, of course, I left early and was still there, but he and I got to be close, even closer after baseball Old-Timers' Games and things of that nature."

FIRST GAME: August 5, 1955 vs. Detroit Tigers at Yankee Stadium

Richardson batted second and was 1-for-3 with a run scored in his first major league game. He did not have a single chance in the field.

"I did fill in. I got a hit in the first game and things looked pretty well, didn't have a ground ball at all but then things got a little worse. They had other infielders beside me. Jerry Coleman was there, Gil McDougald was there and Andy Carey was there early at the time. After about two weeks, I was sent back down. The idea was, instead of going back to Denver, they were gonna be in the playoffs and Richmond was in last place, 42 games out of first place and I would be free to be called up at the end of the season if the Yankees wanted me. So I went to Richmond with Jim Konstanty. He and I were sent down together to Richmond and I did not get called back up."

FIRST IMPRESSION OF HIS FIRST YANKEE MANAGER, CASEY STENGEL:

"My impression was that he was great with the press, but he was smart enough to hire baseball people who would run the ballclub. Frank Crosetti actually ran the club. Jim Turner handled the pitching, and Stengel would be the one that would check with them who's pitching [that day] and they would agree on that. Frank Crosetti would make the lineup out. Any changes you wanna make, see Stengel, but Crosetti basically ran the ballclub. I did see Stengel nodding on the bench. Every now and then, he'd fall asleep during the game. He would stay up all night and was very good with the press. My feeling was he had so much talent that he could get away with, that he could drink. I saw him pinch hit Jerry Lumpe, a left-hand hitter against a left-hand pitcher, but whatever he did, it always turned out right. [Lumpe] got a base hit. He knew how to handle the press, he was very good at that. I'm not sure he ever learned my name the first four or five years. He did pinch-hit for Clete Boyer in the first inning, pinch-hit for me one time in the first inning, first inning! I remember as I walked by him, I said, 'Well, why did you start me if you go pinch hit for me?' and he followed me in the dugout and he said, 'You get your little mitt, go down the bullpen and warm up Ryne Duren. That was my punishment. He knew he'd be throwing hard and throwing it in the dirt a lot, so I didn't say too much after that. Just whatever he wanted, I did."

FIRST TIME BEING HIT BY A BASERUNNER:

"It made me realize that it might be a while, but I have a chance to play some baseball up in the years ahead. I recognize we had some established good players that have been in the service. Jerry Coleman twice called in. He was the finest making the double play I've ever seen. I hung around him and he taught me how to make the double play. I was able to make it very well after he worked with me. Those first years, I don't think there were only two times that I was even hit at second base and both times it was Frank Robinson. He had a little more speed that I had him figured for and both times, I had low throws that kept me down, catching the ball and didn't have a chance to get out of his way. He just was a good hard baserunner. Nothing personal and nothing out of the way but one time I had to have four or five stitches. I didn't [come] out of the game. I got the stitches after the game."

FIRST TIME SEEING HIMSELF ON A BASEBALL CARD:

"The thing I remember the most is because of that card and you could sign a two-year contract with a card company. I was able to buy my dad a color television set so he could see the Game of the Week, which was televised back to South Carolina at that time. No

New York games, but just the Game of the Week would come back and the Yankees were often quite on there so that's what I remember about the cards. I enclosed a couple of my cards when I sent the TV down to my father in South Carolina. It's kind of nice to see your picture that you're a part of a team and then you have your own cards. It was nice. I wasn't thinking monetarily, it's gonna be a lot of money or anything like that. I knew I was a rookie and that I still had a card. That was good enough for me. All these years later, I'm in my 88th year and during [COVID-19], I've been averaging over ten items to sign a day for the last three years. Each one says the same thing. They say, 'My grandfather was a Yankee fan, my father was a Yankee fan, and even though I haven't seen you play, I've gone through the internet and I've seen World Series highlights. I've seen other times when you were playing. Would you sign these?'"

FIRST ALL-STAR GAME: 1957

Richardson made the American League All-Star team but did not make an appearance in the game.

"Al Kaline has been the most consistent ballplayer that I've seen in my career. If I had to pick somebody that I played against, there was an outstanding player to be Kaline and then Nellie Fox. Of course, I looked up to him because I could never win a Gold Glove or anything until he retired. To get on the All-Star team, it had to be the players, but you couldn't vote for anybody on your own team. So Kubek and I would always vote for Luis Arroyo and Nellie Fox. They were considered the best. Evidently, they were voting for us because I did make the All-Star team eight times and I say eight, because one year they had two. They were picked separately, but there were two All-Star teams, so my record says eight times an All- Star."

FIRST WORLD SERIES EXPERIENCE: 1957 vs. Milwaukee Braves

Richardson appeared in two games as a pinch-runner and defensive replacement, but did not get an at-bat in the seven-game loss to Milwaukee.

"Well, there was excitement. I remember that our train, and we were still traveling by train in '57. We stayed outta Milwaukee, [at] Brown's Motor Lodge or something like that. A beautiful place that evidently Mr. Topping [Yankees owner and team president Dan] knew about. He landed his plane on the lake there and in as the owner of the Yankees. I remember that we organized a ping pong tournament out there and that just happened to be my game. Moose Skowron, believe it or not, was a really good ping-pong player and it came down to Moose playing me for the championship. I said, 'Moose, this is really not fair because you don't have a backhand.' He said, 'What do you mean I don't have a backhand?' I said, 'Let's play, I'll show you. Do you ever use your backhand?' I said, 'Well, there's no way you can beat me in that way.' He said, 'Well, let's play,' and of course we played and I keep beating him over and over. That's what I remember. Going in the game, it was a very insignificant time."

FIRST WORLD SERIES WIN: 1958 vs. Milwaukee Braves

The Yankees avenged their loss in the 1957 World Series by defeating the Braves in seven games in the 1958 Series. The Yankees became the second team in World Series history to rebound from a three-games-to-one deficit to win the Series. Richardson appeared in four games and went 0-for-5, but it was the first of three World Series that he would win with the Yankees.

"I remember I thought I'm playing on a championship ballclub with a championship team. The other times, both in '55 and '56, I wasn't on the team, but I'd be hunting back here in Sumter, South Carolina. The Sporting News was the key instrument of information and I read the Yankees had divided up their World Series shares and the veteran players had voted me a one-third share. The check, I couldn't believe. Next year, same thing. They voted one-fifth, even though I was up just a short time at the beginning of the season. So when I had that first full year, it was good. I was a part of that."

FIRST WORLD SERIES MVP:

In 1960, Richardson became the first member of a losing team to be named World Series MVP. During the seven-game series against the Pittsburgh Pirates, Richardson had 11 hits and 12 runs batted in, with an OPS of 1.054.

"I remember that every time I came up to bat, there were a lot of men on base. That first inning in the third game in New York, I hit the ball really good. It was bases loaded, I think it was one out, and Elston Howard got an infield hit, so one run scored. I think I was batting seventh or eighth and I started thinking, you know [Stengel's] pinch-hit for me before in a situation like this in the first inning. The way he did it, he'd holler out, 'Hold that gun.' That meant come on back [and be replaced by a pinch-hitter]. I listened and did not hear it. Walked up and looked down to [third-base coach] Frank Crosetti and Frank gave me the bunt. Well, I didn't think that was a good player. Bases loaded, [two runs] already in, first inning, pitcher coming up shortly. I tried to bunt and fouled it off and I thought, well maybe now I can hit and looked down again. He had the bunt on again so I tried again and fouled it off, not intentionally. Frank Crosetti yelled out, 'Come on, hit the ball to the right side, try to stay out of the double play.' I was trying to hit a ground ball to the right side. Clem Labine had come in [to replace starter Vinegar Bend Mizell] and threw a fastball up and in and I hit it and I knew I hit it good. When I rounded first base, Gino Cimoli in left field had been to the wall and was looking in his glove and I thought he had caught it. Then I saw the umpire doing his fingers around to say it was a home run and it wasn't until I got beyond second base that I realized, 'Man, I just hit a grand slam home run in the World Series.' When I got [to] my teammates at home plate, first comment as I walked into the dugout, 'Good bunt, good bunt.'"

FIRST REACTION TO LOSING WHEN BILL MAZEROSKI HIT THE WORLD SERIES- WINNING HOME RUN:

"We were in the clubhouse after the game and Mantle was actually crying. He just felt like [the Yankees] had a better ballclub, that we scored so many runs and we had reason to believe we should've won because of a double play ball that hit Kubek in the throat, because a pitcher didn't cover first base on a key play that was followed by a three run homer and so forth, but he was actually crying. When the head of *Sport* magazine came in to tell me I had won, Mantle said, at least one good thing. That was his comment, well I was shocked. We figured it would be Mazeroski to be honest, that he'd get it. We did come back the next two years to win world championships. Ed Fitzgerald, editor of *Sport* magazine, and he's really the one that made that decision. Earlier, he'd written a book about a Yankee shortstop (*Yankee Rookie*, published in 1952) and in that book, I would've been about a

sophomore in high school, maybe my freshman year in high school when the book came out. The name of the second baseman for the Yankees was Bobby Richardson."

FIRST REACTION TO WATCHING THE 1961 HOME RUN CHASE BETWEEN MICKEY MANTLE AND ROGER MARIS:

"Most of us were rooting for Mantle because we felt he'd grown up in the Yankee system and he's the one that should break Babe Ruth's home run record. So all of our allegiance was to Mantle. When it got to that point that Mantle couldn't play anymore, at 54 [home runs], they were together, our allegiance went over to Roger. Roger was not used to handling situations like Mantle was. Mantle had been through it before and actually, he was booed until Roger came over. Then, they put to boos in Roger's area and so forth like that. Roger was losing his hair and just a quiet person. One of my close friends, he'd come down, spend a couple of days with me. I remember one time my son was playing Legion ball and that he was a catcher but that night he was playing right field.

Roger was at the game, two thousand people were there. Not one person recognized [him]. In fact, one guy, a friend of mine came up in the eighth inning. He said, 'Boy, you look a lot like Roger Maris.' [Maris] said, 'Thank you,' and that was all that was said. The sport tried to find out the next day he had been my guest at the Legion game. He said, 'Why didn't you tell me he was down there with you?' I said, 'Well, I didn't think of it to be honest.'"

"The record didn't mean that much. He wanted to sit out a game. He said 'I don't care about breaking the record. I just want our team to win.' His attitude was good, but the only peace he had was when he was actually playing the game. The question was always the same, 'Are you going to break Babe Ruth's record?' At World Series time, the little sportswriter who only comes one day a year, will come up, he'll ask that question, then, the next one, the next one, the next one. So he had no peace and it was just wearing on him. Even that last game, he wanted to sit it out, but [manager] Ralph [Houk] said, 'No, you're playing.' I'm so glad he hit the home run. I've got a portrait that somebody did of him with that swing, hitting that 61st home run. I'm gonna give it to Roger's family one of these days. I've got it hanging in my den out there now. Fifty years later when they honored him at Yankee Stadium, they said to Pat Maris, pick any five players that were teammates and we'll invite them to come up and share this day with you and we [him and his wife] were one of the five that were picked."

FIRST GOLD GLOVE: 1961

"Let me tell you what the difference was. The difference was when Stengel eased out of the picture in '60 when he didn't start Whitey Ford in the first game [of the World Series]. When he left, Ralph took over. My whole career was with Ralph, he was my coach in Denver. So my whole career was with him. When he came in, he said, 'Bobby, you're my second baseman. I don't care if you hit .300, .200, you can even hit .150, you're in the lineup and you will stay in the lineup.' We won't be in and out of the lineup. I just had a new air of confidence and I was a pretty good fielder during that time, so it meant a lot."

FIRST COMMERCIAL:

"Gillette. They were paying. I thought it was a lot at that time. It was $1,500 and there were a couple of my teammates, I can't remember who it was but they were trying to tie it in with athleticism. So I was in a swimming pool, two young boys and I was teaching them supposedly how to swim. I think that's what it was. I might have been in the gym, I can't remember, but they came in and gave us one line. After we finished that part of the commercial, went to a different studio downtown to the shaving part of the commercial. I was to look in the camera and realize that I needed a shave and felt my face. Then I was to pick up a can of Gillette Foamy, shake it twice, relay it from my hand to my face, pick up the razor and come down one time and say, smooth. You can hardly tell the blade in the razor. Well, I got through the first part. I didn't need a shave. I took the can of Gillette Foamy, but I forgot to shake it and they had to stop again. Do it again. I shook it twice, but when I started to relay to my hand, I missed my hand. Well, I had to stop and do it again. Next time, I hit my hand just right but when I started to relay to my face, my thumb caught under my neck and it went up in my hair and so the night time, we started over again. The next time, I hit it just right and I picked up the razor and came down one time and said, 'Smooth, you can hardly tell there's a razor in the blazer.' I didn't do it on purpose. I was trying to think ahead and it came out that way. They laughed a little bit but it didn't go over too well with Gillette, but that was my first. I did get some opportunities. Yogi signed me to Yoo-hoo chocolate drink when he was vice president of Yoo-Hoo. He gave us T-shirts, we wore 'em under our uniform. We did have pictures on the cans of Yoo-Hoo. That was good, but the T-shirts we wore, they paid us $300."

FIRST TIME HE CAUGHT THE FINAL OUT OF A WORLD SERIES:

Richardson made a memorable play when he caught the final

out of the 1962 World Series. In the seventh game of the Series, the Yankees led 1–0, but the Giants had runners at second and third with two out and Hall of Famer Willie McCovey at the plate. The Yankees elected to pitch to McCovey, who hit blistering line drive right at Richardson to end the Series.

"First of all, the field was still wet in the outfield and I want to start off by saying Roger made a great play. I saw his foot slip as he was going over, yet he was still able to turn and throw the ball to me. [With two out and Matty Alou on first, Willie Mays hit a ball into the right-field corner. Maris cut the ball off and kept Alou from scoring as Mays took second.] Mays hit the ball to right field and that's the play we're talking about. Maris went over toward the line and he just made a wonderful play without falling and turned and made the throw to me and I was able to get rid of it quick. We knew Roger was having arm trouble, so I went out a little bit extra. Kubek and I had already agreed if it'd gone to Center field, that he would be the one that would take the relay, 'cause he had a stronger arm than I did. But this one, I went out and I made the throw and they in turn kept him on third base.

"The thing I remember the most is that [pitcher] Ralph Terry looked at me where I was playing right before that last pitch, and two things happened. The umpire at second base said, 'Hey Rich, I've got a little cousin. I'd really like to have your cap for my husband after the game's over.' I didn't answer him 'cause it was too close to the ball coming. Then, right before the pitch, Ralph had looked to see where I was playing. I'd moved over in the hole a little more and he took one step out to tell me to get back in my normal position. Then he said, 'Maybe he knows something. He's played 1,400 games there. I'll just go ahead and pitch what I want to do and he'll play where he wants to play. As it turned out, the ball was hit. Willie McCovey told me several times afterwards, we were together, he said, 'That's one of the hardest balls I ever hit.' It had overspin on hit, so it looked like a base hit, but it came down in a hurry. I actually used two hands on it to make sure I had a good grip on the ball going down. Here's the thing. So I caught the ball, flipped the cap to the umpire at second base, went in to give the ball to Ralph Terry, but he was surrounded and up in the air. I waited and kept the ball 'till I got him aside. Then I gave the ball back to him at that time. Three of us had arranged to have an earlier flight to get back to New York. Last day of the season, all my family's packed. So we're going back to South Carolina. Kubek, and I think [Johnny] Blanchard and I believe [Jim] Bouton might have been in there too. We had a police car that was taking us out, but we got caught in traffic. Even though he had a siren, we still got caught. We made our plane but here's the last part of the story.

"Forty-five years went by and they had a new stadium in San Francisco and [Giants manager] Alvin Dark is my friend. He lives in South Carolina. We're close friends. He said, we're having an old tournament game and we can't get the Yankees to come out. They want to have a banquet and they want you and Willie McCovey to speak at the banquet. Then, you two can throw the first ball out the next day. I said, 'Okay, I'll do that.' When I saw [McCovey] for the first time, his response to me was, 'I bet your hand is still hurting.' I said, 'You hit it hard.' Then we threw the ball, first ball the next day. Right before he died, he sent me an autographed picture and said, 'You were playing out of position.'"

FIRST GAME IN THE ASTRODOME:

On April 9, 1965, Richardson and the Yankees played an exhibition game against the Astros in the first game ever played at the revolutionary Houston Astrodome. Richardson batted second behind Mantle, who led off.

"I remember some of our guys that were good with fungoes trying to hit the top of the thing with the fungo. They'd come close. I do remember when you looked up, you couldn't see a fly ball. That was something that was fixed a couple of years later. I do remember Nellie Fox was on that ballclub. They wanted Mantle to be the first one living in Dallas to hit the first home run and he was batting first for that reason. The second time up, he hit a home run. So I've got a picture here at home of Mantle touching home plate and I'm shaking his hand. Mantle always, if you remember, he had his head down and he's not looked up. That's the way he made his trot around. It's a unique trot. I remember that his son, that looked so much like him and playing in old tournaments games, had that same trot."

FIRST TIME HE DECIDED TO RETIRE:

"Actually, it was '65. Tony Kubek and I roomed together in the minors and majors. He and I sat down, we started talking and said, you know, you've got children, I've got children. He said, 'We played 10 years and the Yankees have won nine out of ten years. He said, 'Let's retire together.' I said I wanted to do it because I wanted to spend more time with my family. We played 162 games on the road, we go to Florida for six weeks. We have exhibition games and we're separated from our family. I've seen some of my teammates that stay and they play 20 years, 21 years but their family life's a mess. I would like to spend time taking my boys to Little League ball games, so we agreed we were gonna do it. *Sports Illustrated* heard about it, they sent a photographer. It was all set up. Jim Ogle was the one sportswriter that was in on it and he was to write the story and everything. Then the Yankees signed Bobby Murcer and Ralph now moved up to general manager. He came to us and he said, 'I know you both wanna retire but I want one of you to play one more year and break Bobby Murcer in at shortstop.' I said, 'Well, I really wanna retire.' Tony said, 'Okay, I'll do it,' and Tony was gonna do it. One week later, he got a reserve notice. He had to go in and spend another year with the reserves and wouldn't be back until the end of the season. So Ralph called me up and said, 'Gentleman's agreement, one of you do it. Tony can't, can you play one more year?' I said, 'Sure, I'll be glad to do that. So he handed me a blank contract and said, 'Just fill it in anything you want.' He said, 'You're doing me a favor and I appreciate it.' I said, 'Well, I didn't have too good a year last year, how about the same thing as last year?' He said, 'That's all right with you?' I said, 'That's fine with me,' so that's the way we left it. When he brought the contract back, it was a little bit different. It was a five-year contract, it was my same salary for last year, but it was gonna give me a certain salary for the next four years that would allow me just to decide what I wanted to do and not have to worry about finances. I was actually making a little more than Mantle was making in total. I knew nothing about it and didn't realize that that was Ralph doing that on his own.

"Two years later, I became the coach at the University of South Carolina. I turned them down twice. For the third time [athletic director] Paul Dietzel said he really wants you to coach. I said, let me get released from the Yankees and then I'll be glad to coach. By this time, it was Lee MacPhail [who was Yankees GM]. Lee MacPhail said, 'Hey, listen, if you want to, you can come back and be our major league coach and be our broadcaster, be our Triple-A manager. I said, 'No, the reason I'm getting out is the travel, the separation from family. He said, 'When you get settled down, gimme a call. We'll bring the Yankees down and play your ballclub. Four years later [1974], we lost out to Miami by one run. I called the Yankees and I said, 'Lee, I'm ready for you to come down.' He said, 'Well, we got a little problem.' I thought that was a no. He said, 'We're traveling north with the Mets. I thought, that is the problem? He said, 'Would it be all right if the Yankees and Mets come down and play your ballclub?' I said, 'That'll be wonderful.' Yogi is the manager of the Mets. I drove the bus out and picked the team up and Yogi said, 'Well, what are you doing driving the bus?' I said, 'Well, motor pool I don't trust. I wanted to make sure you're safe and will go at a reasonable speed. The other guy likes to speed too much. I said, 'We'll go play three [innings] against you, three against the Yankees and then we'll all play each other. He said, 'Well, you can't compete with us.' We beat both the Yankees and the Mets. Our guys won the home run contest. We had between 12, 15,000 people come out. The fans stuck with us. The next year we finished second in the nation in the College World Series, 51 and 6, losing just the final game of the College World Series."

FIRST TIME HE HAD A DAY IN HIS HONOR:

On September 17, 1966, the Yankees held Bobby Richardson Day at Yankee Stadium to honor the second baseman. Richardson was in the lineup that day and went 0-for-4.

"I remember first of all the honor of being the 10th Yankee to have a day at Yankee Stadium. I remembered when Lou Gehrig had stood at home plate and here I was standing at home plate. I was to say as Lou Gehrig had said, as Mickey Mantle had said, how fortunate it has been for me to been a Yankee or something like that. The thing I remember most is that I had so many friends. If you look in the record books, the day before we probably had 3,000 people come out. There was a great crowd. It was a wonderful day, some great gifts. [Team president] Dan Topping not only gave me a wonderful gift, but he said I want you to come down and spend a couple of days with my family when the season's over. You've made a film of your life. I'd like to show that film to my son. He had a son named Bobby. Jim Kaat was pitching and he wrote in his book, he picked me on his all opponent team, but he said, on that day, that 'I tried to throw it in there on his day and I told him it was coming in half speed, fastball right there where he wanted it.' I went 0-for 5 [actually, 0-for-4], I remember that.

"I got on a plane and flew home [with] two weeks left in the season. The thing I remember even more than the day was the fact that Ralph [Houk] said, 'Go home and spend some time with your family. We've got a young second baseman, Horace Clarke. I want you to come back, sit down, watch him, observe him, instruct him, help him, but on the last day of the season, I want you in uniform.'

Bobby Richardson by Hideshi Yokoyama

22
DAVE RIGHETTI

Left-handed pitcher Dave Righetti played 11 of his 16 major league seasons with the Yankees. Righetti was acquired in a blockbuster deal that sent 1977 AL Cy Young Award–winning closer Sparky Lyle to the Texas Rangers. In 1983, Righetti was 14-8 with a 3.44 ERA and pitched the first Yankee no-hitter since Don Larsen in 1956. Righetti became the closer out of the bullpen in 1984. In 1986, Righettti recorded 46 saves (a major league record at the time) and is second on the Yankees all-time list behind Mariano Rivera with 224 career saves. After the 1990 season, Righetti signed with the San Francisco Giants as a free agent and later became their pitching coach for their World Series winning seasons of 2010, 2012, and 2014.

FIRST GAME HE ATTENDED AS A KID:

"I'm thinking third or fourth grade. I'm thinking seven or eight maybe and they would take us up in a big bus to Candlestick [Park] and I remember [going] twice. I laugh now because I spent the last 40 years on the field and every ballpark anywhere. Kids are always yelling for a ball from the outfield. My first recollection of that, I don't know if you remember Candlestick very well, but Willie Mays is playing center and you can't take your eyes off him, right? You think he's a cartoon character almost because back then there was no TV and the only games on were the All-Star Game. If the team wasn't in the playoffs, even locally here, we never got Giant games unless they played the Dodgers so you wouldn't see these guys. To see the colors of the field and see the uniforms and watch him running around and every kid yelling Willie, Willie, so that was my first one for sure. I remember going to a Giants game and sitting behind the backstop with a neighbor pretty much around the same time. That's when I think I was hooked. Even though Candlestick was built as a dual purpose or whatever, because the 49ers were there too, the backstop was one of the farthest away from home plate in baseball, much like Oakland is, so you couldn't get close to the guys. The Cardinals had just been in the World Series and to see the Giants playing them. The Cardinal uniform and seeing [Tim] McCarver, [Julian] Javier, I think Orlando [Cepeda], I think [Roger] Maris was out there, [Mike] Shannon, I mean you can remember all these guys. Once I was hooked like that, 'cause that's kind of how I learned to read. My dad would leave the newspaper for me in the morning 'cause he had to go to work early and I'd read the front page of course, but I'd go right to the box scores, see how the teams did. That's how I learned to read and really add. I could add a batting average and ERA, all that stuff. My dad, I asked him how to do it and it got me hooked on reading. I was definitely hooked on a game 'cause I was halfway decent at it too. I think I wasn't great by any means, but I knew I was a little bit good enough to play on the Little League team and start and all that with my brothers. So that was it, I was hooked."

FIRST BASEBALL IDOL:

Leo Righetti, Dave's dad, was a minor league infielder in the Yankees system in the 1940s. Leo spent most of the 1950s playing for Seattle Rainiers and the San Francisco Seals in the Pacific Coast League

"It was my dad 'cause he played. There wasn't a lot of stuff [about his father] around the house. We ended up learning more stuff later, but he came outta the Yankee system. Long story short, being from San Francisco were Charlie Silvera, [Frank] Crosetti,

[Joe] DiMaggio. The grandparents from Italy, they're not gonna let my dad sign and leave high school 'cause he was only a junior, to sign with anybody but it was the Yankees and to them that was like royalty. The [Pacific] Coast League was huge back then, especially the San Francisco Seals so it was all tied in. The DiMaggio brothers all played there, played with the Seals. Because of that, my dad had a trucking company, so he drove a truck. A kid in the sixties, your dad used to play baseball and then find out he's a truck driver. Honestly, I thought he was cool.

"So, he was honestly the guy, but there was no baseball player that stood out. We had colorful guys here [in Oakland], Catfish [Hunter] and Reggie [Jackson] and the swinging A's of the early seventies. The Giants had Mays, [Willie] McCovery and [Juan] Marichal and [Gaylord] Perry and [Bobby] Bonds. I mean we had really a lot of exciting players. The A's, it was hard not to watch 'em with the colors and the white shoes. That was a big deal, right? Then, how good they were for sure. Then shortly five years later, I'm playing with a bunch of them. I didn't have a guy I just had to watch every night. McCovey was the closest, probably my favorite player 'cause I was the first baseman and left-handed. Guys like Wes Parker were playing for the Dodgers. Kind of thinking about guys that you were like. I only pitched a little bit so you never dreamed to do that, but we all tried to copy everybody's swing. Those cards you get, we put 'em in [the] spokes of our bikes. McCovey would've been, I've said that before and I said that when I first got to the big leagues. It didn't really change after that either. Became friends with him and spent a lot of time with him. We were with the Yankees, you were still around some ex-Dodger guys. Jeff Torborg was our bullpen coach and a coach for years. I used to bug him, but he thought McCovey was the most dangerous hitter he ever caught behind. He said [Don] Drysdale couldn't get him out, that kind of stuff. He was definitely one of those players that you never left your seat when he came up to bat for sure."

FIRST PROFESSIONAL MANAGER:

Righetti made his professional career with the 1977 Asheville Tourists of the Class-A Western Carolinas League. His manager was former major leaguer Wayne Terwilliger.

"He was tough too. Did everything. Of couse, all the managers did then, threw BP. I think he was a machine gunner for the Marines. On top of a tank. You just go, there is a man and this is your guy. It was a pretty cool team. There was four or five Californians, so I felt comfortable a little bit and my brother [Stephen, a third baseman] being there. I think all that kind of helped to get my feet off the ground, but Twig was, high pitched voice, 'What are you doing?' He got mad at me a couple of times. You were never allowed to throw a baseball in the stands for fear, number one, you'd hit somebody and you just didn't do that 'cause the balls were like valuable. In the minor leagues, you didn't get baseballs. The team had to pay for 'em or there's no telling where they're gonna come from. Generally, they pass 'em down to the minor leagues. Double A would send them to the A-ball team, things like that. By the time you got 'em, if you're an A-ball team, they were all beat up, so we hit with these older balls. They weren't brand new balls like everybody gets today. A ball came out to me in the outfield and the cover was coming off, so it was flapping around, so I took the ball and in Asheville, which is a neat historic park now, behind the fence was basically the hill and the mountain, so I just threw the ball up there. Holy shit, he stopped batting practice, came running out, yelling at me, 'What are you doing? Did you pay for those balls?' I said, 'No sir, but the cover...' 'I don't care.' He got me good in front of everybody. Anyway, I never did it again.

"He was always good to me and let me pitch and kept me out there and all that, but I blew it one time. I gave up back-to-back home runs against, they were the Greenwood Braves back then. Anyway, my first baseman [said] 'You gotta" [throw at someone], so I'm getting in a fight with my own first baseman. He's mad, I said, I'm the one that gave up the home runs. Anyway, I threw the ball inside of the next guy. I hit him right on the tick of the elbow. It's not like I threw at him, but I hit him. Twig thought I did it on purpose, he chewed me out. Little things you learn and to have a guy like that when you first hit the minor leagues. We talk about it today with these kids. They might get a high school coach no or maybe a guy that's never even coached before. There's no [one] down there anymore that had played the game for years and years and understood it so to get a Twig was, it was perfect because back then we didn't have pitching coaches. You were on your own. Twig hard to forget."

FIRST TIME SETTING A MINOR LEAGUE STRIKE-OUT RECORD:

On July 16, 1978, Righetti set a Texas League record when he recorded 21 strikeouts against Midland. Righetti gave up a leadoff double in the ninth and was pulled from the game.

"It was hot, like it always was in Tulsa in the middle of the summer. I was striking out guys, a lot of guys to that point. I had torn my groin and missed half the year. At that point, I'm not sure how many starts I had in six or seven, couple of rehab starts, but I was averaging 10, 12 strikeouts a game. It was because I had a moving fastball, but could get my breaking ball over behind in the count and I had a changeup. Looking back, I know I had a decent fastball, but I wasn't a blazer by any means. I was just throwing strikes with all my pitches. Then those stupid strikeouts kept adding up and I was blessed. All my years, I was always blessed with great stamina and long games didn't bother me. I threw 130 something pitches that game. What bothered me was not being able to win the game. I mean, I felt bad. The sun got in a couple of guys' eyes. I didn't care. I just wanted to win so I felt bad. Even though I went nine, I just felt like I didn't hold up my end of the bargain.

"I was almost embarrassed by it because the attention. I just was a regular guy with all these guys barely back in the starting rotation. Once the season ended, they shut me down. I pitched another game shortly after that complete game again. I think I had 12 or 13 strikeouts and I had tendinitis in my shoulder. I should have missed a start, but I'm throwing a lot of pitches every game. They just shut me down the rest of the year for fear. Maybe I was gonna hurt myself, so I'm thinking I'm gonna go to the Instructional League again or maybe go to Triple A. The next thing you know, my name keeps popping up in all these rumors for trades and they traded me, so I was never a Ranger again."

FIRST REACTION TO BEING TRADED TO THE YANKEES:

On November 10, 1978, Righetti was traded from the Texas Rangers to the Yankees as part of a blockbuster, 10-player trade. Sparky Lyle. the 1977 American League Cy Young Award winner, went to Texas as part of the deal.

"I thought I was traded earlier 'cause Rod Carew was [rumored] and Bill Buckner was with the Cubs and I was supposed to go to the Cubs. Then, Don Sutton was leaving the Dodgers and he ended up leaving, went to Houston, but I thought they were gonna send me to the Dodgers and my name kept popping up and then bang. The Carew thing was big, it got in the papers. I was at a hot stove dinner and somebody said something to me, 'cause there was a lot of sportswriters at those things back then. I think that was the first time I might have heard but the Rangers never called me and told me I was traded. I wanna say Cedric Tallis was the assistant GM. Bill Bergesch, one of those guys must have called me with the Yankees. I'm not sure if I got a call. The next thing you know, you're getting back then, you would get a letter, an envelope in this one. Instead of Rangers, it said New York Yankees and it tells you you're supposed to report to Fort Lauderdale. [The Yankees] said everything because they just went to three straight World [Series]. I just watched them play in the World Series and played that [tiebreaker] game against Boston. I was working in a sporting goods store and I had a little TV and I left it on and I watched that playoff game. Before I left Tulsa, I had a friend of mine that was a Yankee fan and I'm still a Ranger. He goes, hey, take a picture with, it was Reggie, it was 44. The number and I had it on. Three months later I'm sitting in the locker room with him."

FIRST YANKEES SPRING CAMP: 1979

"My first impression was, 'Okay, don't fall over yourself as you walk in here and people staring at you, you know, who's this guy?' They put me between [Ron] Guidry and [Dick] Tidrow. Unbeknown to me, once I got there, I didn't realize [George] Steinbrenner reached out to my dad or somebody and basically told Guidry to keep an eye on me. I'm not sure, Gator not being pushy or anything like that, he probably just said, whatever, but all I know is I'm next to him and he just won every game in the world that year as a Cy Young winner and Tidrow, who was a tough old guy. I ended up being with Dirt [Tidrow's nickname] the next 20 something years with the Giants. I had that tendinitis in my shoulder, that doesn't really go away. We didn't know it back then. You really have to work tendinitis and stretch that tendon. I'd sit there and there was benches back then in the locker room. It wasn't like you got your own chair or anything. I guess I was touching my arm and Dirt [said], 'Touch your fucking arm!' Basically, he said, don't let anybody see you doing that but it was sore. It was still sore. They were not gonna shut down the whole trade, but rework it 'cause I was damaged goods and did the Rangers know about it, blah, blah, blah. Of course they knew about it. I shut down my arm at the end of the season and I didn't pitch the last month. Now I'm feeling like a weirdo and I'm screwing up this trade. I just got to the Yankees and I'm on this plane with [scouting director Jack Butterfield]. I felt bad he had to fly with me. George probably made him do it all the way back there to get a shot. It did feel better. It took the edge off and it calmed that thing down. There was no damage. It's funny, I pitched the next 16, 17 seasons, never had a shoulder issue at all, nothing. My delivery got a little better.

"Now I start throwing bullpens, back then you went one at a time. So how many pitchers are in camp. Maybe not even 20 but you were last, so you'd sit there for almost two or three hours and you finally got to throw BP or something. I just remembered them telling me they're gonna send me back to Double A. I said, 'What? I was an All-Star in the Texas League last year.' I was hoping for Triple A. They said, 'No, we can't take anybody with a sore arm to Columbus.' I said, 'The team in Double A doesn't mind me having a sore arm.' Basically, they were telling me they had some Triple-A roster guys that they wanted to bring there and they could move me there anytime, blah, blah, blah. Connecticut was closer. I was right there in West Haven. It was snowing but I was closer to New York and they could watch me easier and I didn't know that. I just took it as a demotion. So, I wasn't excited at first but I ended up getting what they told me. Gene Michael was the Triple-A manager then. [Pitching coach] Stan Williams ended up telling me, 'cause he was going to Columbus with Stick [Michael] and he was telling me, 'Listen, you pitch three or four good games, we'll call you right up.' I said, all right, so I kept my mouth shut. I was 3-0 and the phone rang and they said, 'We told you.' So I stayed there a half a year. We had a good team. I really enjoyed being in that, what a big difference in the farm system. Not just players, but attitude and everything and little tougher, little edgier. They were great. It was just nice to be in that winning atmosphere and having to win a little bit, a little pressure. The beginning was a bit sketchy and I finally went to Columbus and end up pitching really good the first two games, almost threw no hitters, both games, but I think my elbow ended up getting sore that year and they shut me down again. Now I've got this label but all my bones weren't down growing. My pain started going away as I finally finished growing, which was weird."

FIRST TIME WALKING INTO THE YANKEES CLUBHOUSE:

"You try to act like you've been there before. You're part of the group but you're tiptoeing. You're just sitting in your locker. My locker, when you were a rookie, you got whatever was left but when you come in through the door, I was the first locker on the right. So, I watched everybody go in but straight down to my eyesight and to the left was Thurman's [Munson] locker and he had just passed away. There was an eerie feeling in the locker room. I didn't feel the excitement or joy. [The Yankees] were out of it, their friend, their leader was gone. Goose [Gossage] had broken his thumb in a fight with Cliff Johnson. The locker room was off so it wasn't a joyous occasion, even though inside I'm jumping around like crazy. You just acted the way everybody acted to so speak. There was a little bit of a pall. You could tell it hurt Lou [Piniella] and Bobby Murcer and those guys. It was different and it took a while for that to go away too, by the way. I think we were excited to be there, the young guys, but weird stuff happened. We were in Cleveland and George and Billy gave us, all the new guys, a hundred bucks each to go to the Theatrical, which was the local big shot restaurant there in Cleveland. A weird strange thing happened out of that. The great writer, Gay Talese, was following the team around and doing an exposé on somebody, probably was Billy, but he was allowed access during the game. He was in the dugout, things like that. We got in a fight with Cleveland. Cliff Johnson was traded away to Cleveland. Now he's catching and he's playing and I guess this is the first time since the fight. Well, Billy yells out of the dugout, he didn't just kind of whisper, he yelled, hit him in the neck is what he said. Plain and simple 'cause I was sitting behind him 'cause I was sitting next to Guidry. I was told to sit next to Gator, so I'm hearing this. So, Bob Kammeyer is a young, he's kind of an older veteran, minor leaguers but he knew he had to do it. Well, he hit Cliff and Cliff turns 'round and was gonna come after Billy. He knew, he could hear 'em too at home plate so that starts the thing. Gay Talese wrote something that Billy paid Kammeyer to hit Cliff Johnson. No, he didn't. He gave us all a hundred bucks to go to dinner, but it made him look that way because he's yelling out there to hit him. So he never paid him to do that, but that got messed up. I just remember, this is crazy and I read, Bronx Zoo [by Sparky Lyle] before I got there.

FIRST MAJOR LEAGUE GAME: September 16, 1979 vs. Detroit Tigers at Yankee Stadium

Righetti received a no-decision in his major league debut. The Yankee rookie lefthander gave up three runs in five innings pitched with six walks and three strikeouts.

"It was '79. We won the championship in Triple A. I've not sure if I've ever had any alcohol ever before in my life. I might have had a beer once and they had champagne. It was late September and I went up with Bob Kammeyer, Paul Mirabella, Rick Anderson, and myself. I think there was four or five of us, so I felt comfortable. George sent us on his private plane from some airfield in Columbus and we flew all night. All I know is when we got to New York [it] took forever to get to the hotel and I'm sure we flew into Newark or something. Ended up in Hasbrouck Heights at the Sheridan, which was the Yankee hotel. I just remember waking up early, excited. You're gonna go to the park. I don't know how we're gonna get there but [hitting coach] Charlie Lau ended up driving. I know I went with him. All I know is I had a hangover and I felt crappy. Dehydrated.

"I get to the ballpark and I went with a coach, we ended up early, right? Billy was there and I saw [pitching coach] Art Fowler and he said, 'Billy wants to see you, boy.' I said, 'All right,' so I went in there and it was like old home week. Billy, Oakland guy, knew my dad and everything. So, I'm just taking it in, keep my mouth shut. He goes, 'By the way, you're starting today,' and I went, 'What?' I said, 'You're kidding me.' So I went to find Gene Monahan, the trainer. I said, 'Is there any way I can get some food? I haven't had any breakfast yet.' They ended up getting me some sort of egg sandwich, but I felt crappy and I started that game.

"I walked down the tunnel and up those stairs. I remember Reggie saying something to me. He goes, 'You look pale.' Again, I kept my mouth shut, I wasn't gonna tell some veteran we had champagne and it got me right. So. in the airplane you fly and you get dehydrated. I felt horrible. I finally got it together enough to pitch and get through it. Billy kind of praised me for being there and all. I didn't take it as bad, but I got a couple more starts. That first game was a little shaky so that was my first experience and it was a whirlwind. It was neat to be up there for the three weeks.

"It was a whirlwind. All I know is my three starts, they were trying to get Ron Davis the rookie record for wins by a reliever or something. I think he ended up winning 15 games. Every fifth inning, I got them coming after me to take me outta the game. I wasn't happy, but I didn't say anything. Now if we had the lead, they would take me out anyway trying to get Ronnie the wins. I didn't care. I was in the big leagues, but I think one game in Minnesota though, I was pitching good, I'd only given up a couple of hits. It was 2–1 in the seventh or eighth, then I got taken out. I wasn't happy about that but at least I got three starts in. I think two months later, Billy got in a fight and he gets fired. My last day in the big leagues that year, he calls me and Guidry into the office. I felt so out of place anyway, but with this star next to me. I said, 'Yes, Billy, what's up?' He goes, 'Gator, what are you doing in the offseason to stay in shape?' and Gator was 150 pounds and could run the 100 in 9.6, a legit track star. Gator goes, 'Well, I hunt.' Billy looked at me and he goes, 'You hunt?' I said, 'No, I don't hunt. I'm from California.' He goes, 'Well, what do you do to stay in shape?' I said, 'Same thing I've always done. I just go play basketball or whatever sport.' Back then that's what you did. You kind of just played other things. I said, 'I'll run around. I'll ride my bike everywhere.' He goes, 'Okay, but make sure you stay in shape. You're gonna be one of my five starters next year.' I went, 'All right.' So I left that meeting thinking I was gonna be the fifth starter with Tommy [John] and myself, [Ed] Figueroa and I don't know who would've been the fifth guy back then. I ended up finding out who they brought in. Gaylord [Perry], Luis Tiant, and Jim Kaat. It wasn't gonna be me so Billy got fired, Dick Howser took over.

"The first day, Dick came up to me and basically told me, you're not gonna pitch, you're not going to the big leagues. I was crushed, but I appreciated him telling me. Of course, I'm sure George had 'em do that and to let me know right away but it took a lot outta me. I thought I was gonna fight for a job, get ready for the season and it crushed me. I don't even get a chance and they had a great team that year. Tommy Underwood was the fifth starter. That was the worst year of my career. Nothing even until the very end. I mean, it was easily the worst. I just took it too hard. We all knew by then, you'd been there enough to know that George wasn't gonna wait for some young guy so they were gonna bring in older pitchers. They won a hundred games and or course they lose to Kansas City. I was bummed because they were pretty left-handed hitting team. I could have helped, but I was crushed."

FIRST POSTSEASON APPEARANCE:

Righetti made his postseason debut in Game 2 of the 1981 American League Division Series against the Milwaukee Brewers and tossed six scoreless innings. Righetti pitched three innings in relief in the deciding Game 5.

"It was a little strange coming off the strike. Even [though] Milwaukee [was a] baseball friendly town, I think half the place was only like 20,000 something people there. I can remember they told me before the series started, Gator was going Game 1. If we won, then I'd pitch the second game. If we lost, Tommy [John] would pitch the second game. Hey, whatever you guys want to do. I pitched really well down the stretch and it was all because we knew we were in. (After a labor issue interrupted the 1981 season, the Yankees were designated the winners of the first half in the AL East and were guaranteed a spot in the postseason playoffs) Everything we did in the second half was really to get ready for the playoffs. In my case, they let me go and pitch, but I ended up getting pulled twice with shutouts. Like six, seven run leads. I just wanted to get my first complete game and shutout and get it out of the way kind of thing."

"We were in Minnesota and Reggie dove for a ball in right field and we were up. I don't know how big we were up. I can remember saying, "Wow, what is he doing?' He didn't have to do it but he was saving a run. I was going for the ERA championship and he knew it. Reggie knew all that stuff. Hell, I didn't even know it hardly in any way. I was just excited for him to do that. I remember [manager] Bob [Lemon] taking me outta the game 'cause they were trying to get Goose right before the playoffs so they wanted him to get an inning and it turned out to be my day. It was two games down the stretch where they took me out in the eighth and I ended up losing the ERA title. I didn't have enough innings. I missed it by I think an inning and a half. It may be a half-inning. It's been cool because Tommy John had won it and Guidry won it in '78. I think Tommy in '79 [actually, Guidry again] and then Rudy May might have led the league in ERA in '80 and it had been the fourth straight year that a left-handed Yankee would've won the ERA title. Bob Lemon said to me, 'Nobody remembers who won the ERA title.' They asked me, 'You want to pitch an inning?' I said, 'No, we can't do something like that.' I said, 'We gotta get ready for the playoffs,' and he didn't really want me to pitch either, but he felt like he should ask I guess. The writers got on it a little bit and they were asking Jim Palmer 'cause we were playing the Orioles. 'Should Righetti pitch an inning,' blah, blah, blah. It was a little bit of controversy, but some of my teammates were coming up to me, 'Hey man, I can't believe they're taking you out.' I didn't care, I really didn't, but I cared later when I became a reliever. It'd been nice to have an ERA title on my resume. We won both games in Milwaukee and then it turned to mush when we got back home. We ran the bases bad, ended up hurting us against the Dodgers [their World Series opponent] in Game 3. We had a couple of bunts that were popped up or did something and George went ballistic. That was my first experience with George in the clubhouse 'cause he didn't come down very much. [Rick] Cerone went off on him and Bobby Murcer had to calm Cerone down. I think he might have made the last out [of Game 4 as Milwaukee tied the series after being down two games to none] and George is crazy. He could have waited 20 minutes but he wasn't in there when we walked in the clubhouse.

"The next day I come to the ballpark. I don't know if Guidry is starting. I'm hoping to pitch in the next series. They called in the office and I think Clyde King might've been the pitching coach with Bob Lemon. They said, 'Hey, Guidry's gonna go four, you're gonna go three and Goose is going two.' I said, 'Anybody tell Gator he's coming out after four innings?' They said, 'Nope, that's the way we're gonna do it.' So now, I'm a reliever again. I really didn't know what to do, how to warm up, nothing. I felt like I was infringing on the bullpen guys a little bit. It was a little bit different, but I wasn't scared and it went all right. We ended up doing exactly, Gator went four, I went three, and Goose pitched the last two. Cerone hits the big home run, George said he motivated him to do that by screaming at him but it's not boring. For them to trust me like, and for Gator to go along with it. I don't know if he felt great or not. I knew I was on short rest but I started getting off my cycle of my arm and I could tell the difference. I wasn't the same guy, even against Oakland. I pitched all right, but I threw more than I pitched, but it was neat to be able to win at home against Billy's A's. It was all surreal. Billy tried to mess with me. I think the first inning, I had a pair of sleeves on. I'm trying not [to copy] a guy, but Guidry always wears the same sleeves underneath his uniform and he got holes in them like we all do and mine did too. So that's what I wore, but Billy saw it and he tried to get me to get nervous or whatever, so I just took my sleeves off and threw 'em away. Gave 'em to the trainer and kept pitching. I didn't care. Anyway, that went good and we won the pennant there. To me today, that's still kind of my biggest thrill. Beating your hometown A's and having family there, going to the World Series. That was pretty good."

FIRST MAJOR LEAGUE HONOR:

Righetti won the 1981 American League Rookie of the Year Award. He was 8–4 in the strike-shortened season with an ERA of 2.05. Righetti pitched 105 1/3 innings and gave up 75 hits.

"It means more as you get older, but even then, I knew it meant something 'cause I think at that point, Thurman might've been the last one to win it before me. A lot of rookies weren't staying there very long to be honest so I took it as a badge of honor. I almost felt cheapest. I didn't pitch my best against the Dodgers and George basically threatened to send me down which he ended up doing anyway. Here I was their best pitcher for almost the whole year. I was counting Columbus and I missed 11 starts. I didn't get one handshake, one clap on the back, nothing. It was, we're gonna send you back 'cause I didn't pitch well against the Dodgers."

"I was disappointed all winter and I've been reading this stuff that George was saying so it was hard to really enjoy the award. I should have, it was at the start of my career in the big leagues and I should have been more proud of myself, but it was the opposite. I almost felt like I let the team down. Then, I got to spring training and the next year in '82 and there was a major fight, like the night before the first day of spring training. All the coaches and GM or whatever, they're all in there arguing. Half their arguments [are] about me and George is mad and he got rid of a bunch of veterans and brought in a different group of guys. Ken Griffey and Davey Collins and all this. It affected me 'cause I knew my coaches were in trouble 'cause guys were siding with me, Yogi, and things like that. That's what George would do. He'd threaten the coaches, if this guy doesn't do this, you're gone. That kind of stuff. When I got sent down, so did my pitching coach. I had three guys out here and they were all sent. You don't fire pitching coaches during the season 'cause the veterans aren't pitching good. Basically, it was 'cause of me and I knew it, so that was a hard burden. I mean, you're just getting into the big leagues, but that's how he worked, that's how he operated. The only way to do is fight back, which I always did. I didn't do it in public. I'd just go right in his office. I said, 'What did I do to you?' That kind of thing.

"A lot of little things would pop up and it seemed like it was about me. [George] traded [Graig] Nettles 'cause he wrote [a] book, but basically, traded them as a gift to San Diego, which was Puff's [Nettles's] nickname] hometown and Goose was already there, so he could finish his career out there. People thought it was because of the book and all. He had it in the paper, it was the first thing out of his mouth. 'Well, you know, I don't know, Puff might be a bad influence on Righetti.' Again, because Nettles was my locker mate on the other side and he did treat me well 'cause he didn't talk to a lot of guys, but we got along good. Joy and excitement of being in the big leagues, I don't think I ever had that 'cause we didn't win. That's all we were trying to do and the pressure didn't matter. You watch [Don] Mattingly win [a] batting title and he couldn't enjoy that 'cause he's fighting [for it] against his own teammate [Dave Winfield] on the last day of the season, so that was odd. Everything was just a little off all those years. It was heartbreaking so it put a chip on your shoulder and he always pitted us against our own fans. He'd badmouth us and he'd get the people thinking the same way. Tell me to go home with the cab driver. Me and Brian Fisher, we didn't finish a game one time in '85 and he told me to go home with the cab drivers and meet with the beer vendors or something."

FIRST TIME SEEING HIMSELF ON A BASEBALL CARD:

"I didn't want to feel like a big shot back then. The big shots were anybody that was drafted like first round. In A-ball, I think it was Asheville. They might have had a card or something of us. I just remember signing something and I said, I hope the guys don't think I'm being a big shot. Isn't that weird? But that's kind of the way it was. I think West Haven did cards my first year with the Yankees and I know there was some in Columbus, but pretty neat. You see your stat line on the back and you're looking for the little blurb that Topps always put down there. Trading cards, they were like a lifeline between the fans and players."

FIRST NO-HITTER: July 4, 1983 vs. Boston Red Sox at Yankee Stadium

Righetti pitched the first Yankees no-hitter since Don Larsen's perfect game in the 1956 World Series and their first regular season no-hitter since Allie Reynolds threw two in 1951.

"You know you always got one. You don't expect to throw one, so you don't care if you give up any hits, 'cause you figured that's inevitable. We were knocked around Friday and Saturday, pretty good. Of course, that year we're fighting not just them, but the Orioles had a great team. I just remember saying, I gotta pitch good today and beat the, keep this game close. Give us a chance 'cause they're killing us and it was hot. I wasn't worried about that but there's a million things that are different in this game. As years go by, there's different things that pop up and where people were and all that. The biggest thing that came out if, unfortunately, I was disappointed I didn't go to the All-Star Game. The reason I didn't back then, like now I'd be on the team, but they only took guys that were gonna pitch in the game and Guidry even backed out. Billy had called MLB and he didn't tell me, he didn't want me to know, but they took Tippy Martinez, they took another reliever. Back then, they wouldn't replace you with another guy. You're still an All-Star and you get to go, back then, you didn't go so I was heartbroken 'cause I couldn't pitch in the game. If I'm starting on Sunday, basically anybody starts on Sunday's probably not going. So I had a chip on my shoulder to show 'em I'm an All-Star, but it wasn't a motivation. The Boston Red Sox were the motivation, I gotta beat 'em, right? Jimmy Rice was my motivation or [Wade] Boggs and [Dwight] Evans and those guys. I'm just trying to beat 'em.

"The biggest thing I knew I was doing was I was starting to overthrow a little bit in the middle of the game and I'm getting these strikeouts early and I said I can't do this. I've gotta get this game to Goose. I gotta touch the eighth inning. For sure, I'd like to go eight full. Generally, they would take us out. Billy let me finish a few games, maybe six or seven, but for the most part you're coming out. So I want to get to Goose. That's my only goal, so I said, I'm gonna throw my other pitches and [catcher] Butch [Wynegar] was great with that. He goes, 'Yeah, let's throw your changeup and curveball a little bit more.' I didn't throw a lot of them, but I threw enough to get some quicker outs and I wasn't laboring as much. That's why I think the seventh, eighth, ninth or the sixth, seven, eight, those went fairly quickly and they saved me 'cause I was on my way to tiring out trying to throw, not too hard, but I'm just throwing fastballs. I think the first three innings, that's all we threw was a fastball and a hard slider that barely broke because I was throwing it too hard. Nowadays, they call it a cutter. That was the only strategy I had during the game was to try to last longer by using my other pitches and getting some ground balls.

"It saved me in the ninth, 'cause that was my worst [inning].

From the first [pitch] to Jeff Newman. He was a low-ball hitter. I said, I got a four-run lead. I know Goose is warming up anyway. I said, if I'm gonna give one up, I know his weakness was up in the strike zone, which is the worst thing. It's like when you're tired and you're overthrowing 'cause you're gonna miss up there. Sure enough, I ended up throwing about six, seven pitches and walking him. I'm saying to myself, that's wasn't good 'cause you don't want it. That's a bad omen. Really, all I'm thinking about is the win. I said I wouldn't think about it unless I had two outs. I think [Glenn] Hoffman, on the second or third pitch, hit a ground ball to short and we almost had a double play and the ball pulled Donnie off first a little bit, even though he might have been out if you watched the game. Jerry Remy hit the first pitch [ground out to second]. So I only threw like four pitches after that, before [Wade] Boggs got up there. Then I said, okay I can go for it. I still got a guy on base and if I lose Boggs by any chance, all of a sudden, the game starts coming into jeopardy. I think it was [Tony] Armas and then Jim Rice [scheduled to bat] and I'm saying, Jesus, you know you can't be walking people but Boggs, I'm not grooving him anything. I always threw balls up and in on Wade. Up on his hands or even move him back, always move him. I didn't want him comfortable 'cause it's a line drive at your chest. My biggest worry was covering first 'cause I had a tendency to fall off towards third base and I didn't want tapper between the mound and me and Donnie. After Remy hitting the fielder's choice to [Andre] Robertson at second, I was doing knee bends and stuff and everybody goes, you do that 'cause you were nervous. I said, no, I want to make sure my legs are ready, if I'm gonna have to go cover first. That's all I was thinking about because if I throw that slider and he gets out in front, he's gonna roll it to first. I knew where the fastball was going. He was gonna line drive that, either up the middle or the other way. He wasn't gonna pull me, 'cause that's how his swing worked. Thank God he missed the sucker.

"There was so much stuff going on. Nettles was sitting next to me [while the Yankees were batting] 'cause he was out. Me and Nettles were going to Atlantic City 'cause it was the All-Star break. He goes, 'What do you want to do?' I saw the Beach Boys are playing Atlantic City. We can go down there anyway, so we were gonna go and Puff was trying to get me to relax and he goes, 'You want me to drive?' I said, 'You can't drive, you got pink eye,' but he ended up driving. That was the only guy that talked to me the last few innings. I'm sitting there in the bottom of the eighth and it's two out. That's when [Lou] Piniella hit the pop up. Jeff Newman went back and made one of the greatest catching plays ever and dove in the stands, come out with a popcorn box. He caught the thing but [umpire Steve] Palermo never saw it and the cameras never picked it up but he was on the ground. He got tangled up when he was going back to the backstop and somehow turned his knee. I don't know if he tore his knee or broke his leg but he got hurt and he was in pain. There was no way he saw Newman catch the ball or if he picked it out of the seats 'cause he was laying on the ground. Lou's just sitting there ready to explode and Nettles goes wait till he finds out that he's out. You know what [Piniella] said? He knew I had the no-hitter and that he didn't want me sitting there forever. He actually tempered himself because he knew that was going on. Otherwise, he said he would've gone ballistic 'cause there's no way Palermo saw the play. So that was kind of a side thing to the game.

"They had [Phil] Rizzuto and Frank Messer and those guys were sitting the stands giving out, it was like a giveaway day or something. In between innings, they were giving off ticket numbers in the stands and people were winning prizes and that's weird for Yankee Stadium stuff. Those in between innings seemed to last longer. Chuck Mangione was sitting in the front row, he had his horn out and playing his songs. It was like a festive day, but I was in the middle of it, so to speak. Those instances happening. [Steve] Kemp made a great play in right field when he did catch that ball up against the fence there in foul territory. I actually had a thing go through me like, maybe that's a good omen. It turned out to be one of the coolest things in my life."

FIRST REACTION WHEN HE LEARNED HE WAS GOING TO BE THE YANKEES' CLOSER:

Following the 1983 season, Rich "Goose" Gossage left the Yankees as a free agent so there was a need for a closer. The Yankees decided to take Righetti out of the starting rotation and make him the closer beginning with the 1984 season.

"We were all disappointed how the season ended. Baltimore, I think won a hundred something [Actually 98] games. We had a great year but they shut me down as soon as we were out of it. I didn't make my last two starts and I went home. I know exactly where I was [when he learned the news]. I was in the bowling alley. We used to go down there a couple of days a week. I grew up around the bowling alley and driving range, this kind of thing and that's where the best food was for breakfast. So me and my parents were having breakfast and there's no phones then, right? But one of our neighbors, my brother must have been home and got the call and told me I had to go. He told a friend of mine who he knew was going down to the bowling alley later and told me I had to go home and I said, 'Uh oh,' and my dad said it immediately. He goes, 'They're gonna ask you to do it.' I said, 'I don't even know, did Goose leave?' That was basically the thought process and I got home and I never heard of this before.

"This is 1984, but they were on some kind of conference call thing. It was [coaches] Jeff Torborg, Sammy Ellis, and Yogi, the three of 'em. I could hear 'em all talking. I didn't find out till later Gator actually told him 'cause they were gonna ask him to do it 'cause he had done it in '79 when Goose got hurt. They went to him first 'cause there was nobody available. I guess Bruce Sutter wasn't a free agent until the next year but Gator said no, Rags ought to do it anyway. I said, I love starting. Not only that, but you got paid a hell of a lot more back then, but I didn't care. I didn't know if I could do it or not, but when Yogi was the first one to mention it to me, he goes, 'I'll take care of you so it's easier on your arm.' I said, 'So, it was all lies.' There's nothing like starting. There's nothing compared to, you can stand on that rubber at the national anthem, Yankee Stadium. You got the ball in the middle of that mound and you go to work for the next three hours. There's nothing like it, but to be the closer in New York and chose me to, in Goose's spot, that's a hell of an honor. So, they didn't know what they were gonna do with me. How they were going to use me, blah, blah, blah, but I was gonna close.

"Back then, there's probably only five relievers. I'm pitching a lot and we all did. I'm sure there was two or three of us every year with 80, a hundred innings, something of course they would never do anymore, but [we] took it as a badge of honor. My demeanor changed. I went from four days a week at least you could relax a little when you were starting, but as the closer for the Yankees, my brain didn't take a day off. I took that job as serious as I could. The only crappy part about the whole thing was people didn't accept it. They were fighting over it till the day I left. 'He shoulda been starting.' Just trying to help the team, but the problem was it permeated all the way down. George, I don't know if he ever wanted me to do it. Billy definitely didn't like me relieving so every time he became the manager, he was gonna use the shit out of me. He never wanted me to do it. He brought me in as early as the fifth inning sometimes, but I pitched and I regretted it when I was 30. I had an old arm and I had a live arm but I just pitched a lot."

FIRST ALL-STAR EXPERIENCE:

In 1986, Righetti was named to his first All-Star Game.

"Yeah, that was fun. So I don't make it in '83 'cause I pitched on Sunday, [In] '84, I'm on the team. Joe Altobelli [of the Orioles] was the manager and he asked me how would you like to go. Be in San Francisco for the All-Star break. Joe was my Triple-A manager and a coach on the team when we went to the playoffs. I said, 'Geez, Joe, I'd love that,' 'cause I lived there. I said, 'I'm not gonna fly all the way, it's only two and a half days. I'm gonna stay in New York.' He goes, 'No, no, no. The All-Star game's in San Francisco this year. How would you like to go?' I said, 'Yeah, I'd love to go.' We got about three weeks left before the All-Star break, I was having a good year and he appreciated it. Here's the manager basically telling me I'm on the team that day. The next day, I sliced my finger open in the bullpen. I missed two weeks and then when I come back off the DL, I don't get invited. So I screwed that one up. Then '85, I'm in Anaheim and I'm having a great start [to the season], gonna be on the team. I broke my pinky toe on my foot going to the bathroom in the middle of the night. I kicked like the edge of the door jamb going into the bathroom just enough where it hit funny and just snapped it. Of course, I didn't tell anybody. I told the trainer and they taped me up and cut a hole in my shoe so my toe would stick out, but it was painful for a while and I pitched on it like an idiot. I didn't want them to find out I got hurt 'cause the year before I got hurt with my finger, well I missed another All-Star Game, so '86 was like, 'Phew, finally. Timmy Raines asked me in the elevator coming back from breakfast or something. Raines goes, 'How many is this for you Rags?' I said, 'It's my first one,' and he goes, 'Holy crap, I thought you were on the team every year?' I said, 'No, thank you.' But it was cool. My parents came and you meet the president back then and all that stuff, but [Roger] Clemens is facing [Dwight] Gooden. This is a big deal. There's two or three things cool things that really come out of it. I felt like a rookie again, which was kind of a neat feeling.

"I felt like a rookie again, which was kind of a neat feeling. True story. I'm sitting in the dugout next to George Brett and we're watching the home run, back then they called it, I don't know if it was home run derby or whatever, but that's when [Darryl] Strawberry hit that back wall of the Astrodome. I'd never seen anything, I thought it was a golf ball. It was incredible. I think the winner hit four and it was like Wally Joyner or somebody. So, Donnie's the reigning MVP and he's having an otherwordly crazy season and he should have been back to back. They gave it to Clemens, but Kirby Puckett walks in the dugout. True story, right in front of George Brett too. Jim Rice was standing nearby and that's the first time I ever heard anybody mention [the nickname] 'Donnie Baseball.' It was Kirby Puckett [who] named him that. He goes, 'Here's Donnie Baseball.' The reason why he said it and maybe
Donnie can, I definitely heard it, 'cause the fans voted Wally Joyner in to be the fan favorite or whatever, because he was 'Wally World' that year. He was a rookie. They put him at first base in the All-Star Game and the players all knew who Donnie was and he

was the best player in the league, our reigning MVP and he's on the bench to start the All-Star Game. That's what Kirby said. Donnie Baseball. I can't remember if he went into another part of 'What are you doing in the dugout?' kind of thing. Joyner probably felt weird too, right? Starting that game, but I remember that was the first time I ever heard that. Donnie, he didn't suck it up or anything. He didn't want to be called Donnie Baseball in front of all those great players.

"Dick Howser was the manager and we didn't know Dick was sick and a weird thing happened. When I went in the game in the eighth, Charlie Hough's throwing his knuckleball and Richie Gedman couldn't catch it. [Howser] got both me and Willie Hernandez up at the same time. Willie was the Cy Young guy, you know, '84 season, but he got us both up, which was weird. He pointed to the dugout. We were just throwing down the side there so you could pop out of the dugout and tell which pitcher to go in and he went to his left arm. Well, we're both left-handed and I ended up going in the game."

FIRST MAJOR LEAGUE HIT: August 8, 1992 as a member of the San Francisco Giants vs. Cincinnati Reds at Riverfront Stadium

In the top of the 11th inning, Righetti singled off Reds pitcher Steve Foster for his first major league hit but he was thrown out at second trying to stretch it into a double.

"Steve Foster. He was pitching and it was a 2-0 count and I hit a line drive into the gap and as I was running, my legs weren't working. I said, you kidding me because you were almost running too hard, instead of just three-quarter gliding and get your legs working. I was locked up, I couldn't believe it. I felt like I was in one of those dreams where you're trying to punch somebody or you're trying to climb out and you can't do it. It was the same stinking feeling. The ball was in front of my eyes so I could see Reggie Sanders picking it up and I said, 'Oh, I'm gonna be out.' So what I tried to do was, if you can imagine running from first to second and the ball's coming in right center there so you could see it. Barry Larkin's at short and you could tell he is getting ready for the throw. I wanted the ball to hit me before it got to Barry's glove, so I tried to slide to the right of second base so the ball would hit me 'cause I felt like I was gonna be out and my only shot was to block him from catching it. So I'm safe, actually, but I can't move the way I slid. I was off, if I roll over either way, I'm out and he had the ball on me and the umpire goes 'Safe!' So I don't know if it's a single or double. I never found out. Yeah, they call me safe first and then I came off the bag. I just got thrown out at second. I gotta go all the way in the dugout and now I gotta come out here and pitch another full inning. You're on the road and the game's tied in extra inning and you're staying out there."

Dave Righetti by James Fiorentino

23
ERIC SODERHOLM

Third baseman/DH Eric Soderholm played his final big league season with the Yankees in 1980. With Graig Nettles manning third, Soderholm saw most of his playing time as the designated hitter. Soderholm played 95 games and slashed .287/.353/.462 for an OPS of .815 with 11 home runs and 35 RBIs. Soderholm was a first-round pick of the Minnesota Twins in the 1968 MLB June Amateur Draft. He also played with the Chicago White Sox and Texas Rangers before finishing his career in New York.

FIRST BASEBALL IDOL:

"When I was seven years old Dad threw me his glove that had no webbing in it or anything. He threw me my first ball and it went right through the fingers and hit me in the forehead. That was a memorable moment but it was good because it created this fire within. Wait a minute, I know I can catch this ball. That was a memorable moment that got me started on my passion, which was baseball. I suppose right about the that time you had [Mickey] Mantle and [Roger] Maris that were getting a lot of publicity. I don't know if idol is the right word but I was intrigued by Maris's home runs and Mickey Mantle's ability to play."

FIRST MAJOR LEAGUE GAME THAT HE ATTENDED:

"We went to a game in Atlanta. Our baseball team in junior college, South Georgia Junior College went to a baseball game in Atlanta and they gave us upper deck seats. That was when Joe Torre was with the Atlanta Braves. I remember Joe Torre that night having a great night. I think he got like three or four hits that night. It's hard to even think about idolizing Joe Torre or anybody. I was just there witnessing and watching and seeing how everybody kind of played the game. How they did the game and I just tried to suck up as much knowledge as I could on how to be a better player.

"I just kind of evolved into the number one draft choice and then just evolved into being a decent major league player. When I first came up, though, I wasn't that. I was scared to death and didn't know if I put my pants on the same way as Harmon Killebrew or Rod Carew or Tony Oliva and it showed. I hit .180 my first year. I hadn't matured into the confident level. Then all of a sudden, I woke up one day and realized I put my pants on the same way as Killebrew. Why can't I play at this level? I just kind of woke up and then started playing a whole lot better and then started looking into the mental aspects of the game, 'cause I realized that everybody at that level was awfully good or they wouldn't be there. The difference between the average players and the good players was their mental toughness, their mental approach to the game, so I began to study a lot about that. I took a course called 'Success Motivation Goal Setting' with the Twins. They paid for the course. Then I got introduced to a hypnotherapist and he began to use hypnosis to help me with my confidence. I had heard that Rod Carew was seeing a hypnotist for his leg issues of pain and confidence. I'm going, 'God almighty, if it's good enough for Rod Carew, it's got to be good enough for me.' So I ended up seeing him. I just learned at a fairly young age that it's really all about the thoughts 'cause my thoughts were creating my reality. I kept thinking all these negative things and I wasn't good enough and it's gonna show in my performance, so I learned how to turn that mental switch on which helped me in my career to end up being a pretty good, pretty decent career for a guy that just had average talent."

FIRST DRAFT EXPERIENCE:

Soderholm was the first overall pick of the Minnesota Twins in the 1968 MLB January Draft, secondary phase from South Georgia College. Soderholm had been chosen by the Kansas City Athletics in the 11th round of the 1967 June Amateur Draft, but did not sign.

"There were scouts obviously coming to the games. We had a couple pretty good pitchers on our team and I was told the scouts were showing up. We were told that there's gonna be several scouts coming to the game and they're gonna be watching the two pitchers that we had. We ended up winning the state championship 'cause we had such good pitching, but found out later they were coming to watch me. I didn't even know that. I think one time my coach came up and says would you be interested in playing professional ball? I said, year, of course I would. I guess the scouts were coming to watch not only the main pitcher but me also. "All of a sudden I got a phone call in the dorm from Sid Hartman from the Minneapolis Tribune, I believe it was. He said, 'Did you know that you're the number one draft choice in the secondary phase of the Minnesota Twins?' I said, no and he said they're gonna be sending a scout to see you and sign you to a contract. Congratulations, you have a chance to be a pro baseball player. I go, oh, great. I told my teammates and they all congratulated me, but I mean it was so low key. I mean, I don't even think I celebrated. I never really drank much anyway so I don't even think I really celebrated other than calling my mom and dad and saying, 'Guess who's the number one draft choice of the Minnesota Twins?' They were shocked too, so it was more of a shock than anything."

FIRST PROFESSIONAL MANAGER:

Soderholm began his pro career in 1968 with the Orlando Twins in the Class-A Florida State League, managed by Ralph Rowe.

"Ralph Rowe was another one of my mentors in the baseball world. The best story I can tell you about Ralph Rowe is that we were in the playoffs and I hit a two-run homer to win the game for us. We were all celebrating in the locker room with champagne and stuff. After it kind of died down, he came over to me, put his arm around me, and said, 'Kid, I gotta tell you. I watched you play all year this year and I really feel you've got the ability to be a major league baseball player.' I remember when he said that to me, it was like a light bulb went off in my head. 'Man, wouldn't it be great if I could be a major league baseball player?' Then, he said something interesting. He said, 'You know, it wouldn't surprise me if you end up having quite a few years in the big leagues and hit .270 and pop a lot of home runs.' Again, the light bulb went on, 'God, wouldn't that be great. I'm a rookie in Class-A ball and a mentor like that is saying those positive things to you. He's planting seeds and I didn't realize that at the time, but he planted a seed. Now, after the fact, after nine years of big leagues, I think my lifetime stats were .264, which would've been over .270 had I not had that first [full] year where I hit .188 with like 300 at-bats. So, he was very prophetic."

FIRST CALL UP/FIRST GAME/FIRST HOME RUN: September 3, 1971 as a member of the Twins vs. Oakland Athletics at Metropolitan Stadium

Soderholm started at third base and batted seventh. He hit his first major league home run in his second at-bat in the fourth inning off A's pitcher Diego Segui.

"I was in Triple-A and the manager called me into the office and just said, they want you up in the big leagues. Harmon Killebrew hurt his knee and they wanna move him to first base. Here's another very lucky aspect of my life. I mean you're in the minor leagues playing shortstop but then as I move through the minor leagues, they moved me to third base. I got a little bigger and stronger. Third base guy named Harmon Killebrew was playing for the Twins. So, it's like you can get buried very quickly in the minor leagues for a long time. Then I just got the call. He hurt his knee and they wanna move him to first base so they wanna call you up. It really caught me off guard. I went up, I wasn't quite ready mentally. Physically, I was but mentally I wasn't ready for the big leagues. Didn't put my pants on the same way as those guys did. It showed, I hit .188, but I showed potential. Pretty good defensive player also and showed some pop in my bat. So they just stuck with me. The next thing I know, the light switch went on and I was there quite a few years.

"Being scared to death, obviously you're very nervous about your first game. I remember it was I believe, Diego Segui. He gave a high fastball and I was a fastball hitter. I think it was my second at-bat, not my first. Home run on your second at-bat, I mean how else can you feel, but totally exhilarated. As I'm running the bases, I didn't feel like my feet was even touching the ground. You're just so excited. You're in that euphoric state of 'Wow.' That was my first home run in the big leagues and it happened to be my first game. So a lot of good things happened."

FIRST TIME HE SAW HIMSELF ON A BASEBALL CARD:

"When I was a kid, we used to have all the baseball cards. I wish I had 'em now, frankly, 'cause they're all worth a lot of money, but you'd have Mantle and Maris baseball cards. Then you'd put 'em on the floor. We had a screened-in porch and we'd take a ping pong ball and we would pitch [to] each other and then take a cigar box top and that would be the bat. We would hit and if it hit up the screen a certain level, it was a double, then triple and a home run. I remember using a lot of baseball cards for that game and then using cards in the spoke wheel of your bike to make the fluttering sound and stuff. What an idiot because all those cards worth so much money now. When I saw my rookie card, it's a good feeling. There's no question about it, but I don't know if I even had a moment where, 'Oh my God, that's my first baseball card.'"

FIRST TIME HE MADE THE FINAL OUT IN A NO-HITTER: September 28, 1974 vs. California Angels at Anaheim Stadium

Soderholm struck out to end Nolan Ryan's third career no-hitter.

"I did not want to be the final out. One of the top five highlights of my career was I hit two home runs off Nolan Ryan, one of the games I drove in three runs and we beat him, 3–2. So there's not a lot of guys on the planet that can say they hit two home runs off of Nolan Ryan. With that said, I was the last out in one of his no hitters. You just don't wanna be that. I think I fouled off, I want to say six or seven or eight balls. I hung in there as hard as I could and then he got me. He was something, man, back in the seventies, you got a guy throwing a hundred. Now it's pretty standard. You know, guys throw 95, a hundred miles an hour. You know how fast that gets on you. I better start my swing before he lets go of the ball. It was that kind of mentality so, yeah, he was one. There's no question in my mind, he was the best pitcher during my era as a player."

FIRST FORAY INTO FREE AGENCY:

Soderholm missed the entire 1976 season due to a knee injury and signed as a free agent with the Chicago White Sox for the 1977 season.

"[White Sox owner] Bill Veeck had a soft spot in his heart for guys that were trying to come back from something 'cause he felt they would be motivated to prove that they still could do it. So, he picked up guys like Richie Zisk who was coming out of Pittsburgh and he was having some injury issues. Alan Bannister, shortstop has rotor cuff surgery. So were like in '77, like the Bad News Bears. It's hard to describe what happened but we jelled and that thing called chemistry. If you could figure out how to get that, you'd make a gazillion dollars. It just worked. We just all seemed like we had something to prove. Ralph Garr came over from Atlanta when his career seemed to be declining. He wanted to show that he could still play. The only really legitimate, solid all-around player that we had, I thought was Chet Lemon in center field. He could cover left center [and] right. He could cover the whole place plus he had speed. He was a great hitter. In my mind, he was the only real solid five-star athlete that we had on the team. The rest of us were just good at parts of the game."

FIRST AMERICAN LEAGUE GAME IN CANADA: April 7, 1977 as a member of the Chicago White Sox vs. Toronto Blue Jays at Exhibition Stadium.

Soderholm went 2-for-5 in the first AL game ever played in Canada.

"I couldn't believe we were playing. I mean, it was literally a snowstorm. It was so cold and when you caught the ball, it'd sting your hand. Doug Ault hit a line drive at me at third base that game. I remember catching it, but, oh my God, my hand hurt for two innings after that. It was just like hitting a brick, my hand was like frozen. Quite honestly, we couldn't wait. We couldn't believe we were playing in the snowstorm, number one and number two, we couldn't wait for the game to end but they wanted to get it in 'cause it was Opening [Day] I think. It was rather crazy."

"They had a couple of situations like that. [Owner] Calvin Griffith on the Twins had a bat night. He gave everybody a bat that came to the stadium, 50,000 people. It was sold out and it rained all day from morning till night. At game time, there was a slight weather break where it was gonna start up again. We had a break of about two hours they thought and he made us play. There was like less than a thousand people in the stands that showed up. They all thought the game was gonna be canceled, but he had made so much money because he had sold out the park with his bat night and he made us play. I remember rounding third base trying to score. I literally slipped coming around this base and almost slid into the dugout, so I was out by a mile. I got in big trouble. The reporters asked me after the game some questions and I quite honestly [said] I can't believe we're even playing this game. I hope, and this was a dumb mistake, I hope Calvin chokes on the money that he made tonight. That did not go over well so that was the beginning of the end for me with Twins, but the problem was Calvin Griffith."

FIRST IMPRESSION OF BEING TRADED TO THE YANKEES:

After being traded by the White Sox to the Texas Rangers during the 1979 season, Soderholm was dealt to the Yankees after the season.

"Texas, there was some talk in the papers about that, that we needed pitching and that Soderholm had a little value, so there was some talk about it. I was hoping that it wouldn't happen, although the magic of the '77 Southside Hitmen team was gone. Now Zisk left and [Oscar] Gamble left. I kind of felt like I was left holding the bag, so I was upset when the guys left. When they announced that I was being traded to Texas, I said that where Zisk and Gamble are so maybe we could recreate the Southside Hitmen in Texas now. I was sad because Chicago had become a home for me, a place where I was well liked. Chicago always felt like home to me."

"When I was in Texas, I was there for just like three months and did pretty well with them. They offered me a three-year deal, $200,000 a year for three years. So it was my biggest contract ever. They offered me to stay but when I got traded down there, it was the first day of 14 straight days of over a 100-degree temperature. I lost like seven, eight pounds in the first week playing down there. It was so hot, so my wife was miserable, our kids were miserable. Ed Farmer, I took his house, he took my house. That's who I got traded for, so we just swapped houses. I wasn't happy because the heat was just unbearable. You're used to playing in Chicago, it's a little different temperatures. So I rejected the offer, then they traded me to the Yankees.

"How many people can say they had an opportunity to play on the

New York Yankees? That is quite a nice little thing on your resume. Yankees was a whole different experience and thank God I was a little more mature by that time. You walked into that locker room, it was just a locker room of huge egos. I guess that's helped them win all the time. Reggie Jackson had 399 home runs and he was hitting fourth in the lineup and I was hitting fifth and he banged out his 400th home run, a line drive to right center field and the place is packed and it erupts and goes crazy. I'm the first guy to meet him at home plate. You know, just shake the guy's hand. I embrace him and I hugged him and we're kinda like jumping up and down at home plate for a few seconds. A photographer from one of the papers down the right field line took a snapshot. In this paper is said, 'Reggie hits 400 home run' at the top and in the small captions underneath and 'Received kiss at home plate from Eric Soderholm.' It looked like the angle he took the pictures, I was sticking my tongue right in his mouth. I was hot about that man. I just thought that was totally irresponsible. The next day I'm screaming and yelling at the reporter and kind of raising hell with the guy. Reggie signals to me, come on over. He puts his arm around me walking a little bit away from everybody. He says, 'Kid, you're on the Yankees, now you gotta remember it's not whether it's good publicity or bad publicity. Just make sure they spell your name right.' That hit me like, oh wow, this is the Bronx Zoo. It's a whole different game in the New York area for sure."

FIRST YANKEES MANAGER: Dick Howser

"I love the man because in spring training he would take each person individually into his office and have a heart-to-heart talk with him about how he was seeing how he was going to use me during the season. He said, 'Eric, listen, I know you like playing third base but we got a guy named Graig Nettles so you're not gonna get much playing time at third, so I'm going to use you as a DH against left-handed pitching. So be mentally prepared when you know a left-handed pitcher is gonna pitch and then [when a right-hander is going to pitch] I'm gonna use you as a pinch-hitter late in the game when they bring in left-handers. So, I'm giving you a little heads up and don't even worry about playing third base.' Well, that was good advice and I was always mentally prepared and I think I did pretty well with the Yankees for the limited time I had. Dick was a great manager that got pushed around by George Steinbrenner. I mean there was a red phone in the dugout that was directly linked to George's suite behind home plate. The phone would ring and one time I heard Dick say, 'George, you hired me to manage the team. Let me just manage the team,' and he hung up the phone on George. I remember seeing that and I was like, oh, wow. Dick, I thought, was a great manager, a great communicator. We won [103] games that year. He was one of my favorite managers only because he had a great personality. He was well liked by the players and the fans. Just dealing with George Steinbrenner during those years. It was so stressful for him."

FIRST REACTION TO PUTTING ON THE PINSTRIPES:

"I think the song that kind of came over me subconsciously was, I guess I've made it. I mean, come on, how many people get to play on the New York Yankees and get to play with guys like Reggie Jackson and Lou Piniella and Ron Guidry and all these great players. It's kind of similar to the first time walking in the Twins' room, but now I was more established as a player and I was able to handle that kind of pressure. Playing on the Yankees is a lot of pressure. It's a whole different ballgame, especially when you got an owner like George Steinbrenner.

"I remember one time. Nettles, I think caught hepatitis. Dick Howser comes up to me and said, 'Eric, I'm sorry to tell you this but he's got hepatitis and he's gonna be out. I'm gonna need you to play third base, so grab your glove and start taking some ground balls. I'd play around a little bit, but I didn't take anything serious 'cause I knew Graig was there and I was not gonna probably get much playing time at third base. So I took a bunch of ground balls and the first game back was in Baltimore and were
battling Baltimore at the time and I made two errors in my first game. Oh my God, George Steinbrenner just ripped me. He goes out, literally within a couple of days and gets Aurelio Rodriguez from Detroit. He has Dick put him at third base and I returned to

my DH job after he got him. I got a chance to play third base, maybe one or two games and then George had seen enough but I hadn't played third base for four months so I was just rusty. It's not that I couldn't play, but George was very impatient and he wanted to win right now. If you weren't gonna be a part of that, then he'd get rid of you. He didn't really get rid of me so he ripped my pretty good in the paper. At the end of the season, I think against Cleveland, I hit a big shot in left center field that drove in three runs and we win. He sends me down a hundred-ounce bottle of champagne, one of those big green bottles. Filled with champagne with a note on it, 'I apologize. GMS.' He wouldn't apologize in the paper for all the things he said."

FIRST YANKEES HOME OPENER:

"There's no question that Yankee Stadium has a mystique about it and it's an energetic mystique. It's like you almost walk into that stadium feeling the energetic vibrations of Babe Ruth and Lou Gehrig and all these great players that the Yankees had over the years. It's palpable. You literally can feel it in your soul, if you will. Even as a visiting player coming into the stadium, you could feel it. You feel it more obviously when you are a Yankee coming into the stadium, but there's a mystique about the aura of the Yankees. The Yankee phenomena, it's like the top of the top."

FIRST GRAND SLAM AS A YANKEE: September 26, 1980 vs. Detroit Tigers at Tiger Stadium

In the third inning of a scoreless game, Soderholm hit his first Yankees grand slam off Tigers pitcher Dan Schatzeder. It was the third and final grand slam of his career.

"It was my hundredth home run. I didn't even know that until somebody got me the ball. I think I hit 102 in the big leagues. So I didn't know it at the time, but that was a monumental home run cause it was my hundredth and it was a grand slam. How many people hit a hundred home runs in the big leagues? I mean, there a lot that do. Obviously, a lot more than a hundred home runs but there's a whole lot of people that don't."

FIRST POSTSEASON EXPERIENCE: 1980 American League Championship Series vs. Kansas City Royals

Soderholm served as the DH in two games and went 1-for-6 as the Royals swept the three-game series.

"I mean I was on the Twins with Killebrew and Carew and those guys and we'd always finish second to the Oakland A's. Oakland was a very powerful team back then and we would always finish second. So I never got a chance to feel the pressure of the playoffs. With the Yankees winning [over 100] games, we thought, at least from my perspective, that we were the best team in either league by far. That just shows you in sports that the best teams don't always win. I mean, on any given day, anybody can win or lose. It was exciting, exhilarating. You could feel the energy in the place was at its highest level but then it was like a balloon getting deflated. George Brett comes out in the first game, hits a home run. I think he hit three home runs that series. I could be wrong [Brett hit two] but I want to say he singlehandedly just beat us. I still think we were the better team. On any given day, you can lose in anything you do. So, it's a lot about momentum in sports. You catch that momentum and you just ride that wave. We got the momentum kind of fizzled very quickly when he started getting real hot during that series. He was a one-man wrecking crew that year. He was one of the best players I've ever seen. George Brett, in my opinion, he could do it all. He was one of the best players I ever played against."

Eric Soderholm by Mark Springer

24
SHANE SPENCER

Outfielder Shane Spencer spent the first five seasons of his seven-year major league career with the Yankees. Spencer was recalled in August 1998 after playing six games earlier in the season and set a then rookie record for grand slams in a season with three. All three of those slams came in the month of September. Spencer is also known for launching the throw that led to Derek Jeter's "flip play" in Game 3 of the 2001 American League Division Series against the Oakland A's. Spencer hit a home run in each of his first two career postseason games and was part of two championship teams (in 1998 and 1999).

FIRST DRAFT EXPERIENCE:

Spencer was chosen by the Yankees in the 28th round of the 1990 June Amateur Draft out of Granite Hills High School in El Cajon, California.

"I had never even thought about baseball. It was all about football. Ever since like young age in Pop Warner, it was all about football. I thought I was gonna play in the NFL and that was my goal. My junior year at baseball, Brian Giles got drafted. I got to see he is a great player and I got to see how he did things. I got drafted kind of late because I was gonna go play football and it was the Yankees. I hated the Yankees 'cause I'm a Padre guy. Tony Gwynn all the way and I was like, 'Why the Yankees? When you start thinking about it, it's like, okay if you're gonna get drafted by somebody, either like the Yankees or Dodgers, two teams I hate. After negotiations, I thought more about the longevity about sports and career and I chose baseball and it was a long, hard road for me.

"I knew I was being scouted. I mean, you always see scouts in the area that I'm in for baseball in San Diego. Obviously, it's a powerhouse. [Scout] Tim Schmidt, when he actually contacted me, he said, 'Hey, this is Tim, familiar with the Yankees? We're just interested if you're interested in playing baseball.' I was like, the Yankees, okay, whatever. Then he came to me and I met him and I talked to him. I said, 'Why are you even looking at me?' He goes, the Yankees draft athletes. That's what they do. I think there's only a few teams at the time that are doing stuff like that. They would draft athletes and have a bigger staff to try and groom into baseball players and that's what happened."

FIRST IMPRESSIONS OF DEREK JETER, ANDY PETTITTE, AND MARIANO RIVERA:

Spencer came up through the Yankees minor league system with three notable players who went on to play on multi-championship teams.

"Of those guys I came up with, Mariano was special, Andy Pettitte was special. Jeter, you could see the talent, he was just so raw. He's obviously a superior athlete. That was one of the good things about coming up with the Yankees was that even the coaches never ever talked about this is what you gotta do to get to the big leagues. It was always about how can we get better that day? That's kind of how I teach now."

FIRST TIME HE SERVED AS A REPLACEMENT PLAYER:

The 1994 strike carried over into the next year's spring training.

At the time, minor leaguers were brought in as replacement players. Spencer and four other players were replacement players which was a tough decision for a 23-year-old who was trying to make it to the big leagues.

"Actually, I had no choice. They asked me before Christmas in the offseason. I said, no. They asked me before spring training. I said, no. They asked me during spring training, I said no. Towards the end of spring training, they told me they're gonna release me if I don't go. So I wasn't even represented. The players' union really wasn't prepared for something like that. Those other guys crossed way before me. I was forced to cross. It ended up working out for me, but I never once was going to do it. I don't even know who Buck Showalter was. When I got to the big leagues, I had to sit down on a plane with like Chili Davis, David Cone, Jeff Nelson, David Wells. Those guys, Bernie Williams and I had to tell my story. You almost get down in tears because you got these guys, your teammates, they look down on you because you did something, but they don't realize really what happened. I never crossed, I was forced to and it was like for a few days only. It is what it is, I can't change it. I talk about it all the time. I do speeches with people and tell 'em, I tell young players, tell 'em like listen, I'm all for the union. I'm all for it. Even though I'm not part of it. I'm 100 percent behind the union. They do the right thing and what happened to me, I have no problems with it."

On mending ways with his teammates:

"I think everybody's a little bit different. I'm really good friends with Jeff Nelson now. I would think he was the hardest on me. He was a firm believer of what the union was about and he was really hard on me. I wouldn't say he was a jerk or nothing. He wasn't like part of his group and I totally accept that. Now we're really good friends. I'm like, 'Listen, I'm here to play baseball. I didn't have anything to do with what happened. Let me prove it. I'm a good teammate. I'm a good clubhouse guy.' Then, everything's good after that, but you can feel the tension. There's no doubt about it. There's tension and it hurts as a player because even though you didn't do anything wrong, but it does hurt. It really does."

FIRST TIME HE REALIZED HE COULD HIT FOR POWER:

After hitting a total of 39 home runs in his first six minor league seasons, Spencer hit 32 home runs with 95 RBIs for two teams, Double-A Norwich and Triple-A Columbus in 1996.

"I was starting to hit the ball good. I've always hit the off-speed pitches good. Obviously, nobody can hit a slider down and away. It doesn't matter what the reports say. Nobody hits the slider down and away, if you swing at it or not. When I got MVP of the Florida State League, the first year I got to play from day one. I was a starter from day one. That's what they told me. [I]f you do good, then we're gonna keep you. If you don't do good, we're gonna release you. I'm like, wait a minute. I get to play every day from day one and they're like, yeah, but if you don't do good. I'm like, no, no, I don't care about that. I get to play every day, that's awesome. When I went to Double A, Darrell Evans was my hitting coach and most of the hitters there did not care for him, but Darrell was a pull hitter and I was a pull hitter but he actually taught me how to straighten the ball out instead of hooking it, topspin hook, whatever. It was a hard process but when it clicked, all of a sudden all those doubles or foul ball home runs, they started straightening out. That's when the home runs came. I always squared the ball up. I just never could keep it straight. So, Darrell Evans had a lot to do with that. A couple other hitting coaches taught me how to stay through the ball in the zone. That's when I started going right center a little more, which is oppo for me, which was crazy. Then everything was fine after that. So it was a long process. I wasn't like, I just came out of my mom's womb and started hitting so it was very hard for me.

"[In] '97, I didn't get called up [for] the playoffs because they told me I couldn't hit for average. It was the best year I ever had hitting the ball. I just could not get a single. I'd line out to center like twice a game. [Minor league coordinator] Mark Newman even called me at the All-Star break. He goes, 'You're hitting .202, what's wrong?' Like, 'Mark, I can't hit a single, I'm sorry.' He goes, 'Well, .202 is not working.' I said, 'Mark, I can't get a single. What do you want me to do? I'm hitting line drives to center field. What do you want me to do?' And he's like, 'Well, it's not working.' Well, I ended up hitting like .300 the second half of the season, but they didn't call me up because of that. I said, 'Okay, I'm gonna go play winter ball and I'm gonna prove to them that I can hit .300.' I went down there and just kind if played pepper with the ball and it ended up being a great thing for me 'cause I actually learned how to use the bat the right way. Then I went to spring training and it was great. The whole year was phenomenal."

FIRST ROOKIE RECORD:

Spencer was promoted to the Yankees in August 1998 and set a rookie record by hitting three grand slams, all in September. The record has since been broken by the Chicago White Sox' Alexei Ramirez in 2008.

"Looking back on it, I think it's kind of ridiculous. At the time, it really wasn't that big of a deal. I was doing it in Triple A. I was having a great year in Triple A. We were raking. Then you go up to the big leagues and they're [the 1998 Yankees] killing people and I'm in the lineup and I have Scott Brosius, who's hitting .290 or something, ton of RBIs behind me. Like, who you gonna pitch to? It's like I got pretty good pitches to hit. You still have to hit 'em but I did and I was locked in and I hit 'em. Trust me, they make adjustments and when you don't play all the time, you look like a fool like I did the next year. People are like, 'How did you do that?' I probably got better pitches than a lot of guys did, it comes down to that. There's no false advertisement about it, but I was hitting the ball. The ball did look like a beach ball, it was pretty sick."

FIRST TIME DEALING WITH SUCCESS:

"When I look back on it now, the one thing I regret and the only thing I regret is not being prepared that off season. I did a lot of signing. Everybody on that team was flying back to New York, wherever you're at. I'm coming from San Diego every other weekend. I'm flying to New York to do signings and you get caught up in it. I don't think you get locked into your training. I feel like when I went to spring training [in 1999], I was behind and didn't click towards the end of the spring training. Then, I just didn't play that much. Really, I didn't. I was just like a spot starter and I don't know why. I just didn't get to play that much and it showed. I was actually a little miffed about it."

FIRST POSTSEASON EXPERIENCE: 1998

Spencer played in two World Series (1998, 2001) with the Yankees and was on two championship teams.

"Obviously, from San Diego. My first year, my rookie year I played against the Padres. Tony Gwynn's my idol. I caught a ball off his first at-bat. I think it was Game 3. It was only the second out and I didn't wanna throw it back. I just wanna put in my pocket. This is the greatest moment of my life. I was so pumped up that I had to throw the ball back in. So I was very disappointed. Then, watching Arizona beat us [in 2001], which sucked, but that whole 9-11 year was very tough on everybody. To see [Curt] Schilling and [Randy] Johnson, you see these guys and they win. Yes, it sucks walking in from right field, the last out of the year and see them celebrating. That sticks in my mind, like that's what it's all about. These guys have waited their whole life to do this and I got to do it three years in a row. It sucks to lose, but those two moments really stick out to me."

You Never Forget Your First: A Collection of New York Yankees Firsts

Shane Spencer by Maz Adams

25
NICK SWISHER

Popular outfielder/first baseman Nick Swisher played four seasons for the Yankees. Swisher, who was a member of the 2009 world championship team and was an All-Star in 2010, was a fan favorite during his time thanks to his wide smile and outgoing personality. The switch-hitter works in the Yankees front office as a special advisor to general manager Brian Cashman.

FIRST BASEBALL GAME HE ATTENDED AS A KID:

"I was five years old, 1986. Waterloo, Iowa, Single A for the Cleveland Indians. I just remember that being my first game. I remember walking out onto the field for the first time as a five-year-old 'cause most kids, you know, during the summer they were playing T-ball or some sort of organized sport. For myself, I was with my dad [Steve] for the summers. He was coaching in the minor leagues, whether it was with the Cleveland Indians, now the Cleveland Guardians, the New York Mets as well, so for myself, I grew up in the minor leagues. I have such fond memories of those times. The first ever game that I can recall had to have been 1986, Waterloo, Iowa. The Waterloo Indians, I'll never forget it."

FIRST BASEBALL IDOL:

"Obviously having a father that played in the big leagues, was an All-Star, was able to accomplish the things you always dreamed of doing. It's easy to be able to have somebody like that as your here and your idol. Also, the fact that my father is as good of a man as he is, always makes it that much easier to love him as much as anybody. Now, as I got older in my life, other players started to come in but my dad was definitely always number. A very close second behind him was the late, great Roberto Clemente. I was never able to see him play but the stories I read and just the knowledge that I gained from reading books and the fact that this man lost his life trying to help others was something that always hit me in the right spot. Since then, I've been able to become friends with the Clemente family, which is like a dream come true for me. To be able to have, in my mind, two of the greatest human being ever created in my father, Steve Swisher, and Roberto Clemente as my favorite players. I think I'm doing pretty good right now."

FIRST COLLEGE EXPERIENCE:

Swisher was undrafted out of high school so he went to Ohio State and played on the baseball team for coach Bob Todd. In 2000, Swisher was named Big Ten Freshman of the Year.

"It was awesome. Probably the first bit of adversity that I dealt with on the sports field had to have been right there after my senior year. When I thought to myself [that] I had the opportunity to get drafted, I thought there was a chance that I'd be drafted into the big leagues. I didn't wanna have to go to college. Not that it's the best thing to be telling people, but school wasn't really my thing. It's hard as hell for me to sit down and take a 45-minute test. I mean, I didn't have a whole lot of opportunities but I could not have asked for a better opportunity for myself. Columbus [Ohio] is an absolutely amazing place. You just learn so much. It's funny. Being a Yankee, now I understand all the things that George Steinbrenner did for the city of Columbus and Ohio State University himself. So there is that correlation between the two which I knew extremely early. I'll just never forget, just going out there and saying, 'You know what? Like, this my time to shine. This is my time to prove to people that I'm better than what everybody's seen. To be able to have that opportunity to start as a freshman is something that doesn't happen a whole lot.

"I've known Coach Todd since I was in elementary school. Him and his daughter, we were best friends all the way up through elementary school. So you never know what's gonna happen, but to be able to get that opportunity to start and play as a freshman, I just knew to myself, 'Man, I better make the most of this opportunity because I don't know how many opportunities I'm gonna get.' People think they're gonna get opportunity after opportunity after opportunity. That's not the case. This world is so cutthroat and sports are so cutthroat. If you don't get it done, there's gonna be somebody right behind you that's coming for your job each and every year. I guess that's kind of one thing you just continue to keep pushing me. Wanting to be a major league baseball player as well. For myself, that's where my chip was built, was when I went to college and my freshman, sophomore, junior year, that chip just kept getting bigger because, in my mind, I had to prove to people that I was good enough to play at the next level. People hadn't seen it and I wanted to make sure that they were able to see that. So I just worked my absolute tail off, had the best time in college, was lucky enough to be around some great coaches, some great mentors. To always be able to have Steve Swisher, my father, in my back pocket at all times is definitely something that I think was definitely an added advantage for me in my career. It's always easier to listen to somebody who's been there and done that rather than no one who's ever been there at all."

FIRST EXPERIENCE IN THE CAPE COD LEAGUE:

In 2000, Swisher played for the Wareham Gatemen of the Cape Cod Baseball League, a well renowned summer league where a number of future major leaguers played.

"Awesome, I was in charge of keeping the field clean. Me and my buddy, Brian, who was a catcher on that squad that year. We were in charge of keeping the field clean. Those outfield lines could not have been straighter. I mean, it was so perfect. The general manager, Mr. [John] Wylde was still there. R-I-P to him. He was so great for the Gatemen. [He] announced the games as well as did everything on and off the field for that organization.

"To be able to go and play with some of the best college players in the country, that in my mind was definitely an eye-opening experience that was right after my freshman year. That was like, 'Wow, I got a lot of work to do, man, because there's a lot of great players around me.' Being able to know those guys and to learn from those guys. I've always been kind of attracted to players that are better than me. I've always kind of leaned my way towards those guys 'cause I wanted to ask them questions. I wanted to learn from them. I feel like in this world, you're only gonna get better from the people who are better than you and you can learn from them and their experiences and they can teach you things that you don't know about. I've always been kind of drawn to those guys, even as a young rookie. I'm always talking with the veterans. I'm always asking those guys questions because they're better than me and they have been part of experiences that I haven't. So, for myself to be able to be on that squad, it was great. Coach [Mike] Roberts, the father of Brian Roberts, a Yankee there for a hot minute, had an unbelievable major league career. Switch-hitter, electric on the base paths, in the field. It was nice to be able to learn from coach. He taught me a lot of things that helped me further my career as well."

FIRST DRAFT EXPERIENCE:

Swisher was a first-round pick, 16th overall, of the Oakland Athletics in the 2002 Major League Baseball June Amateur Draft.

"The night before the draft, we didn't have the internet at the house. We didn't have none of that stuff. We just had the home lines, no cell phones. None of that stuff in the house, so I'll never forget being on the phone with my advisor before the draft, his name was Joe Bick, and remember having the conversation like, Hey, we're still trying to figure out where they think you're gonna go, blah, blah, blah. This is such an amazing time, so excited for you. We got a phone call late that night and I'll never forget Joe Bick saying, 'Hey, talked to [A's GM] Billy Beane. If you're around for pick number 16, they're picking you 16th.' I said, 'Overall!' and he said, 'Yes, 16th pick overall.' At that moment right there, you don't know what to do because it's almost like you've worked your whole life up to this moment right here. You know this is only the beginning, but you also have to get that phone call to be able to continue the journey. To be able to get that phone call from Joe Bick at the time, I still didn't quite believe it, even though my heart is racing a thousand beats a minute.

"I'll never forget the next day the draft comes up. We knew what time it started but we didn't know exactly when we were gonna get a phone call. We're all around my kitchen table at the house on Washington Avenue in Parkersburg, West Virginia. It was my dad, my stepmom was there, my grandparents were there at the time. We're all just kind of waiting to get the phone call. Well, phone call didn't come for a minute. So, we're like, what's happening? Then everybody starts leaving. The next thing I know, I'm at the kitchen table by myself, the phone rings. I answer it, it's Billy Beane. Billy Beane's like, 'Nick, we could not be more blessed to have you. Congratulations, we drafted you 16th overall to the Oakland A's.' I'm like, 'You know, Mr. Beane, I can't thank you enough for this opportunity. I'm so grateful. I can't wait to get there, to get to camp,' the whole nine. Hang up the phone. I'm yelling, I'm screaming. All of a sudden, my dad comes flying down the stairs. He's in nothing but a towel, he was up taking a shower. We like chest bump in the kitchen. It was just a crazy, emotional time. I couldn't even see that from my father's side. You could imagine just having a child that's absolutely just walking in the footsteps of what you're doing and what you already did. I think we're like the fifth or the sixth ever father-son combination to be drafted in the first round, which is something that my father and I hold near and dear to our hearts. Both first rounders, both played in an All-Star Game. Both played for Team USA, a lot of amazing things that I couldn't share with anybody else in the world, other than him. This guy has been by my side from the get go. To be able to have somebody like that in your life, you're pretty blessed to be able to have that."

FIRST PROFESSIONAL EXPERIENCE:

Swisher made his pro debut with the Vancouver Canadians of the short season, Northwest League. One of his teammates at Vancouver was Nelson Cruz, who was entering his 19th major league season in 2023.

"First time I ever ran into Nellie Cruz was in the locker room over there in Vancouver. I hadn't traveled a whole lot up until that point in my life. I lived right there in the Midwest, dude, you know, Ohio, West Virginia. That was kind of pretty much, other than the trip down south to play in Florida with the college team. I'm not really doing a whole lot of traveling outside of that. So all of a sudden they send me to Vancouver, Canada. I'm like, bro, that's like eight million miles away is what it feels like, but to be able to have that opportunity, man and just to continue to keep the journey going. That was like the first moment where you're like, Wow, you're on the road, you're on your own."

FIRST SPRING TRAINING: 2003 with the Oakland A's.

"Come winter time, December, January, back in 2002, 2003, it's snowing where I am. Nobody wants to be there in the winter. Spring training starts up in Scottsdale, Arizona. I'll never forget my grandfather would always have his birthday on January fourth and right after that was when I would head to camp because I could get outside, I could be around the coaches, I could meet the players, I could familiarize myself with the organization, even though it cost me a little extra money to go get an apartment for an extra month. At the end of the day, it was totally worth it because that's why I got my first call up to a big league spring training game because nobody else was there. I was one of the only guys that was there early and they didn't have a choice other than to pick me to go to the games, which ended up working out great. Sometimes you just gotta be in the right place at the right time, but if you're not there, nobody can pick you to go. That's some of the things that I tell my players now, especially with the Yankees. All of a sudden, we've got guys that are here already like the [Anthony] Volpes of the world are here, the Austin Wells [is] here. Jasson Dominguez is right around the corner showing up. It's like we're getting these kids showing up earlier and earlier every year.

"For myself, I'll never forget that first game. I had to play center field. We were playing the Rangers. I forgot where, but it was a long drive, dude. I'll just never forget. I had Terrence Long in left field, I had Ron Gant in right field. You remember Ron Gant, bro, with like huge pipes, dude, you know Miguel Tejada, Eric Chavez. I'm just looking around the field like, 'What am I doing here, man? Like what is happening?' I was a hundred miles an hour all the time. I was so out of control but it was just one of those things where my emotions got so much the best of me because this is where you want to be. I'll just never forget just enjoying every single moment of that.

"I've got a great story behind that. It's the first big league spring training game and I go up for my first at-bat. I'm so nervous. I feel like I'm shaking all over the place and I take three pitches right down the middle of the plate, dude, strike three, no swings, no nothing. Just looked at the first three pitches and started walking back to the dugout. Ron Washington, my father gave Wash his first coaching job in minor league baseball back in the day which was awesome. So I've known Wash ever since I was a little kid. Wash looks at me in the face and he goes, 'Damn, I've haven't seen a motherfucker get a hit with his bat on his shoulder.' I just froze out there. I didn't even know what I was doing, but Wash always knew how to get the best outta me, man. He always knew how to hit me in the right spot. From there, things started to loosen up. Made a great play in the outfield that game. Got a call up maybe like three or four days later and just enjoyed every second of it. I always remember getting that first time to go to the big leagues was only because I was there. It wasn't because I was the best player. It wasn't because I was the top prospect. It just happened to be because I was there. Sometimes all you gotta do is show up and good things happen."

FIRST CALL UP TO THE MAJORS:

Swisher was playing for the A's Triple-A affiliate in Sacramento when he was a September call-up by the A's in 2004.

"I was on a streak. I think I hit like 10 homers in 11 days. Something crazy like that. I was on fire and I'll never forget, man. We're in Tacoma, Washington. I got to the ballpark around 11:30 that day for a seven o'clock game. What else am I gonna do in Tacoma. There ain't a whole lot of things to do, right? So, I'm a gym rat, love being at the ballpark, just love being there. I think that my locker wasn't exactly as clean as I wanted to have it the night before, so I made sure I got to the ballpark before anybody else to make sure I could clean it up. I always thought that was like a huge reflection of me, because if you walk by my locker when I wasn't there, I wanted you to know like, 'Wow, man, that guy, that kids got it together.'

"We're sitting there and all of a sudden, Tony DeFrancesco, who was our manager, walks in the locker room. This is maybe like, 12:15, 12:30. He walks by me and I'm like, 'Yo, hey, what's up, skip?' He's like, 'Hey, how you doing, Swish?' About five minutes later, he goes, 'Hey, Swish, hey you got a second? Can I talk to you?' 'No doubt, Tony D baby, you got it man, what's up?' He's like, 'You know, tomorrow night, Oakland, they're facing Ted Lilly. You think you can hit Ted Lilly? You know, he's really similar to the guy we're facing tonight. What do you think? Kind of like changes speeds on the left side. Nothing overpowering, throws strikes, really utilizes the change up properly. Don't start looking out over the plate, man, and he'll run one up in 'ya.' I said, 'Skip, man, I don't know, bro, but I'd give him a hell of an A-B.' It got quiet for about three or four seconds and he said, 'That's good. That's really, really good. I'm glad to hear that 'cause you're gonna get your opportunity tomorrow night.' I could almost cry right now thinking about the emotions, because once again, it's another rung in the ladder. I'm like, 'Hey man, don't fuck with me, dude. Is this real or not?' He was like, 'No, you're leaving, your flight's later this evening. You can't play tonight's game but you're flying up and you'll be with the team tomorrow.' We're in Seattle, I gotta go all the way across, all the way over to Toronto is where I ended up meeting the team. I go flying out of the locker room. I think I just had a pair of shorts on, I'm like standing out in the parking lot. I'm trying to call everybody I can get a hold of, right? Trying to call my dad, my grandma. Those are the first two people that came to mind. Nobody's answering their phone. I'm like, this is the most important phone call of my life up to this moment and nobody's there to answer the phone. I totally forgot my father had a speaking engagement in Parkersburg that evening. My mom didn't answer the phone. I'm like, dude, I don't even know what's happening. I don't even know who to share this news with. Finally, maybe like half an hour later, my grandma calls. She's like, 'Nick, are you okay?' [In an excited tone] 'Grandma, I'm better than okay. I'm going to the big leagues.' It was just like an emotional moment for all of us. I've always had such a tight-knit family. I think I've been very blessed to be able to have that, because in sports, man, when you're doing well, baby, everybody's cheering you, and when you're not, you're down in the dumps. So to be able to have that rock, that family that was always there for me. To be able to share that moment with them at that time, 'cause I couldn't have done it by myself. To be able to share that moment with them, man, was something I'll never forget."

FIRST GAME: September 3, 2004 as a member of the A's vs. Toronto Blue Jays at SkyDome

"I remember my first a-b. I can almost tell you pitch for pitch. Walked on a 3-2 change up away. I'll never forget it 'cause that was kind of my thing, right? I was an on-base guy, that was kind where the whole Moneyball aspect of it came into play. I was a guy that could get on base and kind of hit homers at the time. And the second at-bat. Got a 2-1 fastball down in the zone, ripped it into left-center for a double. I kept flying around first base and I slid into second and Orlando Hudson was the second baseman for the Blue Jays at that time. He slaps the tag down on me real quick and he says, only 2,999 more to go, kid. Grabbed the ball, threw it into our dugout. 'O-Dog,' if you're reading this, I love that guy, man. He made my first day in the big leagues something that was the most memorable experience and he was a veteran at the time. Those veteran guys are supposed to help the young players and that's exactly what he did for me in the moment, man. I don't think my feet hit the ground the entire time. I didn't even know my parents were coming. I forgot to leave tickets for them. They had to buy their own tickets to my first major league game 'cause I was just like so like crazed out. I had eight million things running through my mind. Totally forgot to leave them tickets.

FIRST HOME RUN: September 5, 2004 at SkyDome

Swisher's first big league home run, a two-run shot, came off of Blue Jays pitcher Sean Douglass in the sixth inning.

"You never forget your first. It's always just something that is just seared into your brain. Sean Douglass, 2-1 fastball, down and away, center field. I'm running around the bases trying to not absolutely just flash the biggest smile ever 'cause we're getting absolutely waxed that that point, so it wasn't like it had anything to do with the final result of the game, but it was my first home run.

"The coolest part of that first home run was for my entire life, I have always been locked and loaded with whatever grounds crew that I've been a part of. Whether it was in high school, whether it was in college, whether it was in the minor leagues. I've always been one of those guys that appreciated working on the field. Whether it was mowing the grass, I can mow the grass, drag the infield with the best of them. They haven't let me do that yet in the Bronx, but one of these days, they're gonna let me do it. I've always been super, super tight with those guys. Guess who ended up bringing me my home run ball. The head groundskeeper happened to be out in center field at that moment. The ball fell down in between the wall and underneath the stands and he was the one that came and brought me that baseball. How much karma is that? How crazy is that? That was definitely one of those things where you were like, 'Oh my gosh, this is really happening. I'm running around the bases at a major league game.' Like I only did this sort of video game before so to be able to do it in real life, it was just like, this is absolutely crazy."

FIRST TIME HE SAW HIMSELF ON A BASEBALL CARD:

"Hey, you're on your way. That was the only thing that really came into play because I've always heard the moment you get a bobblehead, that's when you've made it. Well, I never got a bobblehead until I got to the big leagues. I remember getting that first card and it's funny because it's typical me. The front of my card is I'm trying to be serious, but on the back of my card, it's like I have this huge laugh. I got two bats on my shoulder. It could not be more genuine. Me, on the front trying to put off this tough image, 'cause yeah, I'm here to compete, the whole nine, but in the back, just absolutely pinching myself, like I can't believe I have my own baseball card. I framed it. I think I have at least one baseball card or every one that came out throughout my career. To still be able to have that, like my daughter still has no idea what I did in my life. I think my youngest daughter thinks I was a firefighter for a minute but happy to be able to show, hopefully, my grandkids and my great grandkids."

FIRST TIME HE WAS TRADED:

In January 2008, Swisher was traded to the Chicago White Sox.

"[Two thousand eight] was a year for me, bro. It was probably one of the worst years that I've ever had in my career. On and off the field. I just signed my first contract with the Oakland A's, a long-term contract. I think it's a six-year deal and I'm thinking to myself, Oh my God, if I'm a homegrown kid, I'm gonna be like Cal Ripken. I'm gonna play for the Oakland A's like my entire life.

I bought a place right outside the city of Oakland. I bought a place in Scottsdale [Arizona]. Next thing you know, I get a phone call from Billy Beane saying, 'Nick, it's one of the hardest phone calls I've ever had to make. We're trading you to the Chicago White Sox.' It just felt like somebody just like stuck a knife in my back. It was just one of those things where that was a major understanding for me earlier in my career, how much of a business this was. Loyalty didn't really mean a whole lot from that point moving forward. All of a sudden, I had to sell those places."

"For Oakland, I was a corner outfielder, first baseman. White Sox, like, hey you're a center field now. All of sudden I change positions. I change spots in the lineup. All of a sudden there's just a lot of things that are going on in my head. Me and [White Sox manager] Ozzie Guillen might not see eye to eye throughout the season. It was tough, man, I just couldn't get myself going. I mean, you had to just take it on the chin."

FIRST REACTION TO BEING TRADED TO THE YANKEES:

Swisher was traded to the Yankees in November 2008.

"I'll just never forget the season ending, having a conversation with Kenny Williams, the [White Sox] general manager at that time. They were gonna go out there and shop the market and see if there'd be another team for me to play on. [Yankees GM] Brian Cashman calls. Out of all the things that could have happened in my life, no way did I ever think that the mighty, the evil empire, the New York Yankees, the Bronx Bombers would be the team that would say Nick, last year was a fluke. We know you're a way better player than that. Our metrics show that you were so, here were the percentages of how unlucky you were. Your batting average should have been this, your home run should have been this, the whole nine. He said, 'How would you like to be part of the New York Yankees?' I could have started crying that that moment right there. I was like, thank you so much, I'm gonna be the best player for you. I'm gonna give everything I have for you in this organization.' It's been such a blessing. Now Cash and I have like the greatest relationship. He's like a big brother to me.

"To get that phone call from someone like Brian Cashman, now all of a sudden, things turned around, bro. I came into camp in great shape. I was ready to go at that point. I was the starting first baseman for the New York Yankees until they signed 'Tex' [Mark Teixeira] for like a buck eighty. Then, I'm like, Oh my God, now I gotta go back to the outfield. Now I gotta fight in the outfield against guys like Xavier Nady who hit like .290 the year prior with 30 tanks [home runs]. I'm like, I'm never gonna play. This is outta control, right? Coming to camp and I'll never forget just kind of walking through the locker room and just looking up at all the lockers and seeing Derek Jeter and Mariano Rivera and Andy Pettitte and Alex Rodriguez and Jorge Posada, my guy, Robbie Cano, who I became best buddies with. These are the dudes. These are the GOATs. To be able to be part of all that. It's funny. Sometimes in life, when you think you're in a tough spot, you stress so much over it because you're just like, this is the worst moment because you're so in that moment. From some of the darkest moments of my life have come some of the brightest lights. 2009, I get traded to the New York Yankees. I meet my wife, I fall in love, we win a World Series."

FIRST TIME HE PITCHED IN A MAJOR LEAGUE GAME:

On April 13, 2009, Swisher pitched an inning against the Tampa Bay Rays at Tropicana Field. He also hit a home run and became the first Yankee to do both in a game since Lindy McDaniel in 1972.

"We're facing Scott Kazmir that game. I hit a home run early in the game. They take a commanding lead. It's like 15–5 in the eighth inning. It's top of the eighth inning and I'm sitting there. I think I was in the hole and I'm putting on. I was the wristband guy, dude, I got all the swag, dude, I got the chains. Takes me a minute to get all my gear on, you know? So I'm sitting there and I'm getting ready for my next at-bat. All of a sudden, you know [the] skip at the time, Joe Girardi, man, he was stressed, bro. He's kinda pacing around a little bit and all of a sudden, he turns around and looks at me and he goes, 'Have you ever pitched?' I'm like, 'Oh, hell yeah, Skip.' He's like, 'Good, you're going in next inning.' I'm like, 'Hell, yeah.' The inning ends. I take off all my wristbands, my arm sleeve. I get up there and I'm standing on the mound. Jose Molina was the catcher at the time and I'm just looking around like, bro, what is happening right now? This is almost unheard of. I'll never forget how the whole inning played out, man, gave up a walk, give up a base hit to B. J. Upton. Next thing you know, I got runners on first and second. We got Gabe Kapler coming up. I'm gonna give up like 15 runs, dude, my first ever pitching appearance. It's gonna be miserable. I punch out Gabe Kapler. I don't know how it happened, but he had the best quote after the game. They asked him about it and he said, 'Now when someone asks me what my most embarrassing moment is, I now have an answer.' I thought that was like, so fitting for that moment. Ended up, Carlos Pena almost hit one off the ceiling in the Trop to get the second out. And Patty Burrell flew out to the warning track in left center to end the inning. I'm like a little kid. I'm pitching for the New York Yankees in a major league game, bro. Who does that? I punch out Gabe, I'm like asking for the baseball. I still have that baseball, the lineup card, the whole nine, dude, I've got it all. Even [Rays manager] Joe Maddon gave me the lineup card from their team that night too, which I thought was awesome.

"I'll never forget after the game, I've got like six ice packs on my shoulder, my elbow, my lower back. I'm like a journeyman pitcher that's pitched like, 30 years in the big leagues, right? Because when you're throwing on flat ground all the time, it's so simple. All of a sudden when you put a little tilt to it, just the 25 pitches that I threw, my lower back was absolutely killing me, man. I remember doing the interview after the game and I'm still smiling like, dude, I'm trying to like, you know, create some levity to the situation. Obviously, we just got pounded, like that's the last thing we wanna talk about. I can't believe it. I just pitched for the New York Yankees. I can't believe I'm a 0.00 ERA, like that's unbelievable. Meanwhile, I'm looking out the corner of my eye and Jorge Posada is standing in the corner over there, like giving me the death stare. 'Why are you laughing? Why do you think this is funny?' Right then and there is when I realized, number one, how intense Jorge Posada can be and number two, how important winning was for the New York Yankees. If it wasn't for leaders like Jorge and Derek and Andy and Mo and Alex and all those guys, I wouldn't have understood that you don't just start winning. You have to learn how to win. When you're talking about winning, those individuals right there knew how to win. To be able to have those guys as mentors for me, man, turned me into a winner by following those guys."

FIRST TIME AT YANKEE STADIUM AS A MEMBER OF THE TEAM:

Swisher's first home game with the Yankees was in April 2009 at the brand-new Yankee Stadium that made its debut that season.

"Goosebumps, I got 'em right now. All the hairs on my body are standing up because you're just taking me back to something that meant so much to me at that time. The first time that we were at the Stadium was the night before the welcome home dinner. We played in Miami and then came up to Yankee Stadium. Well, that was when we rolled into the stadium. They had all the lights on in the stadium, bro. We're walking into the locker room, you could play a flag football game in that locker room. It's that big, you know. All of a sudden, we walk out on the field and it was almost like the music that they would've played in Field of Dreams, you know what I mean. The most magical music that you could ever think of should have been playing in the background as we walked down through the tunnel and then up the stairs and out onto the field at Yankee Stadium. To be able to be that first group of individuals to play on that field, it was probably something that I'll never forget.

"Another thing that I'll never forget about Opening Day is I bet you could ask a thousand people who opened up the new Yankee Stadium hitting cleanup for the New York Yankees. I promise you there's not gonna be a whole lot of people that know that answer and the answer was me. It ended up I was hot at the time. I remember Posada hit the first home run of that game 'cause it was against Cliff Lee. I mean we're not gonna talk about the ass kicking (final score was 10–2) we took from the Cleveland Indians that day. It was the seventh or eighth inning of that game [note: it was the third inning], I hit a double in that game. I think I hit the first double in Yankee Stadium, so I'll take credit for that but I'll never forget it was out there. All of a sudden, the entire stadium starts chanting 'We want Swisher, ba, ba, ba, ba, ba, we want. . .' They wanted somebody to go in and pitch. They needed somebody to pitch and I'll never forget just being out there. Are they, that's my name. They're talking to me, bro, like they're talking to me. I think right then and there was maybe when that relationship with the fans was created, because I'm looking around. I'm kind of pumping up the crowd too because I'm like, 'Let's go.' To be able to experience that even though it wasn't the best of first games for us. To be able to experience that first game in Yankee Stadium, something you'll never forget. No doubt."

FIRST WORLD SERIES:

Swisher had three hits in the 2009 World Series but two of those came in the pivotal Game 3 when the Yankees and Phillies were tied at a game apiece.

"A lot more energy. A lot more attention, just a lot more lights. You can feel it, man. You know you're the only game on TV and everybody's watching. You feel that. For myself, looking back on my postseason career, I probably would've attacked it a little different and probably tried to handle it more calmly, but I'm just like, we're in the postseason, baby. For myself, didn't quite pan out for me that postseason in 2009. I'll never forget, I got benched [for] Game 2 of the World Series. That's when we played Pedro [Martinez] at home. Cliff Lee came in for the Phillies Game 1, beat us at home and then they put Pedro in there. Jerry Hairston, who had some great numbers against Pedro, started in place of me. I'll just never forget sitting on that bench, just like devastated. Like wanting to be out there, but also realizing you gotta be the best teammate you can be 'cause this is so much bigger than me. Then Joe Girardi saying, 'Hey, take a mental break today. We're not gonna need you. Jerry's gonna handle this today. Hey, just get yourself ready for Game 3.' That's exactly what I did. I took Game 2 just to get myself more mentally prepared, maybe soak up a little more of what was happening. Pay attention a touch more. Then, in Game 3, to be able to come back, hit a double, a homer, [score] a couple runs in that game and to be able to win a huge game, first game in Philly, was a big deal."

FIRST REACTION TO BEING A WORLD CHAMPION:

Swisher was in right field for the ninth inning of the clinching Game 6 of the 2009 World Series and caught the penultimate out before Shane Victorino grounded out to Robinson Cano at second base to clinch the Yankees' 27th world championship.

"You gotta remember. Jimmy Rollins was talking a little bit, man, saying Phillies in five and the whole night kind of giving us that bulletin board material as if somebody like Derek Jeter needed that. This dude knew exactly what he was gonna do and he did. Once again, had another magical postseason. [Hideki] Matsui, I thank him every time I see him for that 2009 World Series ring man, because his postseason in the World Series was absolutely electric. We're up three games to two at that point and we get the win. I make that second out of the inning. I just remember the emotions, man, because you're like delaying the inevitable and then all of a sudden you look out on the mound and you got Mariano Rivera there, bro. You wanna talk about just the calmness that each and every one of us on that team had every time he was on the mound. Next thing you know, man, Shane Victorino comes, hit a jam job right over to Robbie Cano, right over to Mark Teixeira, New York Yankees 27-time World Series champions.

"From there, I just blacked out. I don't even know what happened. I just remember yelling and screaming and jumping up and hugging as many people as I could because the only thing better than being able to accomplish something as an individual is being able to accomplish something as a team. To be part of group of individuals that have the same goals and thoughts and dreams in mind, and to be able to accomplish them all together, it is so emotional. You go for 162 games during the regular season in 182 days and then you have to go through the grueling grind of winning 11 more in the postseason. It's just such an emotional experience. It's hard to really explain how you feel in that moment because it's like, man, it's like it's over, but look what we accomplished. I can only describe it as probably the pinnacle of my career. The greatest thing I've ever accomplished was with that 2009 New York Yankees. To not only be able to be part of that team, but to also be part of the team that came from a team that didn't make the playoffs the year before. It was almost like, I think of it as my own journey, not being drafted outta high school to becoming a first rounder out of college."

FIRST ALL-STAR GAME:

Swisher was named to the American League All-Star team in 2010, winning the All-Star Final Vote by beating out Red Sox first baseman Kevin Youkilis in the closest vote in history. Swisher promoted his candidacy with a commercial that pictured him holding a surfboard. The game was hosted by the Los Angeles Angels of Anaheim and Swisher wanted to show fans he would be surfing in Southern California. Swisher was a participant in the Home Run Derby.

"Off the charts, just another amazing experience. I can't thank the fans enough. I'm standing there with a surfboard and a Tommy Bahama T-shirt on doing like a little jingle, like trying to get fans to vote for me. It could not have been better that it was a Yankee-Red Sox rivalry, which was so amazing.To be able to be part of that All-Star Game and then finding out the news that Robbie Cano was gonna drop out of the Home Run Derby. It would've taken a million people to tell me not to do that, bro. I was gonna be in that Home Run Derby for sure, because at the end of the day, my philosophy is when am I gonna ever have the opportunity to do something like this? To be able to say yes to those opportunities, just to be part of the overall experience, could not have been more blessed."

FIRST ACTING EXPERIENCE:

Swisher has appeared in a number of sit coms including Better with You and How I Met Your Mother. Swisher's wife, JoAnna Garcia, is an actress who has appeared in Are You Afraid of the Dark?, a horror anthology series, and Sweet Magnolias, a romantic drama TV series.

"Awesome [experience], because you gotta remember, talk about taking yourself out of your comfort zone. When I first did one of the shows, it was How I Met Your Mother.' We had just won the World Series. It was just one of those things where I walked on the set and all of a sudden, I turn and look and there's a group of like 20 people with all Yankee gear on. All of a sudden, they come flying over like, 'Swish, oh my God, man, congratulations on the World Series,' the whole nine, you know, 'Do you wanna be part of the show?' I'm like, 'Oh, hell yeah, dude, who doesn't wanna be part of like, the greatest sitcom ever almost?' To be able to be part of that stuff, you gotta just take yourself out of it. You gotta enjoy the experience.

"I had one or two lines, and I probably ran lines with my wife for two weeks prior, like, 'Babe, should I say it like this? 'Are we all looking for a toothbrush to share?' She's like, 'No, no, no. Say it like this or say it more serious, or whatever.' So just to be able to be part of all this stuff, man, I did get. I'm hoping one of these days down the road, I get the opportunity to host a television show. I think that would be one thing I'd have a lot of fun doing, man. Some sort of a competition-based reality show would be a lot of fun to do. Any chance that I get to do things that take me outta my comfort zone, I try to do that because it always ends up working itself out. If you can just kind of let yourself go for the experience, because everything we do in life, regardless of how big or how small it is, ends up only being a moment in time."

FIRST TIME HE CUT AN ALBUM:

"I'll never forget my guy [noted record producer] Loren Harriet, called me with the opportunity, [he] said, 'Hey, man, [Swisher laughs] would you like to sing on an album?' Well, I didn't know it was gonna be my album. I thought it was just gonna be like me, like, you know, like a little cameo or whatever and they're like, 'No, no, no. This is gonna be yours.' I'm like, 'Bro, number one, I'm not a singer but number two, bro, I could jam in a car, I can get after it.' So I'm thinking to myself once again, when am I ever gonna have the opportunity to sing on an album? So I said yes before he even got the sentence out of his mouth. I remember just going in there and never being more nervous in my life because it was just me in a room with a microphone, a partition behind me, and then a glass window and like 15 people behind there. I'm sure I go to start singing the first song and they're like, this kid can't sing at all, bro, this guy's horrible. I had a couple awesome songs. We had a blast doing it. In my mind, 'Heroes' by David Bowie, I sang that one pretty good and 'Lean on Me.' Other than that, don't pay attention to any other song."

FIRST TIME HAVING A FIELD NAMED AFTER HIM:

In 2011, Ohio State's home ballpark, Bill Davis Stadium, named the playing field "Nick Swisher Field" in his honor.

"So grateful for the opportunity to have gone to school there. Just a way to pay it forward. We always talk about just giving back and help the people who helped you get there. If I didn't have that scarlet and gray running through my blood, I don't know if I would be the athlete that I am today. I learned a lot of things there. You do a lot of growing up when you're in college, especially when you're on your own. I had some great mentors, I had some great friends, and we played a lot of great competition. To be part of that, man, when somebody offers you that opportunity, you jump on it because I wanted to try and leave a legacy. I've always tried to leave a cool legacy and to be able to have your name all over a stadium, especially for something that means so much to you, could not have been more blessed for that. I'm still super close with the university"

FIRST BOB FELLER ACT OF VALOR AWARD:

In 2014, Swisher was named the winner of the Bob Feller Act of Valor Award. The award is presented annually to a Baseball Hall of Famer, a current baseball player, and a United States Navy chief petty officer. The recipients are honored for their support of United States servicemen and women and achievement that represents the character of Bob Feller, who was a US Navy chief petty officer aboard the USS Alabama in World War II. Swisher, whose grandfather served in the military during the Korean War, is a supporter of the "Wounded Warriors."

"You don't do thing for the awards; you don't do things for the recognition. You do things because you want to do them. My love for the military started with my grandfather and always knowing that, there are men and women out there that are giving us what we have here in the United States. In my mind, the United States is the best country in the world. I've been to a couple of other ones and this one right here stands at the top. There's no doubt, no doubt about it. For myself, I always kind of thought, I'm not quite sure that I have the strength and the courage to do what those men and women are doing, so I'm gonna make sure that I can support them in any way possible.

"For my wife and I to go over to Afghanistan in 2010. To be able to experience what that was like during the war at that moment and to be able to give back and to give those men and women a different face to look at from the normal people they were used to seeing on a day in and day out basis. To doing everything I can now to try and help the military with anything I can do, whether that's trying to raise money, whether that's trying to bring recognition to something. Whether that's trying to make a phone call just to let somebody know that you're thinking about 'em, that's what it's all about."

FIRST IMPRESSIONS OF AARON JUDGE:

After stints with the Cleveland Indians and Atlanta Braves, Swisher signed a minor league contract with the Yankees in April 2016. He was never called up to the big club and opted out of his contract in early July.

"If anybody recalls the 'Baby Bombers," that was that year of 2016. For myself, man, I used to always say, Scranton [home of the Yankees' Triple-A farm club] isn't exactly the greatest city, there's not a whole lot of great places to eat. For breakfast, every morning, I used to tell the boys, whoever shows up at the Waffle House at 11:30 every morning, I'll buy you breakfast. So every morning, me and the guys would meet at the Waffle House. We would have breakfast and who was there almost every day, Aaron Judge. To be able to get to know him on more of a personal level early in his maturing process. At that point, he wasn't Aaron Judge, the captain, at that point. He was just like, okay, he's a prospect. He's got power. He's a big kid, but I'm telling you what, man, it's so crazy to see the transition that he had from his overall maturing process from 2016 coming into 2017, all of a sudden, 2017, right? Should have won the MVP as well as Rookie of the Year, as well as one of the more magical runs the Yankees have had, which was so much fun to see."

"I realized at that moment in 2016, it wasn't about me anymore. My career had taken a back seat to, hopefully the knowledge and the things that I was able to teach these young kids. At that point, the Gary Sanchezes of the world came up, the Tyler Austins of the world came up. This is right before Gleyber [Torres] came, but we had Aaron Judge doing his thing up there, man. I'll never forget watching the game Tyler Austin and Aaron Judge went back to back for their first home runs in the big leagues, which was such a magical thing to experience. For myself, man, such a tough point because you're like, I'm trying to get myself back to the big leagues, but also having a realization of, bro, you gotta know where you are in your life.

"That was when my future job now as a special advisor to the general manager, that's when it all started taking place for me. For Cash to be able to bring me back and to trust me enough to know that what I was teaching those guys was gonna be, right? I could not be [prouder] of that, man. I mean, even today, I consider those guys like my little but bigger brothers. Seeing all the things that are happening. Gary Sanchez in Minnesota [later with the New York Mets]. Tyler Austin, he's still playing in Japan. Aaron Judge becoming the new captain to the New York Yankees. Man, could not be more proud of those guys, but also blessed to have known them when. Proud to say that those individuals are exactly the same now as when I knew them back in 2016."

Nick Swisher by John Pennisi

26
STEFAN WEVER

Pitcher Stefan Wever was born in Germany but emigrated to the United States as a six year old in 1964. Following his junior season at the University of California, Santa Barbara, the right-hander was selected by the Yankees in the sixth round of the 1979 Major League Baseball June Amateur Draft. Wever was one of a number of players who played or appeared in only one Major League game. Stefan Wever passed away on December 27, 2022, a few months after being interviewed for this book.

FIRST BASEBALL IDOL:

"I would say Carl Yastrzemski because I grew up right outside of Boston, and that was right around '67. I also loved the way he played left field. I mean, he played it to perfection and he seems like a really classy guy."

FIRST MAJOR LEAGUE GAME THAT HE ATTENDED:

"The first game I attended was with my grandmother. She lives in Philadelphia and I went to a Phillies game against the Mets. I didn't know it until later, but Tom Seaver [was] the pitcher for the Mets. I would say, maybe 1968."

FIRST HIGH SCHOOL CHAMPIONSHIP GAME:

Wever attended Lowell High School in San Francisco. As a senior, Wever pitched in the championship game, a 5–4 loss to Washington High.

"It was exciting. The team we were playing, the Washington Eagles, had a pitcher who was a thorn in our side all year. He was a very tough left-handed pitcher. He didn't throw hard, but threw a lot of curveballs. I remembered [how] the winning run scored. There was a runner on second with two outs and he tried to steal third. The catcher threw the ball into left field, so the run scored and that was the game."

FIRST EXPERIENCE WITH THE DRAFT:

Wever was chosen by the Yankees in the sixth round of the 1979 Major League Baseball June Amateur Draft out of the University of California, Santa Barbara.

"I knew I'd be drafted, but I actually though it would be either the Angels or Dodgers because they're both Southern California teams and they had expressed an interest. So I was totally shocked when it was the Yankees, especially being a Red Sox fan. I think I just got a call. I forget the name of the scout. He goes, 'I'd like you to know, we selected you in the sixth round.' Which, I mean I was happy but a little surprised. It was kind of strange because I did not expect to go to the Yankees. There was really no one else around, just my college roommates."

FIRST PROFESSIONAL MANAGER:

Wever began his pro career with the 1979 Oneonta Yankees of the New York-Penn League. His manager was Art Mazmanian.

"Art was great. He'd been there forever. He was like an older man. Totally a baseball guy. He was just a great guy. A very, very nice guy. Very easy to like."

FIRST PRO CHAMPIONSHIP EXPERIENCE:

Oneonta played the Geneva Cubs in the finals. In the first game, Wever pitched a shutout with nine strikeouts as the Yankees went on to win the championship.

"Do you remember [Geneva] had Mel Hall that played for the Cubs? He was on the team and I faced them before and he just talks a lot of smack. So when we faced them for the championship, I struck him out three times, which is fantastic."

FIRST IMPRESSION OF DON MATTINGLY:

Wever and Mattingly were teammates at Oneonta.

"We roomed together, but you know, we'd heard about this guy that they signed. He was kind of a scrawny, little left-handed hitter, couldn't pull the ball, just kept flicking the bat, hitting it to left field. Steve Balboni was ahead of him. The next year, Mattingly came back, we went to the Instructional League and he started hitting singles. He started to definitely hit for average. He hit about .330. The next year, he came back and he was all bulked out and he started hitting doubles and home runs and RBIs, which allowed them to trade Balboni."

FIRST EXPERIENCE WITH HALL OF FAMER HOYT WILHELM AS HIS PITCHING COACH:

In 1981, Wever played for the Yankees' Double-A affiliate at Nashville. His pitching coach was Hall of Famer Hoyt Wilhelm.

"He was great. Because he was a knuckleballer, he couldn't really teach me much about my stuff, because he didn't have any stuff. He just taught me a lot of mental toughness and [perseverance] and stuff like that."

FIRST TIME HE WAS TOLD HE WAS BEING CALLED UP TO THE MAJORS:

After posting a 16–6 record with a 2.78 ERA for Nashville, Wever was called up to make his major league debut in September 1982.

"Well, the [Nashville] manager was Johnny Oates, the late Johnny Oates. He and Hoyt called me into their office. I had been planning to fly back to San Francisco the next day. They said, 'You're going to be flying tomorrow, but not to San Francisco.' So, I'm kind of like, what? 'So, you're gonna be flying to New York.' Anyway, that was pretty exciting.

"I took a taxi from the airport to Yankee Stadium. I got to the players entrance, which was kind of exciting as it was, and the game hadn't started yet. It was still lined with the fans that were up there and they knew exactly who I was. They knew my stats, I mean, they are really knowledgeable. They knew all about me. Then, I walked through the tunnel and it was like dark and a long walk. I forget who walked me through, one of their staff guys, front office guys walks me down the clubhouse to the locker room. Then I opened the door and there was a beautiful locker room."

FIRST TIME HE WALKED INTO YANKEE STADIUM:

"I expected [to be given] a number like 89 or something, they usually get rookies and a locker tucked away in some corner. So they brought me to my locker which was right in the middle of the locker room and [there was] a jersey hanging up there, number 25. My name above it, 'Wever'. I looked at the locker to my right and it said, 'Gossage' and I looked at the locker to my left and it said, 'Winfield,' so I was in heaven."

FIRST TIME PUTTING ON THE YANKEE PINSTRIPES:

"Up until that point, I was a die-hard Red Sox but the Yankees do a really good job of brainwashing you. By the time I was in the big leagues, I was all Yankees. I bought all the gear, 10 Yankee jackets and T-shirts back to my friends in San Francisco. I mean, I totally drank the juice."

FIRST MAJOR LEAGUE MANAGER: Clyde King

"I didn't really talk to him that much. He didn't really deal with rookies that much. I knew some of the players out there. I knew Dave Righetti because we played together [in the] Instructional League, so it wasn't like I went up there cold. I knew the pitching coach, Sammy Ellis, from Instructional League. It wasn't like I was totally out of my element. It was actually nice, those guys up there."

FIRST ROAD TRIP:

Wever's first road trip with the Yankees took him to Baltimore and Milwaukee. During the trip, Wever ended up with his own room at one of the hotels, which was unheard of for a rookie.

"It was kind of interesting. The traveling secretary of the Yankees, his name was [Bill] "Killer" Kane. Apparently, he took a liking to me because Barry Foote was on the team and he had taken off because his wife was having a baby. So he wasn't on the trip, so they game me his room. Apparently, he had reserved a private room, so I got the private room. When word got out that the rookie had a private room, the players just kind of congregated there and we started playing poker."

Reportedly, the players who were playing included Lou Piniella, Bobby Murcer, Oscar Gamble, Willie Randolph, and Dave Winfield.

"First of all, I don't know how to play poker. I think they figured that out pretty quick because they wanted me to keep playing so basically lost all my money, like any of these guys need my money."

FIRST GAME: September 17, 1982 vs. Milwaukee Brewers at County Stadium.

Wever was named the starting pitcher and tossed 2 2/3 innings, giving up nine runs (eight earned) in his one and only appearance in the major leagues, a 14–0 loss.

"I was kind of walking around all day in Milwaukee. Went to a mall, kind of walked around, looking at newspapers and stuff, listened to what people were saying. Probably around that afternoon some time, it hit me."

FIRST REACTON TO TAKING THE THE MOUND FOR THE FIRST TIME:

"Well, it was slow. I tried not to look at the scoreboard because it had [a] big picture of me up there, but I took a little glimpse. I mean it was pretty amazing. Something I'd been dreaming of ever since I got to this country. As a six-year-old boy, I put a ball in my hand and never put it down."

Wever faced a Brewers lineup that had three Hall of Famers— Robin Yount, Paul Molitor, and Ted Simmons— among its first four hitters.

"I remember they were good hitters. I remember the first guy was Molitor. He kind of bounced one through the right-hand side. Kind of like a ten hopper, but then Yount, Yount was amazing. I threw him a good fastball up and then he just kind of inside outed it and got a double to right-center which is kind of like his trademark."

Wever threw three wild pitches in the game, two in the third inning when he was taken out of the game by manager Clyde King.

"I had that last inning was pretty rough when I threw a bunch of wild pitches, so I kind of expected it. He was very nice when he came out because our defense was really shabby that day. It wasn't all my fault. I don't like it. I know a lot of people say that but it really wasn't because there were like three times when there was a ground ball with a man on first, where a double play should've occurred. We only got the lead guy, didn't get the hitter. A lot of runs scored after a couple of double plays should have been turned."

FIRST EXPERIENCE AS THE CO-OWNER OF A BAR:

In 1991, Wever and a friend purchased a bar in San Francisco's Marina District and named it the Horseshoe Tavern.

"I had been bartending at another place and a friend of mine was bartending at yet another place and we kind of been talking and we decided we didn't want to work for other people anymore. We just kind of wanted our own place. I lived in the marina at the time, so I've been to pretty much every bar in the marina and someone said I heard the Horseshoe might be for sale. I said, 'Oh, that place is a dump.' The guy had been there like 38 years, it was really dark. Couldn't even look in because it was so dark, just look like a tiny little hole in the wall. The guy said, 'No, no, go to the back.' So I went in, went to the back, it was huge. It really opened up huge. We have two pool tables there now. The owner was kind of a cantankerous old guy, former Marine, Portuguese, but he was a tough guy, but very popular. He really didn't want to sell it. He threatened to sell it several times before, but he really didn't want to. What me and my friend did, we just kept going in, we kept buying his regulars, he was very concerned about his regulars. We kept buying them drinks, we actually made him like us. When he actually signed, you can see his hand was he really didn't want to sign, but eventually he did."

Stefan Wever by Eric Kittelberger

27
PAUL ZUVELLA

Infielder Paul Zuvella spent parts of two seasons with the Yankees, who acquired him to fill a void at shortstop. Unfortunately, Zuvella got off to an 0-for-28 start with the Yankees and played a total of 35 games during his Yankee tenure.

FIRST BASEBALL GAME HE ATTENDED AS A KID:

"I remember going to Candlestick Park, obviously in San Francisco, I see the Giants play. They were my parents' favorite team. They were both from San Francisco. I remember coming up, onto the concourse and they had these orange doors that you'd open up. I remember when they first opened the doors and just the greenness of the field. It was just eye-popping to me. The contrast between the green of the baseball field and the stadium. The rest of the stadium, the concrete at the stadium. That was my first real memory I think that first time at a big league game."

FIRST BASEBALL IDOL:

"Willie Mays. I just loved the guy. Just loved the way he played. Played with such joy, always seemed happy and he was just a good player. Still to me the best that's ever played."

FIRST YEAR AS A COLLEGE PLAYER:

Zuvella played on the baseball team at Stanford University

"The upperclassmen knew how to play. You tried to keep your head down and learn as much as you could from 'em, but you also had to have that cockiness, that I belong here. For me, I was an infielder. I guess I played outfield when I was young in little league and what not. Then I became an infielder when I was 13, 14 years old. As soon as I got to Stanford, to get in the lineup, I was playing left field. Wherever I could play, you just got in the game.

"Gordy King, remember that name? The offensive tackle or whatever, he's a Stanford guy. I vividly recall going into the training room as a freshman. Hamstring deal or something, using some ice or whatever. I remember the football players in there, seniors and these guys, I mean they were huge. Their biceps were bigger than my thighs. You're just like, whoa, this is real."

FIRST AMATEUR WORLD SERIES:

In 1978, Zuvella played for the United States team in the Amateur World Series that was held in Italy.

"It was a great experience. You're a little bit overwhelmed as this was the first time I'd been out of the country. We had played up in Alaska the previous summer so kind of knew each other. Of course, I knew Terry [Francona]. Terry and I were pretty good friends back in the day. We played against each other when he was at Arizona and [Tim] Leary was at UCLA. It was a really good collection of talent. Some of the foreign teams weren't real good but you had your Cubas and we were 22-year-old kids. I was 19 or whatever and you're playing against these guys and they're in their mid-thirties and these guys are throwing like 94 miles an hour. Fastballs and these nasty sliders that are on these Cuban teams. So that was a little eye-opening as well, but it was a great experience."

FIRST DRAFT EXPERIENCE:

Zuvella was originally taken by the Milwaukee Brewers in the 11th round of the 1979 MLB June Amateur Draft but he did not sign. In the 1980 MLB June Amateur Draft, Zuvella was chosen by the Atlanta Braves in the 15th round.

"At that time, there weren't many Stanford guys that were getting drafted. If I remember right, they just kind of assumed that Stanford guys are gonna go back and get their degree, you know guys from really good schools. It's certainly not like that now but there's a lot of these really good programs or these really good schools, they're not really good baseball programs. The kids go in there thinking, I just need to go play two years or three years and I'll sign professionally. So the idea back then was that if we draft these Stanford kids, we don't want to take them too high 'cause they may not sign and we'll waste the draft pick. I just think I wanted to go back to school. I didn't think I was ready for pro ball. I could have done it, I'm sure, but I wanted to get my degree. I just figured, you never know if baseball's gonna pan out. I wanted to make sure I got my degree, so I went back, got that degree and I don't think it really mattered."

FIRST PROFESSIONAL MANAGER:

Zuvella began his pro career in 1980 with the Gulf Coast League Braves where he only played two games before joining the Durham Bulls. His manager at Durham was Al Gallagher.

"You get into pro ball with a guy like 'Dirty' Al and it's like, 'Hey, this is the way the game's played.' He was a no-nonsense guy. I mean, everything you hear about him. From what I recall, he was a little hard-nosed and he went after it. He kind of led by example a little bit. It was just getting yourself ready day to day. I mean, that's the number one thing a manager of a young player, a new player, that's the number one thing they want to instill in them. Hey, this is a marathon, it's not a sprint and you've gotta prepare yourself every day."

FIRST SPRING TRAINING:

"In a way, you feel like you've arrived a little bit, like you're good enough. You also have that confidence that, 'Hey, I belong here and I gotta prove myself.' It's a pretty cool feeling. I used to idolize a lot of these guys and maybe not the guys you end up playing with. You see some of these guys and how far they hit the ball and how consistent they are. You gotta remember as you're coming up through the minor leagues, you're around some pretty good players. You see some of these guys, 'Oh, that guy's a really good player.' Then you get to the big leagues and now you're around guys that have established themselves and you know it's just all part of that process. You feel like you're at the that point in your career where you want it to be. Now you had to go out and prove that you belong there."

FIRST REACTION FOR BEING CALLED UP TO THE MAJORS:

Zuvella was playing with the Braves' Triple-A affiliate at Richmond when he was first called up to the major leagues in September 1982.

"I believe Eddie Haas, who was my manager, just pulled me aside and I don't even remember where it was. Might have been after a game or something. If I remember right, the Richmond Braves were in the playoffs and we had a chance to win the [International League] championship. Obviously, I didn't care about that once I heard I was called up. I shouldn't say I didn't care about that. I felt bad 'cause a lot of the guys weren't gonna be there for this and they ended up winning it. Just excitement, this is great. This is a kind of culmination of everything I've been working toward. You're hoping during the year that maybe you'll get called up [in] September and everybody's doing the math and they're seeing this. Atlanta at the time was in the playoffs and maybe they are gonna need some extra guys. Sure enough, that's the way it played out and very excited about it."

FIRST MAJOR LEAGUE MANAGER: Joe Torre

"Obviously, you remember him as a player when I was a kid. I probably had Joe Torre baseball cards, you know, he was a good baseball guy. I was in a different position. He knew me from spring training and he knew I was a good player. He's a good manager and I was fortunate to be there but you're thinking, 'Okay, how am I gonna get him to think he needs to play me more?'"

FIRST MAJOR LEAGUE GAME: September 4, 1982 vs. Montreal Expos at Olympic Stadium.

Zuvella made his major league debut in the seventh inning when he pinch ran for Bob Watson.

"I remember running out there. I do remember sitting in the dugout when you're first in the big leagues before I played and think, 'Okay, now I know why they called it The Show.' There's a lot of stuff going on. It's not like your Triple-A games. Yeah, get a helmet, go run for him. They give you the heads up. If he gets on, you'll be running for him. I remember running out there thinking, 'This is different,' but it was cool. It was really, really cool."

FIRST AT-BAT: September 18, 1982 vs. Cincinnati Reds at Riverfront Stadium.

Zuvella entered the game in the fifth inning as the Braves' shortstop. Zuvella faced Reds pitcher Brad Lesley in the eighth inning and flied out to left field in his first big league at-bat.

"Excitement, obviously. You're just trying to remember the things that got you there. Okay, this guy's a fastball pitcher I'm looking for. I got a pretty good pitch to hit and I got under it and tossed it up.
Anyway, you're just excited. You try not to live in that moment too much. It's just like, okay this is another at-bat, it's just on a

bigger stage. Again, you think back to the things that got you there. I picked the ball up out of his hand and stay inside the ball, but it was exciting. I just wish I'd hit it better."

FIRST TIME HE SAW HIMSELF ON A BASEBALL CARD:

"That was pretty cool. A lot of guys that you've talked to, I'm sure they collected cards when they were a kid. Of course, back in those days you didn't get to see these players very much. The cards were really all you saw of them or knew of them. When I started playing and got to the big leagues, you had the 'Superstation' and our games [Braves] were televised every time, every game. It was a little different. Getting a card for the first time, I remember thinking I finally arrived. It's you have your own baseball card. That's something that resonated."

FIRST MINOR LEAGUE ALL-STAR NOD:

In 1984, Zuvella was named to the International League All-Star team.

"Again, you felt like I'm being recognized by the sportswriters or whoever it was, maybe it was the managers that chose you. It was a good group of players and, at that time, none of us know how our careers are gonna go. You're still relatively young in the whole process but these are guys that go out there and they play hard every day. It feels pretty darn good to be considered as one of the top at that position in any league that you're in. I ended up being an All-Star a number of times in Triple A and it was always a nice feeling. You're recognized by your peers, other managers, and sportswriters and everybody else, they recognize what it I that you bring to the table."

FIRST TIME HE APPEARED IN A MOVIE:

Zuvella appears in the movie, *Ferris Bueller's Day Off.* Zuvella is seen on first base in game footage when a foul ball hit by Claudell Washington is caught by Ferris Bueller (played by Matthew Broderick) in the stands at Chicago's Wrigley Field. The footage is from a game played on June 5, 1985.

"It's funny but we had gone in to Chicago and I think the next time we came in, our PR person came up to us and said 'Hey, we need you guys to sign these waivers.' They're thinking about making a movie and they may use some of the footage. Claudell, I think he's the one that fouled the ball off. I don't know, it's [Glenn] Hubbard, and [Rafael] Ramirez and some of these other guys they may have used some of the footage for. You're a player and you think, well if we don't sign the waiver, they won't use the footage. So, you sign this waiver. Think back, wow, I wish I wouldn't have signed that waiver. You'd get a dollar for every time someone watches that movie. I wouldn't need to sell real estate anymore, but it was pretty cool. I still get people asking me about it. It's funny, it's pretty crazy. Hey, did you know you were in *Ferris Bueller's Day Off?* I kind of knew. I do remember the play, though. I had just gotten a hit off off [Cubs pitcher] Lee Smith. He tried to sneak a fastball by me and I got a base hit to left field and that's how I got on first base. It's kind of cool how it all played out."

FIRST TIME BEING TRADED:

On June 30, 1986, Zuvella was traded to the Yankees, along with Claudell Washington, for Ken Griffey and Andre Robertson.

"I was in Triple A, had gotten to the ballpark. Roy Majtyka was our manager and he called me into the office and he wasn't happy. I'm just thinking, what's going on this time? I screw something up. This was, I think it was before the game. He wasn't happy 'cause he was losing his shortstop as it turns out. 'Hey, you've been traded to the Yankees and they need you to get there first thing tomorrow morning.' Yeah, I'm in a bit of a shock. My wife and I just found out that she was pregnant and now we're getting traded. It's like, whoa, there's a lot of stuff going on in your life. Brian Fisher was a good friend of mine from my Atlanta days. I knew him from the Yankees and I was excited to team up with him again. So, it was an exciting time."

FIRST TIME PUTTING ON THE PINSTRIPES:

"I was a student of baseball. You knew the [Mickey] Mantles and the [Lou] Gehrigs and the [Babe] Ruths, you knew all those guys. You knew the history of the game and you know what it meant to people, what it meant to the country and as a pastime. Coming out onto that field for the first time and just going into the locker room. Walking past some of these guys and it was Don Mattingly, of course. I'd come up against Mattingly and [Dave] Winfield was on that team and Ron Guidry. Donnie I knew from having played against him in the minor leagues and it's an adjustment [coming from the National League to the American League], so you kind of had to adjust to that. It was really cool running out of the field for the first time. Those monuments are out there and it's just a really cool feeling."

FIRST YANKEES MANAGER: Lou Piniella

"Lou was a hard-nosed guy. He thought things needed to be done a certain way. That might have been his first year as a manager, so he's kind of acclimating himself to being a big league manager. He was a good guy. He was a crusty baseball guy, that's a guy with a very successful playing career. We were all in the George Steinbrenner under his eye kind of thing. You really felt that as a young player. Lou was a good guy and I just wish I would've gotten off to a better start in New York. Kind of getting acclimated to everything and living in the city and having a pregnant wife. It was a lot at that time and it took me a little while to adjust."

FIRST YANKEE HIT: July 12, 1986 vs. Minnesota Twins at the Hubert H. Humphrey Metrodome

Zuvella ended an 0-for-28 skid with an infield single in the sixth inning off of Twins pitcher Allan

Anderson.

"It was a big relief, obviously. It's kind of all you think about for a while. If I'm not mistaken, I think I pounded it off the plate and bounced about 30 feet in the air. That's the kinda hit I got but yeah, it was a big relief. I think if remember right, I got three or four more hits over the next 10 or 12 at-bats. I felt like, okay, I'm starting to come around. I got the monkey off my back and then they traded for somebody else. I think I would've really kind of started to establish myself had I been given a little bit more time."

FIRST TIME HE HEARD THE LEGENDARY PUBLIC ADDRESS ANNOUNCER, BOB SHEPARD, ANNOUNCE HIS NAME:

"I mean, he would say it. How would he do it? He would be, [imitates Shepard's voice] 'Now batting, number twenty-six, Paul Zuvella, shortstop,' something along those lines. You kind of repeat something and yeah, it was really cool. He actually came up to me before the first game, I mean, in pregame, and wanted to know how I pronounced my name. I told him, 'Zu-vell-ah.' I said thank you and he walked off. I don't even know that I knew who it was at the time 'cause you're getting ready for your first game in the American League. Yeah, it was pretty cool."

FIRST IMPRESSION OF GEORGE STEINBRENNER:

"I don't know if I ever did [interact with George]. I remember watching him walk through the clubhouse. He had his little entourage with him and I saw that a few times. I just stay under the radar and stay on the field if I could. Again, it was just a tough start for me. I wish that would've played out better 'cause I was a much better player than I showed when I was in New York. For sure."

Paul Zuvella by Jared Kelly

28
THE ARTISTS

The following artists were kind enough to supply amazing portraits for each of the Yankees in this book, over and above the written word, we think you will agree that every picture tells a story.

MAZ ADAMS:

Maz supplied the artwork for Wade Boggs, Al Downing, Jim Leyritz, and Shane Spencer.

Maz was born in Queens and spent the early innings of his life in Canarsie, Brooklyn, New York. Hailing from the birth state of baseball, and having a die-hard Yankees fan for a father, it was inevitable that he would fall in love with America's pastime.

A 2010 graduate of the prestigious Joe Kubert School of Art, Maz takes his comic book-inspired line work and uses it to create unique pieces of art, paying homage to the legends of both today and years gone by.

He has appeared on the YES Network, in *Beckett* magazine, various articles, podcasts, and interviews. He is the official artist of the Latino Sports Awards. His clients include Topps, Beckett, Fanatics, the Ed Lucas Foundation, the Isaac Bruce Foundation, the Negro

League Museum, Rod Carew, Don Mattingly, Mariano Rivera, and Bernie Williams, among many others.

He resides in Pennsylvania with his wife/best friend Danielle, and his sweet French Bulldog, Bram.

JAMES FIORENTINO

James supplied the artwork for Tony Kubek and Dave Righetti.

James Fiorentino is a master in watercolor. His works of art have been internationally recognized since he was young. At the age of 15, he became the youngest artist ever to be featured in the National Baseball Hall of Fame and Museum for his likeness of Reggie Jackson. In 1998, James became the youngest artist to be inducted into the prestigious New York Society of Illustrators, along with such artists as Norman Rockwell and Andrew Wyeth. He has painted for many legends of the past and stars of today, including Ted Williams, Joe DiMaggio, Cal Ripken Jr., Arnold Palmer, Muhammad Ali, Derek Jeter, Mariano Rivera, and Tiger Woods. James's work has won numerous awards and can be seen nationally in books and magazines, as well for national products including trading cards for Topps, Upper Deck, and Kellogg's.

JARED EVAN KELLY

Jared supplied the artwork for Doc Medich Mike Pagliarulo.,and Paul Zuvella

Jared Evan Kelley is a portrait artist by trade and resides in Alabama. He earned a Bachelor's of Fine Arts degree from Auburn University in 2008 with an emphasis on Studio Painting. He has been working professionally as a portrait artist since 2010. His sports art has been featured in many trading card products produced by Upper Deck, Sport Kings, In the Game, Inc., and Sage. Since 2021, he has worked on Topps' MLB Living Set, which features weekly portraits of major league players from the past and present. Apart from his sports art, Kelley has also been the official portrait painter for the National Trial Lawyer Association Hall of Fame since 2009.

Kelley's biggest influences on his art career have been Norman Rockwell, Drew Struzan, James Knight a.k.a Fourhundred ML, Alvin Chong, Robert Barrett, and renowned sports artist Dick Perez.

The artist may be reached by visiting www.JaredKelley.com.

JAMES KIMBALL

James supplied the artwork for Mike Heath and Dennis Rasmussen.

James Kimball is a chef and up-and-coming artist out of St. Louis, Missouri. A Cardinals fan since birth, he moved to the Lou in 2017 where he was married in front of Busch Stadium and now has a son, Ozzie, named after his idol Ozzie Smith. He began drawing as a child, but only five years ago began pursuing art again and his style is constantly changing from realism to abstract to anime. He has recently completed pieces for Nolan Arenado and UFC fighter Tyron Woodley.

Twitter: @papabadbird
Instagram: @realtimeJKsportsart

ERIC KITTELBERGER

Eric supplied the artwork for Charlie Hayes and Stefan Wever.

Eric is an award-winning creative with nearly 35 years of advertising and design experience. He received his BFA in Graphic Design from Kent State University in 1989. After graduation, Eric worked for an advertising agency in Akron, Ohio, for five years before starting the Triple Play Design Company in 1995. Throughout his professional career, Eric has worked on projects for companies such as Guinness and Bass Ale, Swedish Fish, Sour Patch Candies, American Heart Association, the National Park Service, Evenflo, Avery Labels, Bubblicious, Banana Boat, Autism Speaks, Ocean Spray, and TDK to name a few. You can see more of his work at www.TriplePlayDesign.com.

JOHN PENNISI

John provided the artwork for Stan Bahnsen, Ron Blomberg, Joba Chamberlain, Rocky Colovito, Johnny Damon, Tommy John, Fritz Peterson, and Nick Swisher.

Throughout the years, John has been influenced by many cartoonist/illustrators including Mort Drucker (*MAD* magazine), Joe Giella (comic book legend), sports cartoonists Willard Mullin and Bill Gallo as well as his main influence, Bruce Stark. After seeing Stark's impressions in the *New York Daily News* when he was 10 years old, John knew what he wanted to do the rest of his life. Studying under Tom Gill of Lone Ranger fame, John's illustrations have become a staple of numerous publications such as *New York Sportscene*, and both the *New York Post* and *New York Daily News*. For the past 15 years John has done the art for the yearly Baseball Writers Association of America Scorecard following in the footsteps of Mullin and Gallo who illustrated the it for the previous 49 years. He has also illustrated for the Baseball Hall of Fame, the Babe Ruth Hall of Fame, and the Phil Rizzuto, Gene Michael, David Cone Celebrity Charity Golf Classic for the benefit of the Ed Lucas Foundation for the past 20 years.

ERIC RALEIGH

Eric supplied the artwork for Steve Balboni and Jake Gibbs.

Eric Raleigh is a self-taught artist. He specializes in black and white acrylic paintings as well as pyrography. Eric is legally blind in one eye and is able to create his amazing pieces despite his lack of depth perception. Eric is a firm believer that if you work hard at it, you can accomplish any goal you set your mind to

MARK SPRINGER

Mark supplied the artwork for Jack McDowell and Eric Soderholm.

Mark Springer is a graphic artist and co-owns a screen printing, embroidery, and marketing company in Goshen, Indiana, where he lives with his wife and two children. Drawing and baseball have always been two passions of his, and he loves combining the two. Around 2010, Mark began illustrating some of his favorite baseball players in his current style using bold lines and minimal colors. Since then, numerous players and personalities have commissioned portraits or implemented his illustrations on social media.

HIDESHI YOKOYAMA

Hideshi supplied the artwork for David Aardsma and Bobby Richardson.

Hideshi Yokoyama is a Sports illusrator/Artist based in Japan. Instagram : hide.yokoyama

Made in the USA
Monee, IL
26 August 2023

41690815R00201